The
Research-Productive
Department

The
Research-Productive
Department

Strategies From Departments That Excel

Carole J. Bland
Anne Marie Weber-Main
Sharon Marie Lund
Deborah A. Finstad
University of Minnesota

ANKER PUBLISHING COMPANY, INC.
Bolton, Massachusetts

The Research-Productive Department
Strategies From Departments That Excel

ISBN 1-882982-74-6

Composition by Deerfoot Studios
Cover design by Jennifer Arbaiza Graphic Design

Anker Publishing Company, Inc.
P.O. Box 249
Bolton, MA 01740-0249 USA

www.ankerpub.com

Library of Congress Cataloging-in-Publication Data

The research-productive department : strategies from departments that excel / Carole J. Bland . . . [et al.].
     p. cm.
Includes bibliographical references and index.
   ISBN 1-882982-74-6
   1. Universities and colleges—Departments. 2. Learning and scholarship.
3. Universities and colleges—Faculty. I. Bland, Carole J.
   LB2360.2.R47 2005
   378.1'2--dc22   2004010642

Dedication

We dedicate this book to all those individuals who make a department excel—staff, faculty, and department heads and chairs—through their commitment to discovering new knowledge, providing quality education, and serving their community. They continually improve the world for us all.

On a personal note, two of the department heads/chairs whom we interviewed for this book have since passed away. Mary McEvoy, professor and chair of educational psychology, was an internationally known researcher and political activist who died on October 25, 2002, in a plane crash in Eveleth, Minnesota, while on campaign with Senator Paul Wellstone. She was a passionate advocate for the rights of young children.

Joe Warthesen died on January 31, 2003, having been a faculty member in the Department of Food Science and Nutrition since 1974 and its chair since 1997. His research focused on understanding the chemical reactions in foods during processing, storage, and preparation. His work contributed significantly to one of humanity's most basic needs: a safe, wholesome, and quality food supply.

About the Authors

**Carole J. Bland** is professor and director of research in the Department of Family Medicine and Community Health, Medical School, and member of the Department of Educational Policy and Administration, College of Education and Human Development, both at the University of Minnesota, where she has been a faculty member since 1974. She received an M.A. in experimental psychology and a specialist degree in behavior modification from Drake University in 1970 and a Ph.D. from the University of Minnesota in 1974 in educational psychology with an emphasis on measurement, evaluation, and adult learning. During 1989–1990, she was an American Council on Education Fellow, learning about higher education's administration, organization, and funding. She has been active in university-wide governance, having served on the Senate Faculty Affairs, Judicial, and Faculty Consultative committees. She has served as special assistant to the provost and has codirected a three-year university initiative to assist departments in solving complex academic issues. In the Academic Health Center she has served on the Faculty Consultative Committee and has chaired the Faculty Affairs Committee. Currently, she directs the following: a university-wide study on the characteristics of research-productive departments, a departmental division that provides consultation, resources, and programs to support research; a three-year Clinical Investigator Fellowship for family physicians; and a one-year national fellowship to prepare family medicine educators for the deanship or higher-level administrative positions. She also teaches courses and workshops on education, administration, research, evaluation, and faculty vitality. She has served as a consultant in these areas, as well as on physician specialty choice, to departments, universities, foundations, professional associations, and the federal government. She served as chair of the board of directors of the Alfred Adler Graduate School, is currently serving as a regent for Augustana College, and has chaired or served on numerous other organizational and editorial boards, national peer review committees, and task forces. Her research focuses on the development and productivity of faculty, administrators, and institutions. She is series editor of the Springer Series on Medical Education

(Springer Publishing Company), and has written more than 80 publications, including an award-winning book, *Vitality of Senior Faculty Members: Snow on the Roof—Fire in the Furnace.*

Anne Marie Weber-Main is assistant professor and associate director of research in the Department of Family Medicine and Community Health at the University of Minnesota Medical School. With Carole Bland, she helped develop a three-year Clinical Investigator Fellowship for family physicians and codirects a departmental research division that provides consultation, resources, and programs to support faculty-led research. In this capacity she consults with faculty and fellows on their research goals and plays a substantial role in assisting researchers with their scholarly writing projects, that is, the development of grant proposals, journal articles, book chapters, and other research-related manuscripts. She lectures on scholarly writing in a family medicine research course and cofacilitates a participative writing seminar for family medicine and pediatrics fellows. To these academic roles she brings a diverse blend of educational and professional experiences that span the physical sciences, technical writing, and communications. She received a Ph.D. in chemistry (analytical emphasis) from the University of Minnesota in 1997. Her doctoral research was funded by the National Institutes of Health and has been published in several peer-reviewed journals (*Biochemistry, Journal of the American Chemical Society,* and *Archives of Biochemistry*). In 1995 she was awarded a Mass Media Fellowship by the American Association for the Advancement of Science. Through this program, which places scientists in media settings to promote the public understanding of science, she researched and wrote science news stories that aired on CNN. She has been active in Graduate Women in Science, serving a three-year term as editor of its national newsletter. In 2000 she completed a core curriculum in medical editing offered by the American Medical Writers Association (AMWA) and is continuing her training as a participant in AMWA's advanced curriculum.

 **Sharon Marie Lund** resides in St. Paul, Minnesota, where she is a Ph.D. candidate in nutritional epidemiology at the University of Minnesota. She received her B.S. in nutrition and dietetics from the University of Minnesota and an M.S. in nutrition and dietetics from New York University in Manhattan. Her expertise is in diet assessment—measuring the impact of diet on health and diseases in large populations. Her professional experience includes directing a Women, Infants, and Children (WIC) Program in the Lower East Side of Manhattan and developing policy in maternal and child health at Minnesota's state health and human service agencies. She has lectured and conducted research in the University of Minnesota's Division of Epidemiology. She is also collaborating with international foundations and agencies in East Africa to develop a comprehensive public health program, which would include a food supplementation program, designed to serve vulnerable populations in developing and war-torn nations.

 **Deborah A. Finstad** is director of research services in the Department of Family Medicine and Community Health, University of Minnesota. Since 1986 she has consulted with faculty and fellows on their research projects and assisted with instrument design, collection, management, analysis, and interpretation of quantitative and qualitative data. The projects cover a diverse range of research areas, including cancer prevention, smoking cessation, sexual health, women's health, and faculty vitality. She lectures on instrument design and database management for the fellows' seminars.

Table of Contents

Foreword

The Research-Productive Department: Strategies From Departments That Excel takes aim at the critical role the department (or similar immediate collegial environment) can play in encouraging and supporting excellence in research. Many of us have observed that certain departments seem to achieve exceptional levels of research productivity and to have a culture that inspires and sustains excellence in research. The interviews the authors have conducted, within a conceptual framework based on their review of the literature, help us better understand the dynamics of the microenvironments that encourage and support such productivity and excellence. The authors have identified an important set of factors that operate in the range between the creative individual and supportive institutional policies. This book deserves attention by all who are involved in ensuring research productivity and excellence in our universities.

Nils Hasselmo, President
Association of American Universities

Preface

Motivation for This Book:
Supporting the Research Mission of Academia _____

Many authors writing for academic department chairs and deans have taken a broad-stroke approach, choosing to address the full range of leadership and management tasks that routinely befall this extensive readership. Few published works have narrowed their scope, as this book does, to the important leadership tasks influencing an academic department's overall excellence in one critical area—research. It is in this context that our book, aimed specifically at helping academic leaders to facilitate their faculty's productivity in research, takes on particular significance.

For decades, the creation of new knowledge through research has been an integral, valued part of postsecondary education. Faculty in all disciplines are eager to put their hypotheses to the test, to answer some of society's most pressing questions, and to try out their most inspired, creative ideas. For many faculty, this stimulating process of inquiry and discovery is precisely what drew them to their profession. It is also what informs, enriches, and keeps current their teaching. In short, it helps satisfy and sustain them over their long careers as academicians.

A high quality and quantity of faculty scholarship also directly affects the institutions where these faculty work. From a financial standpoint, faculty-acquired grants can bring in external funding for direct and indirect research costs. Concomitant discoveries can yield new inventions and patents, generating additional revenue. Departments, colleges, and universities with the earned reputation of being "research-intensive" have a leg-up in attracting outside funding for future initiatives. They are also alluring environments for talented, research-oriented faculty and postsecondary students—people whose work is likely to further propagate high-quality research and scholarship.

Finally, we as a society depend on our faculty researchers to advance knowledge in countless areas. We demand innovations that can improve and enrich our lives—from finding new vaccines or developing more sustainable agriculture to understanding and alleviating gang violence, creating new music to soothe or excite the soul, or informing international policies to make this a safer world. Simply put, we all have a vested interest in facilitating the research productivity of our higher education faculty; their achievements can dramatically affect our quality of life and that of many generations to come.

Our Audience and Purpose

We recognize that the important task of nurturing and sustaining faculty research productivity typically falls on the shoulders of individual department heads or chairs. Our purpose in creating this book was to provide these busy but very influential leaders with two pragmatic and intimately intertwined tool sets: 1) an overarching, literature-based framework for thinking about and attending to faculty research productivity, and 2) a set of diverse, concretized strategies—best practices, if you will—for making an academic "home" in which faculty can achieve excellence in research.

Our method for identifying these best practices was to interview the department heads/chairs of 37 highly research-productive and highly ranked departments at our institution, the University of Minnesota. We designed our semi-structured interviews around the many characteristics known from prior literature to be associated with high productivity in research—characteristics such as strong professional networks, sufficient time for research, brokered opportunities for faculty development, the targeted recruitment of highly motivated faculty, and many more. With this body of literature as our guiding framework, our goal was to learn how research-facilitating characteristics such as these are actually manifest in currently productive departments, whether through specific programs, policies, allocation of resources, and so on.

Having successfully completed this project, we now share with readers our qualitative findings. We prepared this book primarily for deans, department heads/chairs, or others responsible for maintaining or increasing faculty research productivity. Indeed, the many diverse voices readers will hear in the ensuing pages are from this particular peer group. We expect, however, that the information we present will provide tangible benefits to other audiences as well. These might include current faculty looking for ways to increase their own research productivity; future faculty searching for the academic home that will, by virtue of having certain desirable environmental features, best facilitate their research careers; and scholars investigating ways to develop and sustain research-conducive work environments.

In addition, although the emphasis of this book is on sharing strategies for ensuring the highest levels of faculty productivity in research, there is applicability to other areas of institutional vitality as well. For example, all work environments, research-focused or otherwise, are likely to benefit from having clear goals that coordinate individual members' work, regularly rewarding work that achieves these goals, creating a work culture that embodies the goals, and maintaining a positive work climate conducive to meeting these goals. Thus, we anticipate that this book, which shares specific strategies for creating and maintaining this type of productive work environment, will have wide-reaching utility for people seeking to improve their organization's overall vitality, not just research vitality.

Unique Contributions

We Let the "Experts" Tell the Story

This narrative is unique in encapsulating the opinions and practices of not just one authority, but nearly 40 leaders with extensive experience within the trenches of academia. The participants in our qualitative study came from diverse disciplines, college types, and community settings. Some are chairing departments with a long history of excellence in research. Others have guided their departments through recent initiatives that helped earn their departments' now-strong research reputations. But all hail from one of the most comprehensive and highly ranked research institutions in the country, and specifically from highly ranked departments and schools where faculty excel in research. Most important, all offer up specific, useful ways by which other academic leaders can help foster high levels of research productivity in their own settings (e.g., through specific recruitment practices, formal and informal mentoring programs, rewards systems, culture-building activities, distribution of fiscal and human resources). Taken together, our study participants' responses constitute a very practical set of hands-on lessons learned which readers can apply as is or otherwise adapt for use in their own institutions.

We Ground Our Practical Findings in a Well-Established Model

Our rich body of qualitative data takes on greater clarity and importance when cast within the framework of an existing literature-based model for understanding how to maximize research productivity. This model, described in Chapter 1, asserts that research productivity rests on three foundations: the characteristics of the individual researcher, the characteristics of his/her home institution, and the characteristics of the institution's leadership. Together, these features act to facilitate research and to support the overarching, yet delicate research enterprise. This model undergirded our qualitative study and provided us with a blueprint for clustering our qualitative findings of best practices.

To our knowledge, this is the only book to bring together 1) a user-friendly summary of the literature on the characteristics of research-productive organizations, and 2) highly descriptive examples of how these characteristics are actually manifest in a large number of highly research-productive academic departments/schools.

Structure of This Book

Chapter 1 provides an overview of salient literature on the correlates/predictors of research productivity. It constructs this information into a model of "the research-productive organization" that encompasses 1) the individual characteristics of the highly productive faculty researcher, 2) the environmental characteristics of the institution in which the faculty member works, and 3) the leadership characteristics of the organization in which the research is being conducted.

Chapters 2–14 are organized thematically, such that each addresses a single feature of the research-productive organization:

Chapter 2: Faculty Recruitment and Selection
Chapter 3: Clear Goals That Coordinate Work and Emphasize Research
Chapter 4: Shared Culture and Positive Group Climate
Chapter 5: Mentoring
Chapter 6: Interdisciplinary Collaboration
Chapter 7: Communication With Colleagues: Professional Networks
Chapter 8: Resources
Chapter 9: Teaching
Chapter 10: Sufficient Time for Research
Chapter 11: Rewards
Chapter 12: Brokered Opportunity Structure
Chapter 13: Faculty Size and Diversity: The Right Mix of Expertise and Experience
Chapter 14: Leadership and Governance

This structure allows readers to dig deeper into each research-facilitating characteristic. Each chapter begins with a particularly salient quote about the chapter's theme from an interviewed department head/chair. The subsequent chapter text is divided into three major sections:

1) *What Does the Literature Say?* This section serves the important purpose of placing our qualitative findings into the broader context of what is already known from previous literature about research-facilitating practices across many institutions.

2) *Department Practices.* This section provides a detailed narrative of our qualitative findings. The text is organized thematically under topic questions, the answers to which include numerous illustrative responses from the interviewed department heads—wonderfully concrete examples of how these departments manifest all the characteristics of a research-productive organization.

3) *Review.* For readers who want to get right to the punch line and/or see a review of the narrative they have just finished reading, this section provides a bulleted abstract summarizing the core research-facilitating practices that emerged from our study and prior literature.

Chapter 15 serves to summarize the book while reemphasizing the key overarching themes. Five take-home lessons are presented which span the more detailed qualitative findings presented in Chapters 2–14.

Lastly, eight appendices supplement the main body of the text.

Appendix A: Study Origins and Methods (design, participant selection, data collection, analyses)

Appendix B: Pre-Interview Survey (completed by participating department heads/chairs)

Appendix C: Semi-Structured Interview Protocol

Appendix D: Senate Working Group Project on Research Productivity

Appendix E: Demographic Survey Results of Participating Departments (completed by participating department heads/chairs)

Appendix F: Brief Narrative Description of the University of Minnesota

Appendix G: Leaving the University of Minnesota (Executive summary of an exploratory survey study of tenure-track/tenured faculty who had voluntarily left the University of Minnesota for other academic positions (1997–2000). These results highlight the importance of environmental features in maintaining a highly productive and satisfied faculty.)

Appendix H: Related Works (sample list of other published works on academic leadership)

Portions of the literature review sections were drawn from:

Bland, C. J., & Ruffin, M. T., IV. (1992). Characteristics of a productive research environment: Literature review. *Academic Medicine, 67*(6), 385–397. With permission of *Academic Medicine.*

Bland, C. J. (1997). Beyond corporate downsizing: A better way for medical schools to succeed in a changing world. *Academic Medicine, 72*(6), 13–19. With permission of *Academic Medicine.*

Bland, C. J., & Bergquist, W. H. (1997). *The vitality of senior faculty members: Snow on the roof—fire in the furnace* (ASHE-ERIC Higher Education Report, Volume 25[7]). Washington, DC: George Washington University, Graduate School of Education and Human Development. Also, February 2000, Jossey Bass. With permission of John Wiley & Sons, Inc.

Carole J. Bland
Anne Marie Weber-Main
Sharon Marie Lund
Deborah A. Finstad

Acknowledgments

This project could not have succeeded without the financial support of the University of Minnesota's Office of the Executive Vice President/Provost. We particularly thank Robert J. Jones, vice provost and executive vice president for student development, for his commitment to finding ways to help faculty succeed and his unwavering support of our efforts.

This book would also not have happened without the vision of the chair of the Senate Committee on Faculty Affairs, Richard Goldstein, who initiated this project with Robert Jones, and the commitment of the members of the University of Minnesota Joint Senate/Administrative Working Group on Faculty Development. It is they who designed this project, carried out the interviews with department heads/chairs and deans, and reviewed initial drafts of the results. We thank each of the following members of the working group:

Sandra O. Archibald (associate dean, Hubert H. Humphrey Institute of Public Affairs)

Carole J. Bland (professor, family medicine and community health, working group chair)

Eugene Borgida (professor, psychology)

Carol A. Carrier (vice president, Office of Human Resources)

Esam E. El-Fakahany (assistant vice president and associate dean, Graduate School)

Richard J. Goldstein (regents professor, mechanical engineering)

David W. Hamilton (professor; genetics, cell biology, and development)

James C. Hearn (professor, educational policy and administration)

Robert J. Jones (vice president and executive vice provost for faculty and academic programs)

Victoria M. Mikelonis (professor, rhetoric)

James A. Parente (associate dean, College of Liberal Arts)

Angelita D. Reyes (associate professor, African-American and African studies)

Virginia Seybold (professor, neuroscience)

Janice A. Smith (program director, Preparing Future Faculty, Office of Human Resources)

Paul J. Strykowski (professor, mechanical engineering)

Peggy A. Sundermeyer (coordinator, Office of the Vice President of Research, Graduate School)

We extend a very special thank-you to the many staff members who contributed so much of their time and talents to this project: Jody Burrows, Laura Feiker, Barbara Fox, and Liz Greene, who arranged and transcribed the interviews; Ross Johnson, who acquired literature; Barb Hartman, who coordinated and staffed the working group; Liz Greene who created and maintained our references database and edited the final drafts of this manuscript; and Libby Frost, who lent her artistic vision to the book's graphics.

Finally, but above all, we are incredibly grateful to the many department/school leaders who, by participating in our qualitative study, gave graciously and generously of their time and ideas. The following are alphabetical listings of our study participants by name and discipline.

Study Participants, Alphabetized by Name _____

Name	Discipline (Title)	Institute, School, or College
Ames, Trevor R.	Clinical and Population Sciences (Chair)	College of Veterinary Medicine
Archibald, Sandra O.	Public Affairs (Associate Dean)	Hubert H. Humphrey Institute of Public Affairs
Ascerno, Mark E.	Entomology (Head)	College of Agricultural, Food, and Environmental Sciences
Basham, Katherine	English (Head)	College of Liberal Arts, Duluth Campus
Bates, Frank S.	Chemical Engineering and Materials Science (Head)	Institute of Technology
Bearinger, Linda H.	Center of Adolescent Nursing (Director)	School of Nursing
Ben-Ner, Avner	Industrial Relations Center (Director)	Curtis L. Carlson School of Management
Bernlohr, David A.	Biochemistry, Molecular Biology, and Biophysics (Head)	College of Biological Sciences; Medical School

Name	Discipline (Title)	Institute, School, or College
Boyd, John H.	Finance (Chair)	Curtis L. Carlson School of Management
Campbell, John P.	Psychology (Chair)	College of Liberal Arts
Collins, Terence G.	Academic Affairs and Curriculum (Director)	General College
Eidman, Vernon R.	Applied Economics (Head)	College of Agricultural, Food, and Environmental Sciences
Ek, Alan R.	Forest Resources (Head)	College of Natural Resources
Farber, Daniel	Law (Associate Dean for Faculty and Research)	Law School
Feldman, Roger D.	Health Services Research and Policy (Professor)	School of Public Health
Garavaso, Pieranna	Philosophy (Assistant Chair of Humanities Division)	Division of Humanities, Morris Campus
Gengenbach, Burle G.	Agronomy and Plant Genetics (Head)	College of Agricultural, Food, and Environmental Sciences
Gladfelter, Wayne L.	Chemistry (Chair)	Institute of Technology
Hicks, Randall E.	Biology (Head)	College of Science and Engineering, Duluth Campus
Hogan, M. Janice	Family Social Science (Head)	College of Human Ecology
Houston, Michael J.	Marketing and Logistics Management (Chair)	Curtis L. Carlson School of Management
Klinger, Eric	Psychology (Discipline Coordinator)	Division of Social Sciences, Morris Campus
Knopp, Jr., Lawrence M.	Geography (Head)	College of Liberal Arts, Duluth Campus
Leppert, Richard	Cultural Studies and Comparative Literature (Chair)	College of Liberal Arts
Loh, Horace H.	Pharmacology (Head)	Medical School
Luepker, Russell V.	Epidemiology (Head)	School of Public Health
Maheswaran, Samuel K.	Veterinary Pathobiology (Acting Chair)	College of Veterinary Medicine
Masten, Ann S.	Institute of Child Development (Director)	College of Education and Human Development

Name	Discipline (Title)	Institute, School, or College
McEvoy, Mary A.	Educational Psychology (Chair)	College of Education and Human Development
McMurry, Peter H.	Mechanical Engineering (Head)	Institute of Technology
Moller, James H.	Pediatrics (Head)	Medical School
Pharis, Mark W.	Art (Chair)	College of Liberal Arts
Ravdin, Jonathan I.	Medicine (Chair)	Medical School
Simone, Donald A.	Oral Sciences (Chair)	School of Dentistry
Sterner, Robert W.	Ecology, Evolution, and Behavior (Head)	College of Biological Sciences
Sullivan, E. Thomas	Law (Dean)	Law School
Vayda, Patricia M.	Diagnostic/Surgical Science (Chair)	School of Dentistry
Warthesen, Joseph J.	Food Science and Nutrition (Head)	College of Agricultural, Food, and Environmental Sciences; College of Human Ecology

Study Participants, Alphabetized by Discipline _____

Discipline	Name	Institute, School, or College
Agronomy and Plant Genetics	Gengenbach, Burle G.	College of Agricultural, Food, and Environmental Sciences
Applied Economics	Eidman, Vernon R.	College of Agricultural, Food, and Environmental Sciences
Art	Pharis, Mark W.	College of Liberal Arts
Biochemistry, Molecular Biology, and Biophysics	Bernlohr, David A.	College of Biological Sciences; Medical School
Biology	Hicks, Randall E.	College of Science and Engineering, Duluth Campus
Chemical Engineering and Materials Science	Bates, Frank S.	Institute of Technology
Chemistry	Gladfelter, Wayne L.	Institute of Technology
Child Development	Masten, Ann S.	College of Education and Human Development
Clinical and Population Sciences	Ames, Trevor R.	College of Veterinary Medicine

Discipline	Name	Institute, School, or College
Cultural Studies and Comparative Literature	Leppert, Richard	College of Liberal Arts
Diagnostic/Surgical Science	Vayda, Patricia M.	School of Dentistry
Ecology, Evolution, and Behavior	Sterner, Robert W.	College of Biological Sciences
Educational Psychology	McEvoy, Mary A.	College of Education and Human Development
English	Basham, Katherine	College of Liberal Arts, Duluth Campus
Entomology	Ascerno, Mark E.	College of Agricultural, Food, and Environmental Sciences
Epidemiology	Luepker, Russell V.	School of Public Health
Family Social Science	Hogan, M. Janice	College of Human Ecology
Finance	Boyd, John H.	Curtis L. Carlson School of Management
Food Science and Nutrition	Warthesen, Joseph J.	College of Agricultural, Food, and Environmental Sciences; College of Human Ecology
Forest Resources	Ek, Alan R.	College of Natural Resources
General College, Academic Affairs, and Curriculum	Collins, Terence G.	General College
Geography	Knopp, Jr., Lawrence M.	College of Liberal Arts, Duluth Campus
Health Services Research and Policy	Feldman, Roger D.	School of Public Health
Industrial Relations	Ben-Ner, Avner	Curtis L. Carlson School of Management
Law	Sullivan, E. Thomas	Law School
Law	Farber, Daniel	Law School
Marketing and Logistics Management	Houston, Michael J.	Curtis L. Carlson School of Management
Mechanical Engineering	McMurry, Peter H.	Institute of Technology
Medicine	Ravdin, Jonathan I.	Medical School
Nursing	Bearinger, Linda H.	School of Nursing
Oral Sciences	Simone, Donald A.	School of Dentistry

Discipline	Name	Institute, School, or College
Pediatrics	Moller, James H.	Medical School
Pharmacology	Loh, Horace H.	Medical School
Philosophy	Garavaso, Pieranna	Division of Humanities, Morris Campus
Psychology (Morris campus)	Klinger, Eric	Division of Social Sciences, Morris Campus
Psychology (Twin Cities campus)	Campbell, John P.	College of Liberal Arts
Public Affairs	Archibald, Sandra O.	Hubert H. Humphrey Institute of Public Affairs
Veterinary Pathobiology	Maheswaran, Samuel K.	College of Veterinary Medicine

1

Blueprint for This Book: A Literature-Based Model of the Research-Productive Organization

While at a distance the research enterprise looks like a highly robust entity, upon closer inspection it is revealed to be a delicate structure highly dependent on the existence and effective working of numerous individual, organizational, and leadership characteristics.

(Bland & Ruffin, 1992, p. 395)

This book evolved from a desire to help higher education faculty remain vital, stimulated, and highly productive in their work life, particularly in their role as researchers. How is faculty excellence in research nurtured? What specific strategies can leaders in academia use to create an environment in which their faculty researchers will not just survive, but thrive, and do so continually, year after year? These are the pressing issues addressed in this text.

In ensuing chapters we describe a diverse array of structures and practices (e.g., in areas such as faculty recruitment, goal setting, mentoring, faculty rewards, and resource allocation) for creating a work environment that strongly supports its faculty's research-related activities. We collected this information by tapping into the shared experiences of nearly 40 leaders in higher education (department heads/chairs and deans), all of whom hail from highly research-productive, and highly ranked, departments. We conducted semi-structured interviews with these leaders to probe for specific research-facilitating strategies that they considered critical to their faculty's success. Taken together, our qualitative findings constitute a very practical set of hands-on lessons learned or best practices which readers can apply as is or otherwise adapt for use with their own faculty, in their own institutions.

Our Blueprint: A Model of the Research-Productive Organization

The personal accounts of research-facilitating practices that we present in Chapters 2 through 14 have intrinsic value, but they take on greater meaning when cast within the empirical framework that guided our qualitative research. This framework is an existing literature-based model for understanding how to maximize research productivity in a group or organization (Bland & Bergquist, 1997; Bland & Ruffin, 1992). The primary purpose of this introductory chapter, therefore, is to briefly acquaint our busy readers with this model of the research-productive organization. The model undergirded our qualitative study design and is subsequently reinforced (and expanded on) in the remaining chapters of this book.

In essence, this model serves as the blueprint linking the multiple themes that come to bear on the research productivity of an organization and its members. According to the model, previously developed by the first author and her colleagues and based on more than 40 years of empirical work by many researchers, there is a defined set of research-facilitating characteristics which, when carefully attended to by any number of diverse strategies, can yield high levels of productivity that are sustainable over time. These research-facilitating characteristics fall into three general domains:

1) The characteristics of the individual researcher (faculty member)

2) The structure/environment in which the researcher finds himself or herself (department, college, or university)

3) The leadership of the organization (department head/chair, dean, etc.) in which the research is being conducted

These three "pillars of productivity" act together as an interdependent whole to support the overall structure of the research enterprise. They influence one another, and all characteristics need to be present to create the most productive research organization. A brief overview of the literature from which the model was created is provided next.

Individual Characteristics That Facilitate Research

Numerous studies outline the characteristics of successful researchers (Blackburn, Behymer, & Hall, 1978; Bland & Bergquist, 1997; Bland & Schmitz, 1986; Pelz & Andrews, 1966; Taylor et al., 2001; Tschannen-Moran, Firestone, Hoy, & Johnson, 2000; Wheeler & Creswell, 1985). They include such factors as socialization to academic values and norms, a strong motivation to create new knowledge, competence in their content area, well-developed research skills, engagement in simultaneous projects, committed involvement in both institutional and discipline-specific activities (i.e., orientation), a balance between institutional commitment and individualism or autonomy, and scholarly work habits. Each of these characteristics is defined in Figure 1.1.

Figure 1.1

Individual Features

I N D I V I D U A L

1) *Socialization.* Understands the values, norms, expectations, and sanctions affecting established faculty (e.g., beneficence, academic freedom)

2) *Motivation.* Driven to explore, understand, and follow one's own ideas and to advance and contribute to society through innovation, discovery, and creative works

3) *Content knowledge.* Familiar—within one's research area—with all major published works, projects being conducted, differing theories, key researchers, and predominant funding sources

4) *Basic and advanced research skills.* Comfortable with statistics, study design, data collection methods, and advanced methods commonly used in one's area

5) *Simultaneous projects.* Engaged in multiple, concurrent projects so as to buffer against disillusionment if one project stalls or fails

6) *Orientation.* Committed to external activities (e.g., regional and national meetings, collaborating with colleagues) and activities within one's own organization (e.g., curriculum planning, institutional governance)

7) *Autonomy and commitment.* Has academic freedom, plans one's own time, and sets one's own goals, but is also committed to and plays a meaningful role within the larger organization

8) *Work habits.* Has established productive scholarly habits early in one's career

Environmental Characteristics
That Facilitate Research

Although these characteristics of the individual researcher are essential to one's productivity, they are not sufficient in and of themselves. Of all the factors that affect an academic's productivity, none are as powerful as the environmental features of the workplace (Clark & Lewis, 1985).

Work by Pellino, Boberg, Blackburn, and O'Connell (1981) is illustrative of the studies in this area:

> [In higher education, the] place of employment is the single best predictor of faculty scholarly productivity.... Faculty [members] who come to productive surroundings produce more there than they did before they arrived and more than they will later if they move to a less productive environment. Resources, support, challenge, communication with producers on other campuses, all correlate with a professor's productivity. (p. 26)

Other studies have echoed this (Blackburn, 1979; Bland, Hitchcock, Anderson, & Stritter, 1987; Bland, Seaquist, Pacala, Center, & Finstad, 2002; Dundar & Lewis, 1998; Long & McGinnis, 1981; McGee & Ford, 1987; Perkoff, 1986; Perry, Clifton, Menec, Struthers, & Menges, 2000; Teodorescu, 2000). Their results reveal that productive academic organizations have a consistent set of features: targeted recruitment and selection of driven faculty researchers; clear goals that serve a coordinating function and heavily emphasize research; a strong academic culture; a positive group climate; mentoring for junior faculty; frequent communication between faculty and their professional networks; sufficient and accessible resources; substantial, uninterrupted time for research; a critical mass of faculty who have been together for a while and who bring different perspectives to the mix; adequate and fair salaries and other rewards; proactive brokering of opportunities for all faculty; and a decentralized organization. Each of these environmental characteristics is defined in Figure 1.2.

Leadership Characteristics
That Facilitate Research

Effective leadership is a particularly important characteristic of research-productive organizations. To quote Blackburn (1979), when it comes to research

Figure 1.2
Institutional Features That Facilitate Research Productivity

1) *Recruitment and selection.* Great effort is expended to recruit and hire members who have the training, goals, commitment, and socialization that match the institution.

2) *Clear goals.* Visible, shared goals coordinate members' work; research has priority greater than or equal to other goals.

3) *Culture.* Members are bonded by shared, research-related values and practices, have a safe home for testing new ideas.

4) *Positive group climate.* The climate is characterized by high morale, a spirit of innovation, dedication to work, receptivity to new ideas, frequent interactions, high degree of cooperation, low member turnover, good leader/member relationships, and open discussion of disagreements.

5) *Mentoring.* Beginning and midlevel members are assisted by and collaborate with established scholars.

6) *Communication.* Members have frequent and substantive (not merely social) communication, both impromptu and formal, with research peers inside and outside of the institution.

7) *Resources.* Members have access to sufficient resources such as funding, facilities, and especially humans (e.g., local peers for support, research assistants, technical consultants).

8) *Work time.* Members have significant periods of uninterrupted time to devote to scholarly activities.

9) *Diversity (expertise, size).* Members offer different perspectives by virtue of differences in their degree levels, approaches to problems, and discipline backgrounds; the group is stable, and its size is at or above a critical mass.

10) *Rewards.* Research is rewarded equitably and in accordance with defined benchmarks of achievement; potential rewards include money, promotion, recognition, and new responsibilities.

11) *Brokered opportunities.* Professional development opportunities are routinely and proactively offered to members, assuring their continued growth and vitality.

12) *Decentralized organization.* Governance structures are flat and decentralized, but supported by clear and common goals, assertive and participative leadership, and feedback systems.

productivity, "Nearly every positively correlated factor resides in administrative hands" (p. 26).

Prior studies of research-productive organizations have found that effective leaders are themselves highly skilled researchers, with the ability to influence members' knowledge and values, to facilitate contacts and networks, to help colleagues who are stalled in their research efforts, and so on (Andrews, 1979; Dill, 1982, 1985, 1986b; Drew, 1985; Sindermann, 1985). Other studies report that the background and leadership behaviors of the leaders can have an influence on members' satisfaction and the overall group climate (Andrews, 1979).

Notably, it is the leader who influences the presence or absence of all of the other institutional characteristics. For example, leaders can play key roles in facilitating a clear vision for the organization. They might be called on to raise funds to ensure that faculty have the necessary resources for their research. And they manage the day-to-day workings of the department, from budgets, to space, to people.

Leader-member relations are, ideally, based on mutual confidence in one another's competence, rather than on power (Pineau & Levy-Leboyer, 1983). Effective leaders use an assertive participative governance style, in which there are formal mechanisms and expectations for all group members to participate in decision-making. High-quality information about the organization is readily available. Members feel their ideas are valued, and they have a sense of ownership and involvement in the future of the organization.

The overarching profile of the effective leader is one who facilitates group productivity through the pairing of common goals (and some structure) with highly participative governance (Birnbaum, 1983; Dill, 1986a, 1986b; Epton, Payne, & Pearson, 1983; Hoyt & Spangler, 1978; Locke, Fitzpatrick, & White, 1983; Pelz & Andrews, 1966; Pineau & Levy-Leboyer, 1983). This profile is summarized in Figure 1.3.

Putting It All Together

On the whole, this body of literature on research-productive organizations can be distilled down to two key messages:

- First, a diverse set of individual, environmental, and leadership characteristics contributes to the research productivity of an organization. Individuals' success in research depends on their knowledge, skills, and motivation, but also hinges on the depth and breadth of support provided by their home institutions. This support can take the form of resources (personnel,

---

Figure 1.3

Leadership Features That Facilitate Research Productivity

1) Highly regarded as a scholar; serves as a sponsor, mentor, and peer model for other group members

2) Possesses a "research orientation"; has internalized the group's research-centered mission

3) Capably fulfills all critical leadership roles (e.g., manager of people and resources, fundraiser, group advocate, keeper of the vision)

4) Keeps the group's mission and shared goals visible to all members

5) Uses an assertive, participative style of leadership:

- Holds frequent meetings with clear objectives
- Creates formal mechanisms and sets expectations for all members to contribute to decision-making
- Makes high-quality information readily available to the group
- Vests ownership of projects with members and values their ideas

6) Successfully initiates structures for attending to the many individual and institutional features that facilitate research productivity

---

funding), protected work time, culture-building activities, coordinating goals, leadership styles, and a host of other environmental factors—most of which are leveraged by department heads/chairs and other academic leaders.

- Second, and most important, these many individual, environmental, and leadership characteristics operate as an interdependent whole. They are broad-reaching, mutually reinforcing, and synergistic. In other words, the highest levels of research productivity are achieved when all characteristics are present and when there is a successful interplay between them.

Figure 1.4 encapsulates how all of the individual, institutional, and leadership characteristics work together to facilitate high levels of research productivity. In academic settings this productivity is manifested in the form of innovations, grants, articles, books, discoveries, creative works, a satisfied faculty, and more.

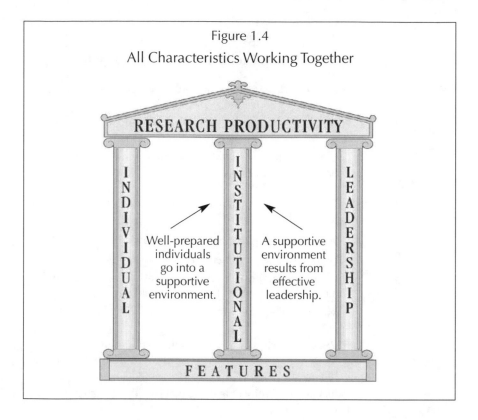

Figure 1.4

All Characteristics Working Together

Why Read On?

Thus far we have provided readers with the proverbial big picture—an overarching model of the research-productive organization, derived from the scholarly literature defining the many correlates/predictors of research productivity. However, naming a correlate/predictor of research productivity is one thing; putting it into practice is quite another. Consider the following:

- We know from the model that having clear organizational goals that guide members' work is an important environmental characteristic for facilitating research. But how, in practical terms, are an academic department's goals and research priorities established? How are they communicated and reinforced?

- We know that researchers need sufficient work time. But what specific strategies do highly research-productive departments actually apply to maximize the time their faculty are engaged in research-related activities? How is a workable balance between research and teaching achieved?

- We know that productive faculty need to have frequent, substantive conversations with their research peers. But how do departments actively
  promote this type of regular interchange within their walls and halls?
  How do they help faculty to expand and strengthen their professional
  relationships with colleagues in other institutions?

Finding answers to these and a host of other pragmatic questions was the
driving force behind our research. What we found is that there is no single path-
way by which a department achieves research excellence. Rather, as will be
shown in the chapters to come, academic leaders can (and do) draw from a wide
range of structures and strategies to facilitate their faculty's success in research.
Moreover, their choice of strategies depends on a host of local factors such as the
type of academic discipline, the size of the department, available funding for
research-linked initiatives, and even the proximity of faculty members' offices.

We know, from previously presenting the research-productivity model to
different audiences at higher education conferences, that faculty and administrators are eager for these kinds of strategic details. They want to know not
just the characteristics of research-productive institutions, but also *how* other
departments have successfully adopted these essential characteristics. They
want examples of specific strategies they might use or adapt to increase
research productivity in their setting.

We also know that department heads/chairs—those typically responsible
for facilitating research—are among our busiest faculty. As such, most have
had little opportunity (beyond their personal, on-the-job experience) to learn
about the many diverse, oftentimes creative methods that are being successfully applied by their peers. This book represents an effort to meet this important need. In these pages, readers will find numerous examples of how academic leaders from a wide range of disciplines have actually put into practice—to good effect—this set of research-facilitating characteristics.

Overview of Our Qualitative Research Methods _____

Our experimental approach was to interview the leaders (heads, chairs, deans)
of 37 highly research-productive and highly ranked departments/schools at
our institution, the University of Minnesota. Interviews were conducted
between April 2001 and November 2001. Using a semistructured protocol, we
asked the leaders of each of these distinct academic units to tell us which of the
research-facilitating characteristics they deemed most important, and how
these characteristics are actually manifest in their settings, whether through

specific programs, policies, allocation of resources, and so on. Interviews were taped and transcribed. We coded participants' responses into themes and wove them into a narrative that is rich in detail and experience based.

A full description of our study design, analytic methods, pre-interview survey, interview protocol, and participant demographic survey is provided in Appendixes A–D.

How Can I Apply These Lessons Learned to My Own Institution?

Although our data are drawn from academic leaders at one institution, our findings have relevance to other postsecondary colleges and universities. Consider the following:

- First, ours is a very large, comprehensive institution, comprising 23 colleges on four campuses in urban, semi-urban, and rural settings. The participants in our study represent a wide range of college types: a two-year general college, a rural four-year liberal arts college, a land-grant school, a branch campus, and multiple professional schools in areas such as dentistry, law, and business. A further description of the University of Minnesota is provided in Appendix F.

- Second, the interviewed faculty represent a highly diverse set of disciplines. Our sample includes scholars in liberal arts, the humanities, engineering, physical science, public health, social science, education, biological and natural sciences, economics, medicine, law, agricultural science, veterinary science, and more. Additional diversity in our sample makeup is evidenced by large differences in important demographic characteristics such as size (number of faculty), student population (undergraduate and/or graduate), annual budget, and geographic makeup (proximity of faculty offices). Descriptive statistics for these and other characteristics of our sample are provided in Appendix E.

- Third, although these departments differ in discipline, size, resources, college type, and location, they all have one very important thing in common: By the standards of their field, their faculty are not just productive in research—they excel in research. In other words, these departments were not drawn as a representative sample of departments at the University of Minnesota; rather, they are examples of departments ranked nationally

> At the time of the interviews, 9 of the 37 participating departments were rated in the top 5% in their field, and 14 were in the top 10%.

for their research capacity and accomplishments—the very source from which strategies for facilitating research can be drawn and disseminated.

- Finally, and perhaps most important, we are confident that others will benefit from reading this body of work because members of our intended readership have repeatedly told us so. In the course of analyzing our data, we presented our preliminary findings at several national meetings on higher education. Each time we made it a point to ask our listeners, "Is this information useful to you and others in your college or university?" The response was a consistent and overwhelming "yes." Our listeners told us they were able to use our information in one or more of the following ways:

1) They picked out several research-facilitating strategies that they could immediately take home and use as presented.

2) They thought of ways to readily adapt information from our study to fit within their particular organizational culture.

3) After hearing about a particular finding, they were led to conceive of an entirely different strategy that would work best in their setting.

4) They used the research-productivity model to do a needs assessment of their department and identify areas needing improvement.

Encouraging this type of inspired yet practical thinking is the desired outcome of our work.

That said, context is important to consider, particularly in qualitative research where the context is part of the data and where a description of the context is a required component of study reports (Creswell, 2002; Miles & Huberman, 1994). Recognizing this, we made a concerted effort in creating our narrative to facilitate readers' interpretations of our findings. For example, when the interviewed department leaders explained their rationale for adopting a particular approach or strategy, we provide that information. Each time a participant is quoted, we identify his/her home department, institute, or school to provide a disciplinary context. Lastly, in Appendix E we provide descriptive statistics for our study's participating departments, and in Appendix F we include a brief description of the University of Minnesota—its many campuses, colleges, and schools. In doing so, we provide readers with a flavor of the type of setting in which our study was conducted. We anticipate that this will help readers judge how best to apply the described strategies to their unique environment.

A Preview of Chapters 2–15 _____

The remaining text is organized into chapters which mirror the many environmental characteristics from the research-productivity model described above, as well as two new themes (the importance of teaching and collaborative research) which emerged from our qualitative data set. In each chapter, additional literature related to that characteristic is presented. This is followed by a description of ways in which that characteristic is implemented in the highly research-productive departments from our study. In some instances, we also describe the implementation challenges that they face. Each chapter concludes with a more generic overview of our key qualitative findings.

Although this book focuses primarily on the environmental characteristics of research-productive departments, it does not neglect the many individual and leadership characteristics that also contribute to an organization's success. The individual characteristics predictive of research productivity are addressed in this book, most substantially in Chapter 2. Leadership and governance are also addressed separately, and quite extensively, in Chapter 14.

We ordered the chapters so that the first five (2 through 6) reflect the characteristics most frequently cited by our study participants when asked the initial interview question, "In your assessment, what are the key factors that contribute to the research productivity of your faculty?" The dominant characteristics that emerged are as follows:

Chapter 2: Faculty Recruitment and Selection (24 responses)
Chapter 3: Clear Goals That Coordinate Work and Emphasize Research (16 responses)
Chapter 4: Shared Culture and Positive Group Climate (10 responses)
Chapter 5: Mentoring (4 responses)
Chapter 6: Interdisciplinary Collaboration (4 responses)

The remaining chapters were placed in no particular sequence:

Chapter 7: Communication With Colleagues: Professional Networks
Chapter 8: Resources
Chapter 9: Teaching
Chapter 10: Sufficient Time for Research
Chapter 11: Rewards
Chapter 12: Brokered Opportunity Structure
Chapter 13: Faculty Size and Diversity: The Right Mix of Expertise and Experience

Chapter 14: Leadership and Governance
Chapter 15: Final Take-Home Lessons

Each chapter can successfully stand alone, but we strongly encourage readers to review this book in its entirety. Many of the research-facilitating characteristics, though separated into discrete chapters, overlap extensively with one another. Moreover, as demonstrated by the literature-based model that undergirds this study, research productivity cannot be maintained by focusing on just one characteristic (e.g., setting clear research goals, attending to group climate). Rather, all must be nurtured to create the *most* research-productive organization.

2

Faculty Recruitment and Selection

In real estate, what is important is location, location, location.
For research productivity, it is the people, people, people.

(Horace Loh, Pharmacology)

LITERATURE SUMMARY
Research-productive departments spend extraordinary time and effort recruiting faculty whose specific training, socialization, commitment, and goals match those of the department.

DEPARTMENT PRACTICES COVERED IN THIS CHAPTER
1) What individual characteristics do departments look for in faculty candidates?
2) How common is it for departments to hire faculty whose expertise meets certain needs or aligns with certain priority areas? How are such areas selected?
3) What strategies are used to identify the best faculty candidates?
4) What strategies are used to attract the best faculty candidates?
5) How do departments successfully retain their faculty who are being recruited away by other institutions?

What Does the Literature Say?_____

According to the literature, a defining environmental characteristic of research-productive organizations is their practice of spending extraordinary time and effort in recruiting new members (Dill, 1985, 1986a, 1986b; Zuckerman, 1977). Particularly notable is that these organizations go to great lengths to recruit members who possess precisely those individual traits shown to predict research productivity (e.g., strongly motivated to conduct research, highly skilled in research, well-socialized to the academic environment). Departmental leadership also comes into play, given that the successful recruitment of desirable faculty candidates can depend heavily on the research reputation of the department head, as well as his/her demonstrated ability to leverage research resources, keep research goals visible, and routinely use a participative governance style. (For additional literature on leadership's influence on an organization's research productivity, see Chapter 14.)

These findings illustrate a key point: With respect to recruitment, there is a particularly vivid interplay between the three components of the literature-based model of the research-productive organization presented in Chapter 1. In light of this, it is not surprising that faculty recruitment and selection emerged as the dominant theme in our qualitative study of highly research-productive academic departments. When department leaders in our study were asked to name the top three factors that contributed to their unit's productivity, their most frequently cited response was the appropriate selection of new faculty. "That is the thing we obsess over the most," said one. Another noted, "When we haven't made a good hire, the person hasn't worked out no matter what we have done."

Our primary goal for this chapter is to describe the many specific strategies used by these highly research-productive departments to recruit and select promising faculty researchers. In doing so, we are focusing on recruitment as an environmental characteristic. Yet, our description of these recruitment practices would be incomplete without first summarizing for readers the salient literature that defines and identifies the many individual characteristics of the productive researcher. Why? Because a key determinant of whom these departments ultimately hire is their assessment of whether a faculty candidate possesses these correlates/predictors of research success (Bland & Schmitz, 1986). In other words, departments looking to hire strong researchers want to know:

- Are the candidates socialized to academic values and norms?

- Are they highly motivated to conduct research?

- Do they have an in-depth knowledge of their research area, plus basic and advanced research skills?

- Do they plan to engage in simultaneous research projects?

- Have they demonstrated an internal and external orientation, that is, a commitment to activities both within and outside of their organization?

- Do they exercise autonomy in their work, but also have a meaningful commitment to their host institution?

- Do they have productive work habits?

This is the only chapter that explicitly focuses on these individual characteristics from the research productivity model. Thus, the literature review for this chapter is the most lengthy. Nonetheless, we highly recommend that readers take the time to explore this overview, because it sets the stage for the subsequent Department Practices section. In that section, we describe, using our qualitative data from the interviewed department leaders, an array of best practices which can be applied to actually find, attract, and retain faculty members who possess these desirable qualities.

Socialization

The successful faculty member, especially the successful researcher, has learned and embraces the values, norms, expectations, and sanctions of the academic profession. One dominant value of academics, for example, is serving society through objectivity, truthfulness, beneficence, and academic freedom. Several studies find that a faculty member's level of academic socialization is the fundamental and most powerful predictor of his or her research productivity (Wheeler & Creswell, 1985). For example, Corcoran and Clark (1984) studied two faculty groups—63 faculty members who were "highly active" in teaching, research, and service, and 66 randomly selected tenured faculty who were matched to the highly active faculty on rank and age. There were significant differences between these two groups with regard to socialization. For example, when asked what was satisfying about work, the first group consistently reported two things: academic freedom and the ability to contribute through research. These aspects of faculty work were not, however, regularly cited by the representative group. The impact of professional values on productivity cannot be underestimated. In highly developed professions, these unwritten rules, concepts, values, and behaviors undergird nearly every action.

Personal Motivation

The productive researcher is driven to explore, understand, and follow his or her own ideas and believes he or she has a responsibility to advance and contribute to society through innovation, discovery, and creative works. Studies of scientists have found that internal motivation plays a pivotal role in their productivity. Those researchers who are driven in their work by a personal desire are more productive (Tschannen-Moran, Firestone, Hoy, & Johnson, 2000). This was vividly illustrated in a recent survey of 465 faculty in a highly research-oriented medical school (Bland, Seaquist, Pacala, Center, & Finstad, 2002). One item in the survey asked how strongly a faculty member agreed with the statement, "I am driven to conduct research" (1 = strongly disagree, 5 = strongly agree). The most common response to this item was "4." However, those faculty who were highly productive (had published over five articles in the last two years) consistently perceived their research drive to be "very strong" and marked this item "5." This difference in passion for research was so consistent for highly productive researchers, compared to other faculty, that of all the items on the survey, a faculty member's rating on this one item turned out to be the best predictor of his or her level of research productivity. The development of strong inner motivation is important in ensuring productivity over a life span. Pelz and Andrews (1966) reported that older scientists who maintained their productivity also had maintained their high level of motivation.

In-Depth Knowledge of Research Area; Basic and Advanced Skills in Research Area

Without question, to be a highly effective faculty member one needs to be up to date and knowledgeable about one's content area and in one's skills relevant to teaching, research, and service (Lee, Ognibene, & Schwartz, 1991; Taylor et al., 2001). Productive faculty members are familiar with all major published works in their area, with the current major projects being conducted, and with differing theories, key researchers, and predominant funding sources. Moreover, they are comfortable with basic statistics, study design, and data collection methods, and with more advanced design and data collection strategies commonly used in their research area. Studies do not find that age is the major predictor of being less up to date. In fact, studies have found age to be a positive predictor of research productivity, and that with regard to intellectual ability, currency, and motivation, there is no reason to expect less because of age (Bland & Bergquist, 1997; Lawrence & Blackburn, 1988; Perry, Clifton, Menec, Struthers, & Menges, 2000; Tosti-Vasey & Willis, 1991). Still, it is becoming increasingly difficult for all faculty to stay abreast of the exploding knowledge in most fields and the enormous continual changes in technology. In a matter of years, at any age, one can quickly be left behind in one's field. Thus, this is an area of concern for the continual vitality of all faculty. It is important to maintain a sense of momentum and growth among faculty members in order to avoid having to develop programs later to deal with disconnected, out-of-date, burned-out faculty.

Simultaneous Projects

Productive researchers are engaged in multiple, simultaneous projects. Evidence suggests that faculty are more productive if they pursue several research projects at once. If one project stalls or fails, another may prove successful, and faculty are thus buffered against the disillusionment that can occur when roadblocks appear during a difficult project (Hargens, 1978; Stinchcombe, 1966; Taylor, Locke, Lee, & Gist, 1984).

Orientation

Productive faculty are committed to both external and internal activities. External orientation involves attending regional and national meetings and collaborating with national colleagues. Internal orientation requires involvement within one's own organization, including curriculum planning, institutional governance, and similar activities. Early research suggested that prolific researchers were predominately externally oriented, rather than being oriented toward their institution; however, more recent work finds that these faculty, while highly active in external institutional activities such as disciplinary societies and conferences, are no less involved internally (Blackburn & Lawrence, 1986; Finkelstein, 1984). The Corcoran and Clark (1984) study described earlier, for example, revealed that highly active faculty were heavily involved with major decisions on campus such as governance and curriculum redesign.

Autonomy/Organizational Commitment

Productive faculty have academic freedom and the ability to work independently to plan their own time and set their own goals. They also play meaningful roles within their organizations and are valued as important contributors to the institution. Autonomy and independence are highly valued aspects of academic life. At the same time, being committed to and feeling a part of one's institution is a characteristic of productive faculty at any age, but particularly so for senior faculty (Braskamp & Associates, 1982). This tight-loose arrangement between an organization and its productive members is noted by several authors in business and higher education (Cole & Cole, 1967; Peters & Waterman, 1982). For example, studies on work commitment and involvement revealed that workers who keep progressing up the professional ladder maintain a higher level of work commitment compared to those who do not (Baldwin, 1990; Howard, 1984; Kanter, 1979). To quote Votruba (1990):

> ... faculty who conceive of themselves as among the "moving" rather than the "stuck" will be likely to keep their aspirations high, have positive self-esteem, work hard, take

appropriate risks, remain engaged in their interests, remain involved with their students and colleagues, and advocate constructive organizational change. (p. 218)

There is one exception to the positive impact of autonomy, and that is for new faculty. Katz (1978) found that having complete autonomy during a researcher's first year was a "most significant negative correlate."

The tie between productivity and commitment was recently highlighted in the corporate literature by Reichheld and Teal (1996) in their book, *The Loyalty Effect*. They describe a study that compared thriving companies with those that failed in our turbulent times. Companies with the highest employee retention rate earned the best profits. Notably, retention explained profit better than market share, scale, cost position, and other variables usually associated with competitive advantage.

Work Habits

It is essential for a faculty member to establish productive scholarly habits early in one's career. Evidence suggests that unless productive work habits take hold within the first five years of a junior faculty member's appointment, they

---

How Did Our Departments Match on These Traits?

All of the department heads/chairs in our study were asked to complete a pre-interview survey (Appendix B) that asked, "To what extent do each of the following research-facilitating characteristics [of the individual, institution, and leader] describe your department?" The six-point scale ranged from 0 = Not at all, to 5 = Completely.

For nearly all of the individual characteristics, participants' responses had a mean of over 4 indicating that their faculty did indeed match the profile of the highly productive researcher.

Characteristics of the Individual That Facilitate Research Productivity	Mean of Responses*
Socialization	4.03
Personal motivation	4.19
In-depth knowledge of research area	4.08
Basic and advanced research skills	4.29
Simultaneous projects	4.06
Orientation	3.86
Autonomy/organizational commitment	4.25
Work habits	4.19

* Six-point scale ranging from 0 = Not at all, to 5 = Completely.

are unlikely to be developed later. Lightfield (1971) looked at the publishing records of young sociologists in the first five and ten years after the completion of their doctorates. He found that frequent publications and numerous citations in the first five years predicted output in the second five years. Studies in other disciplines, such as physics and chemistry, have similarly found that few researchers who start their careers slowly ever become highly productive (Cole & Cole, 1967; Reskin, 1977).

Department Practices

We know from the literature summarized above that the research excellence of a department depends heavily on the quality of its faculty. This was confirmed in our interviews with the leaders of highly research-productive departments, who resoundingly declared that hiring the right faculty candidates is the key factor to developing and maintaining an environment conducive to research. Consider these illustrative comments from Houston (Marketing and Logistics Management):

> I spend a lot of time on hiring, because being a great department all begins with that. I am not talking about a department that is good for a couple of years—I am talking about a department that sustains research productivity over decades. An excellent department for research develops well-regarded, highly visible senior faculty, and then hires junior faculty who are better than them.

The question then arises, how *do* highly research-productive departments approach the recruitment process to ensure they attract faculty with the personal characteristics that predict productivity in research? The answer to this important question extends beyond the routine mechanics that lay the groundwork for any hire (e.g., setting up a search committee, developing a position description, and placing national advertisements). What makes the difference, as will be shown below, is that these departments apply very strict criteria in assessing candidates. They take care to determine, in advance, the areas in which they need to hire. They adopt multiple strategies for identifying and attracting the best candidates. And they make retention a priority, so as to keep current faculty with successful research records from being recruited away by other institutions.

What Individual Characteristics Do
Departments Look for in Faculty Candidates?

Certainly, the specific content knowledge and research skills looked for in new faculty hires vary with the type of department and position. But there are common criteria that these highly research-productive departments seek. Not surprisingly, several of these mirror the individual characteristics that the literature finds associated with research productivity. Chief among the criteria identified by the interviewed department leaders were the following:

- Strong motivation to conduct research

- Demonstrated research experience (seasoned researchers)

- Good fit between candidate and department

- Ability to collaborate

- Highest standard of excellence

- Strong teaching skills

Strong motivation to conduct research. All departments, when seeking to fill a faculty position that involves research responsibilities, include "high research motivation" in their search criteria. But in the most highly research-productive departments, search committees look for an important order-of-magnitude difference in a candidate's passion for research. One department head in our study said that when he asks potential faculty members about their future goals, he expects to hear them talk about wanting to be the leading researcher in the world or planning to solve the key problem in their content area. In contrast, candidates are not thought to be sufficiently research driven—and thus not a good fit for the department—if they say they merely want to be good in research or to have a balanced career in which they are effective in both research and teaching. Ravdin (Medicine) put it this way: "I only recruit faculty who are as interested, motivated, and committed to the academic mission as I am." This essential quality in a recruit was reiterated again and again by the department leaders in our study, as illustrated by these quotes from various disciplines:

- "Passion for research is critical." (Family Social Science)

- "The key factor is to have motivated faculty who are ambitious." (Entomology)

- "This department looks for new faculty who are very creative, interesting thinkers, first and foremost, as well as high-energy and passionate about what they are doing." (Child Development)

- "The key factor is hiring very good people who are motivated to do research." (Applied Economics)

Seasoned researcher. Coming into a faculty position with a high motivation for research is, without question, essential to one's productivity. But also needed is the ability to successfully persevere and follow through on that motivation, that is, to transform one's energy and creativity into a tangible research plan, completed projects, new knowledge, grants, research articles, books, patents, and so forth. Several department leaders in our study described having learned the hard way about hiring faculty with research potential but only a limited record of research success. Hogan (Family Social Science) recalled hiring a recent graduate of an excellent program in a research-oriented institution who had not yet published much or acquired grants. She found that this faculty member could not hit the ground running as could other new faculty members with more experience. This lesson has changed their approach to recruitment: "Now we are a lot more cautious about assuming that they can succeed just because they came from a 'good' institution. . . . Now we look for experience."

Often, highly research-productive departments are looking for candidates who have research experience as demonstrated in an actual faculty role, not just work as a graduate student. To quote McEvoy (Educational Psychology): "Our preference is to recruit midlevel people who are young in their career, meaning three or four years . . . and have demonstrated an ability to secure external funds, and have a clearly defined line of research." This is not to say that these departments never hire recently prepared faculty. But this is less often the case, and when it is done, it is done very carefully. For example, McEvoy explained that if they do take a recently trained person, it is one who has demonstrated his or her ability to succeed within the demands of a research-oriented institution.

Good fit between candidate and department. Departments leaders spoke with particular passion about the importance of assessing how a potential faculty member will fit into their organization. Leppert (Cultural Studies and Comparative Literature) said he stresses the importance of fit very explicitly in their department's pre-interview process and in the manner in which he charges the search committee: "I instruct the committee that, at all levels, they are to look for a clear indication of collegiality." Others expressed a similar view:

- "We hire people who can be catalysts for other people. There is a certain amount of citizenship that goes into being a faculty member. We try to hire people for the long term, who will be good citizens—effective, supportive, helpful." (Forest Resources)

- "Once upon a time, we didn't pay a lot of attention to whether they [faculty members] were team players, a supporter of peers. Then we had two unfortunate hiring experiences. They were good scholars, but were unsupportive of graduate students and colleagues. Fortunately, they had offers from other institutions and left." (Psychology, Twin Cities campus)

- "In the interview stage we have taken people with the best written record and considered them unacceptable because they are not interactive enough.... I ask everyone I meet with, 'What are you looking for in a university?' If they don't say being interactive, or having diverse colleagues, or something like that, they get scored way down in my book." (Ecology, Evolution, and Behavior)

Some departments assess the fit by first interviewing candidates at national meetings and then bringing them to campus. The onsite visit provides additional opportunities to observe potential faculty members in person and across different settings. In most departments, candidates are given the opportunity to present their research and teach a seminar where they can be observed interacting with students and faculty. The visit usually includes a social event at which faculty can further familiarize themselves with the candidate and thus more carefully assess the suitability of the match.

Because the match involves two parties—the faculty candidate and the department—it is vital for departments to share with candidates their institution's defining culture and scholarly expectations. These discussions can help a candidate to decide if the position is an appropriate match for him or her. Sullivan (Law) said that when he is interviewing and extending an offer to candidates, he makes it clear what the school's values and behavior expectations are for faculty:

> I am very direct about [saying] if you are not comfortable with this image that I am portraying, then maybe this is the wrong place to be.... The fit is important. Maybe we are not the right place, but at least we have put it right out there up front.

Study participants also pointed out that it is a difficult balancing act to search for faculty who will fit well into their culture and environment, while at the same time wanting very much to bring in faculty who are passionate, creative, and have skills and perspectives not already present in the department. As Farber (Law) said,

> It is a collegial institution . . . and you don't want somebody who will destroy that. On the other hand, we are not primarily a social club. If somebody is really good, you strive to find ways to include them.

Ability to collaborate. Collegiality is clearly a desirable quality in faculty members working in highly research-productive departments. So, too, is a clear willingness to collaborate with other researchers. Numerous examples of this viewpoint were expressed in our interviews, including the following:

- "When we recruit a person, yes, we want to recruit a person for our own program, to strengthen that. But at the same time we have to think more broadly. What kinds of people can this person interact with across the university? I think that's very important." (Oral Sciences)

- "I tell new faculty this is a good place to work with other people. The fact that we put together a group makes us highly competitive for big grants. If you want to go off in a corner and do your own thing, there are plenty of positions in academe where you can do that, and they'll merit you for doing that. But that will not work here." (Epidemiology)

A few department heads/chairs commented specifically on the funding advantages of collaboration—and the importance of finding this quality in faculty recruits. For example, some departments frequently recruit jointly with other departments or research centers at the university. Through such partnerships, academic units can leverage resources and increase the attractiveness of faculty positions.

Even in the absence of formal partnerships, search committees can act informally to facilitate future collaborations involving their new faculty hires. Simply identifying (during the recruitment process) other local researchers who share the scholarly interests of a candidate can prove fruitful down the line. Smaller departments and schools seem particularly attuned to this practice. Their faculty members are, typically, less likely to have similar research interests to their immediate colleagues. Accordingly, these departments take extra care to locate and link their new hires with potential collaborators, be they internal or external to the institution. Consider these comments from Hicks (Biology):

> We are a small enough campus and department that they [faculty] may not have collaborators in the department. So we look for people who can find collaborators around our campus—for example, in the Natural Resources Research Institute or the School of Medicine, or in the larger research community such as NIH or the regional EPA research laboratory. We look for a good fit—not only how they fill a need in the department, but also how they may fit into the bigger community of researchers here.

The leaders in our study deemed collaboration to be so important to their faculty's productivity that collaboration surfaced as one of the dominant qualitative themes in our data set, despite its absence from our original literature-based model of research productivity and the interview protocol. The whole of Chapter 6 is devoted to this important environmental feature for promoting research productivity.

Highest standard of excellence. Hiring the best may seem an obvious recruitment tactic. Who wouldn't try to hire excellent faculty? But when these departments say they search for excellence in new faculty, they mean the best in the world. To quote Ben-Ner (Industrial Relations):

> The excellence that we sustain is attained through two measures—how hard we work on hiring the best people, and how hard we work on weeding out through the tenure process. . . . We seek excellence, and we recruit people on this criterion primarily. We retain people on this criterion primarily.

One specific mark of excellence that many departments look for in recruits is their involvement and expertise in research that matters. Houston (Marketing and Logistics Management) said, "We look for a person investigating something that is meaningful and worthy . . . worthy in terms of being an interesting issue, one we would hope would have impact on the field." Leppert (Cultural Studies and Comparative Literature) echoed this, saying, "The first criterion is what these folks bring to us intellectually. . . . Is their research not only going to generate new knowledge, but new knowledge that will actually matter to somebody?"

When recruiting new faculty, all of these highly research-productive departments set the research bar high—an order of magnitude higher than other departments. Their expectations for a faculty member's research productivity are demanding, and so they hire candidates who share and aspire to these same goals. Campbell (Psychology, Twin Cities campus) stated that a department's success in research hinges on hiring "people who fully intend to be world-class researchers. And they know that from the first day they walk through the door. Six years from now when their tenure consideration takes place, they will be known worldwide for something."

Strong teaching skills. Of course, a faculty member is not only a researcher—he or she also has interests and responsibilities in teaching, outreach, and service. Although this study focused exclusively on the research role of faculty, it was nonetheless quite clear that these highly research-productive departments look also for candidates who possess good teaching skills. For example, Campbell, who just above spoke of only hiring faculty who wanted to be world-class researchers, also said, "We expect faculty to be good teachers. All of our courses are taught by tenured or tenure-track faculty." Houston (Marketing and Logistics Management) agreed with this expectation for high-quality teaching, noting that, "the dominant focus in our hiring [process] is candidates' research qualifications, but this is not at the expense of teaching."

As will be described in Chapters 9 and 10, most highly research-productive departments use specific strategies to attend to the educational part of their mission. They strive to carefully manage their faculty's time in research and teaching so that both roles are done well, despite the challenges that this can incur.

How Common Is It for Departments to Hire Faculty Whose Expertise Meets Certain Needs or Aligns With Certain Priority Areas? How Are Such Areas Selected?

We learned from our interviews that the process of conducting a faculty search often begins with one key decision: Is the department focused on hiring someone with expertise in a particular content area, or is a more general, open-ended search within the broader discipline the best approach?

In some settings, focused searches are not the norm. Within the Law School, search committees do keep certain areas in mind, particularly if there are identified curriculum needs, but they prefer, explained Sullivan, to "focus more on finding a star and fitting around what he or she might teach." Similarly, in Chemical Engineering and Materials Science, "we generally like to recruit wide-open," said Bates. "We just want to hire smart and promising people. We would rather not specify an area."

These examples notwithstanding, the predominant practice among the departments that we studied was to recruit faculty within a specified area of need. Defining these areas can be difficult, however, and reaching agreement on them is no easy task. Even when faculty can agree on the hiring priorities, there are seldom enough funds to address them all. Department leaders shared some of the ways in which they define their hiring priority areas. Three common strategies and considerations emerged from our qualitative data set:

- Long-range strategic planning
- Potential for external funding
- Curricular needs

Long-range strategic planning. In our study sample, the most common approach to identifying a hiring area is long-range strategic planning. Precisely how this planning is done and the factors considered can vary by discipline and by the current situation.

The long-term hiring plans of the Department of Medicine were significantly shaped by factors unique to its local environment. These included the recently identified priority research areas of its larger organizational entities (the university's medical school and academic health center), as well as input collected from community-based physicians.

The priority faculty recruitment areas within General College were largely determined by external forces. Spurred on by an institutional reorganization plan in the late 1980s and by a threat to close the college in the mid-1990s, the faculty shifted to more of a research focus. Because the college is committed to underprepared students, their recruitment plans focused not just on faculty who were skilled in research, but more specifically on those whose research contributed to developmental education.

In Family Social Science, the hiring priorities in their strategic plan were influenced by their anticipated faculty retirements and the future need for new master's degree programs. Having defined hiring priorities in the long-range plan avoided possible conflict over which area would get a new position when a faculty member retired. This structure also allowed them to take advantage of an available person early, because they already knew the future areas in which they had planned to recruit.

In the Department of Psychology (Twin Cities campus), the chair and executive committee drafted a position paper that described the goals and initiatives the department should pursue during the next 10 to 15 years. This was used to stimulate conversation among faculty, and the final synthesis will be used to determine the areas in which future faculty are hired. This strategy should result in faculty being aware of future faculty needs for years to come.

Consequently, the department can avoid the problem of divisions vying for positions as people retire.

Potential for external funding. The availability of extramural funding in a potential recruit's research area is another important hiring consideration. In some departments, search committees pay close attention to whether the primary research interest of their faculty candidates are fundable:

- "If they are in areas that society has decided don't get money for whatever reason, or if that person has not been able to demonstrate who would ever fund their area, that is a consideration. No matter how good the idea is, unfortunately, if it's not fundable, we have to be very careful." (Food Science and Nutrition)

- "If you hire someone into an area that you think you or society needs, but there isn't any money out there, you are setting them up for failure." (Entomology)

According to Ascerno (Entomology) it is also important to keep a department fairly balanced in terms of its faculty's research interests. "It's like a portfolio of stocks," he explained. "It's useful to be diversified. For example, in the 1960s and 1970s, toxicology was a hot area. But hot areas change, so the department needs to be diversified so that indirect costs keep coming in to allow people to shift a bit when an area becomes cold." The value of having a diversified faculty with regard to their research interests, skills, and experience is discussed more fully in Chapter 13.

Curricular needs. Without question, the areas in which departments recruit can also be fiercely driven by their curriculum. In our study sample, this seemed particularly common in the professional schools, for example, in Medicine, Law, and the Veterinary Sciences. Ames (Clinical and Population Sciences) said, "We are so tied to curriculum and the needs of being AVMA accredited that if we're down a surgeon, then we are going to hire a surgeon. . . . I would say a lot of our hires in this department tend to be more driven by the clinical teaching demands."

What Strategies Are Used to Identify the Best Faculty Candidates?

When planning to fill a faculty position, these highly research-productive departments take the typical recruitment steps: they develop a position description, set up a search committee, and place ads in professional publications. What is notable about their recruitment approach, however, is their proactive engagement of additional strategies, all of which are aimed at identifying the best faculty candidates. These strategies, as identified by our study, are as follows:

- Extensively use networks.

- Use national recruiting mechanisms.

- Host visiting scholars.

- Hire in bunches.

- Adopt multiple approaches.

- Spend enormous attention and time on recruitment.

Extensively use networks. All successful researchers have an extensive network of colleagues with whom they regularly communicate. Departments can use these networks to good effect, tapping into them as a way of identifying possible new hires. Campbell (Psychology, Twin Cities campus) said, "We are mandated to use certain advertising outlets, of course, but we ourselves contact every place and every person who might have likely candidates in their own organization or who know of somebody." For the last search in the Department of Biology, they sent 375 email messages to colleagues and contacts. The head of Chemical Engineering and Materials Science tries to track promising candidates early in their careers (i.e., as undergraduate or graduate students), a practice that helps years later when it comes time to recruit junior faculty.

The use of networks can work particularly well when searching for specific characteristics in a faculty member. For example, at one point the Department of Family Social Science was searching for a marriage and family therapist, female, of color, with high research ability and potential. Finding such a candidate was facilitated by the department's existing collegial relations with several faculty of color around the country (developed largely through their summer teaching program that brings in outside faculty as guest teacher/scholars). In addition, faculty members personally called members of their professional network, asking for the names of people who matched this description. These people were then personally contacted and, if not themselves interested, were asked to suggest other potential candidates.

Use national recruiting mechanisms. Some departments are based in disciplines that have national mechanisms for assisting with recruitment. The American Association of Law Schools, for example, has centralized entry-level recruitment. All first-time candidates interested in a new faculty position complete the same application, and all law schools have access to the complete set of applications (via a printed compilation or a searchable electronic database). All recruiting law schools meet with candidates on a common weekend at a hotel in Washington, DC. This culminates in the schools inviting the few they are most interested in to visit their campus. Other disciplines use a similar approach, with search committees interviewing candidates at national meetings such as the American Marketing Association Educators' Conference or the Modern Language Association. This helps departments to narrow the applicant pool before extending invitations to visit the campus.

Host visiting scholars. Several department heads/chairs described their practice of periodically bringing visiting scholars into the department. This not only enriches their faculty's collegial network, but also helps to identify future faculty candidates. In some settings, all external faculty members brought in to make a presentation or to consult with the faculty are alerted to position openings at the university. This provides a safe mechanism for departments and candidates to try each other out.

Hire in bunches. Cohort recruiting is another successful hiring strategy used in General College. Collins described the advantages of this approach:

> We hire people in bunches, four or five at a time, and then we facilitate them to work in bunches, so they immediately have a very vital social connection. We bring them in a couple of weeks early on payroll so they can learn about the institution and each other before the rest of the faculty are around and school starts.

Adopt multiple approaches. All of the departments in our study are flexible in their approach to recruiting, taking different approaches when, for example, there are many candidates available versus a limited pool or when the timeline is constrained. Bernlohr explained that his department (Biochemistry, Molecular Biology, and Biophysics) had two search models in progress. One is a traditional search, in which a search committee is appointed in the fall, advertisements are placed, candidates are brought in during the year, and the position is filled by summer. For another position, they are running an open search whereby they are "simply beating the bushes, talking to people, bringing people in, until they find the right person."

Spend enormous attention and time on recruitment. One final, important commonality is that these highly research-productive departments have adopted a comprehensive, intensive approach to recruitment. This typically involves the collaborative efforts of faculty on the search committee and the department chair/head. Here is one example, from Bates (Chemical Engineering and

Materials Science) of the type of attention paid to their most promising faculty candidates:

> In the process of hiring _____, the last time he came back
> with his wife. I spent three or four solid days with them—
> showing them houses, having them to my home, going to
> other faculty members' homes—to help them understand
> who we are culturally. That part was the most time-inten-
> sive, and you do that for everybody. That kind of attention
> is not always going to work, but it gives you an opportunity
> to influence the candidate's decision, including the spouse's.

The consistent, substantial involvement of the department head in faculty recruitment was evident even in large departments. For example, in Medicine the division head and search committee manage the search, with guidance from the head and the human resources office. But when a short list of
potential faculty is asked to visit the department, the department head meets
with each one. Over the last five years, this involved 400 interviews to fill 50
positions.

The careful checking of references is one detail that is particularly worth
the time and effort, according to Sullivan (Law):

> We do not hire anyone, whether a secretary or a professor,
> without a thorough check of background references. Our
> culture here is to be very careful. If a candidate for a posi-
> tion has waived the confidentiality arrangement, we check
> all references that the individual has given us as well as other
> people in that person's prior employment. Given the fact
> that there are only 185 law schools, among the faculty and
> staff, we know many people at each institution. We try to
> ask very thorough questions to make sure that there are no
> surprises. When I am making phone calls, there are two
> general questions I always ask at the end of the inquiry, "Is
> there something important about the individual that I have
> not asked that I should know? Knowing everything you
> know about this person, would you hire him or her for this
> position?" Very often, if earlier questions had not drawn out
> a thorough description of the person's strengths and weak-
> nesses, these questions will. One, in good faith, cannot fail
> to answer thoroughly and accurately given the sweep of
> these questions.

What Strategies Are Used to Attract the Best Faculty Candidates?

At the same time that a department is looking for the most qualified new faculty member, potential recruits are looking for the best department in which to launch/continue their academic careers. Thus, another essential step in the faculty recruitment process is to effectively sell the position to desirable candidates. The interviewed leaders of highly research-productive departments described four primary strategies for attracting, and ultimately hiring, exceptional future faculty:

- Highlight the department's reputation.

- Emphasize the unique qualities of the department.

- Accentuate the unique qualities of the community.

- Provide a generous, detailed, and firm letter of offer.

Highlight the department's reputation. Nothing draws high-caliber faculty to a department as strongly as a department's reputation. Bates said, "In Chemical Engineering, we are recognized as being the number one department in the country, so we get an easier time of recruiting." This reputation, he said, has helped them to be competitive with institutions that offer considerably higher salaries.

Moller (Pediatrics) has also found that lower salaries can be overcome by a program's quality, its people, and the opportunities it offers for new hires to work with highly regarded researchers. He recalled what led a recent faculty hire to join their ranks: "The attraction for her was our having a top-notch adolescent program, where there are people who could help in her type of research, secretarial support, and a collaborative network."

Ben-Ner made an important point related to reputation: You should never assume the best in the field won't come to your institution. The Industrial Relations Center recently made offers to two faculty candidates who were ranked very highly. Although in the end these exceptional candidates did not come to the university, the very fact that they seriously considered the offer enhanced the center's ability to land the next person.

Emphasize the unique qualities of the department. Each department has its own positive features that can be highlighted during the recruitment process. For the departments in our study, collegiality and culture are particularly important features—recruits are excited about the opportunity to work in an enjoyable place, with outstanding colleagues, and to be recognized and assisted by these colleagues. This is illustrated in the following quote from Masten (Child Development):

> Our reputation does a lot of the work for us, because not only is this a highly rated department, but it also is a very nice place to work. When people come here, they all tell us the same thing: "You have wonderful graduate students. This is a great place to visit." There is a warmth and intellectual openness here that people sense, and they send their undergraduates to us. In this way the culture attracts people who perpetuate it.

Many departments market the quality of their students, since high-caliber students contribute to both the joy of teaching and one's ability to do research. For example, Garavaso (Philosophy) tells her new faculty "you will have to be productive, and you will be able to do that because we have very good students." On her campus, the Academic Partners Program provides a stipend for students to work with faculty on research. Indeed, many departments provide graduate student support as part of faculty start-up packages. The availability of graduate assistants, teaching assistants, and other vital resources—such as support staff, technical personnel, and flexible funding streams—is itself a characteristic of highly research-productive departments. Our qualitative findings for this important environmental feature are described in Chapter 8.

Accentuate the unique qualities of the community. Every department exists in a larger context, be that an academic division, school, college/university, or the surrounding community. Highly research-productive departments take stock of their broader environment and make sure to point out its attractive features to faculty candidates. As Maheswaran (Veterinary Pathobiology) explained, "We sell the department, the program, the college, being part of the Academic Health Center, the University of Minnesota, the close proximity of the Twin Cities' campuses, and the metropolitan area. We accentuate all of the positives."

Hicks (Biology) also spoke of selling the campus:

> [The] Duluth [campus] is in a unique situation. Some people feel like it's the edge of the world. We try to change their mind-set—that it is really the Gulf Coast of Canada. People from Canada come down here to shop, vacation, and swim in Lake Superior. The setting is an asset to people who want this environment and would like to live in a town this size rather than a large metropolitan area.

Many departments emphasize the collaborative opportunities that the university has to offer. Others point out its policies and benefits, such as the faculty leave policy, the opportunities and support for spousal hires, and the ability to step off the tenure track for such things as a new child or the need to care for an aging parent. These and/or other attractive features are present in every institution. What is striking about the approach of highly research-productive departments is that, no matter what college or campus they are part of, they systematically identify their location's positive aspects and strategically use these in their recruitment efforts.

Provide a generous, detailed, and firm letter of offer. Closing the deal is the crucial final step in the faculty hiring process. When extending an employment offer to a faculty candidate, it is essential to consider the overall attractiveness of the hiring package. As Boyd (Finance) aptly stated, "These people are hired in at least a national market, really a world market. So you have to have somebody (whether it's a dean or a school or some other administrative unit) give you the money."

In addition to salary, nearly all of the departments in our study offer some kind of start-up package. These act as a financial incentive to potential faculty hires, and they provide key resources needed to jump-start their research programs. "We really do try to set people up to win . . . since it's just more work for us down the road if they don't get tenure," said Hicks (Biology). "So we ask them what they need in the way of research start-up in order to do the job they want to do. If it's within our power, we try and meet those needs."

The content of these start-up packages varies by discipline and the needs of each new faculty member. Often they include access to a research assistant, travel funds, computer equipment, and a reduced teaching load for a specified period. Here are some specific examples provided by the interviewed department leaders:

- New faculty in the Department of English are given computers, a small amount of money for travel, and, occasionally, teaching release time to facilitate the revision of dissertations into articles or books.

- In the Institute of Public Affairs, faculty start-up packages include summer money, a computer, and research assistantships.

- With the aid of Agricultural Experimental Station money, all new Family Social Science faculty have a reduced teaching load (one less class), a part-time research assistant, computer hardware and software, and usually summer salary support for two years.

In science and medical departments, particularly those whose faculty are heavily engaged in laboratory or "bench" research, the start-up package must be sufficiently large (with respect to funds, space, and other resources) to launch the new faculty member's research career. Consider the following examples from our study:

- "We were talking the other day about somebody we'd like to hire as an assistant professor. It will probably cost us $300,000 start-up. That's what people in basic science expect." (Pediatrics)

- "For one of our recent hires, we renovated the whole laboratory, provided technician support for three years, and equipment support." (Veterinary Pathobiology)

- "We provide them with seed money, from $200,000–$300,000. Then they use the seed money to hire people and to buy some simple equipment. We provide the lab and the big equipment." (Pharmacology)

Our interview protocol did not ask specifically about the sources of funds for start-up packages, but a few department leaders volunteered this information. One spoke of including monies for general faculty support in her institute's capital campaign. Others described their efforts to specifically recruit faculty whose research interests match the priority areas of their university or college (e.g., microbiology, translational research). This allows them to receive money allocated to these initiatives.

Attractive, competitive start-up packages can be financially difficult to put together, but in nearly all cases, these department leaders thought these start-up investments eventually paid for themselves. Hicks (Biology) expressed this well: "Usually they [faculty] more than pay back for their research start-up through indirect costs before they come up for tenure."

Two final, yet crucial points were voiced by several department leaders. First, the letter of offer must be very explicit in laying out the expectations for new faculty and the arrangements and resources that will be provided to them. Second, departments must honor those commitments explicitly. In the Law School, the dean reiterates in the letter of offer the values and culture of the school, as well as the scholarly expectations for each rank of faculty. Similarly, in the Department of Medicine, "each new recruit receives a letter that has a complete plan with goals and how they're going to spend all their time for the first three years, who's their mentor, financial resources, space, what their developmental resources are, and so forth," explained Ravdin. "We prepare a draft letter, then a lot of people, including the candidate, review it. So by the time the final letter goes out for signature it is a fait accompli." He also emphasized the importance of sticking to this written offer: "We keep every commitment we've ever made. It is essential . . . that we keep commitments with the faculty we recruit. Otherwise, it is pure poison."

How Do Departments Successfully Retain Their Faculty Who Are Being Recruited Away by Other Institutions?

Of course, departments that are successful in hiring exceptional faculty cannot end their efforts there. As indicated by the literature, departments must also ensure that the many other environmental features that facilitate research productivity—all of which are described in great detail in the remaining chapters of this book—are both enacted and regularly attended to. To do so is to create an environment where research-productive faculty will want to stay, in spite of attractive offers from other institutions.

Still, as junior faculty achieve growth and prominence, there is an increasing likelihood that they will receive compelling offers to move to other institutions. Indeed, institutions trying to recruit away established faculty will apply many of the same tactics described above. The pervasiveness of this practice is illustrated in a survey of faculty at the University of Michigan, which found that 62% of the faculty respondents reported receiving at least one retention offer to stay at Michigan (Center for the Study of Higher and

---

The 1998 NSOPF questionnaire* provides some insight into how many and which type of faculty are considering leaving their institution. The survey asked, "During the next three years, how likely is it that you will leave this job to accept another full-time position at a different postsecondary institution?"

Full-time faculty in research institutions (n = 5,226) answered:

	All Faculty		Faculty Who Listed "Research" as Their Primary Role		Faculty Who Listed "Teaching" as Their Primary Role	
	Very Likely	Somewhat Likely	Very Likely	Somewhat Likely	Very Likely	Somewhat Likely
Professors	5%	25%	5%	26%	5%	23%
Associate Professors	8%	35%	14%	42%	7%	32%
Assistant Professors	16%	43%	6%	18%	3%	15%

*National Study of Postsecondary Faculty (NSOPF) conducted by the U.S. Department of Education National Center for Education Statistics. The 1998 NSOPF sampled 960 institutions from 3,396 degree-granting postsecondary institutions. All Carnegie Research I institutions were sampled.

Postsecondary Education, & Center for the Education of Women, 1999). Faced with this reality, departments seeking to retain their faculty must be willing to put together attractive retention offers as needed.

In our study, the heads and chairs of highly research-productive departments echoed again and again the importance of protecting their initial recruiting investment. "Our greatest challenge is to retain the faculty whose careers are really skyrocketing," said Gladfelter (Chemistry). "Those recruited by others are outstanding scientists and educators. In the end, it is often more expensive to hire an equivalent replacement than to retain someone." Importantly, retention offers aren't just for faculty. Several department leaders also described their successful efforts to retain staff that are critical to their faculty's research productivity (see Chapter 8).

The University of Minnesota expects a faculty member to have a formal letter of offer from another institution before a retention offer can be made. This can be a problem, however, since "by the time the faculty have an offer in black and white, they are already very deep in negotiation with the other school, and it is too late," said Loh (Pharmacology). Fortunately, the department leaders we interviewed do have strategies for retention, which oftentimes have worked. Leppert (Cultural Studies and Comparative Literature) described how his college addresses this difficult issue:

> Sometimes our dean has made what you would call a preemptive strike, when he gets wind that a really top-quality senior or early-career person is being courted.... He understands full well that this could be a slippery slope. But in given instances, and it isn't just our department, he has acted in a preemptive fashion to stop a process that might otherwise go too far and be too inviting, and frankly even more expensive.

Sterner (Ecology, Evolution, and Behavior) talked about being proactive with regard to retention, and the need to "open up the vault" as needed. "There is a lot of competition out there, and we know it," he said. "These individuals all have their own needs, wants, and desires; and most of them are expensive. But if we want somebody, we try to keep them." Sullivan (Law) agreed:

> I have a philosophy—and I have told the faculty this—that I will not lose a faculty member to any institution on salary, period. If we want to keep that faculty member, I will outbid that school.... In every case the other dean knew that he/she was not going to beat me on salary or financial support because I told the faculty member and they didn't.

How departments get the resources to handle a retention varies by college and by case. If a retention offer is approved in the College of Liberal Arts, for example, the college covers 66% to 75% of the cost; the remaining 25% to 33% comes from the department's merit pool. "I think in the end this is a good policy," said Leppert (Cultural Studies and Comparative Literature). "Requiring a significant department contribution encourages departments to weigh retentions very carefully." Other departments have successfully used donor support to acquire funds. Occasionally, departments have used unfilled salary lines or a portion of the indirect dollars from grants. Ravdin (Medicine) sees retention offers as an opportunity for both the faculty and the institution. He uses the ideas in the competing institution's offer to develop a similar counteroffer, working closely with the dean, center leaders, division leaders, and, in one case, the president of the university. "It [retention] is good for the research enterprise," he said. "We keep them [productive faculty], and if you look at what it is going to cost to replace them, it ends up being economical."

Chapter 2 Review:
Faculty Recruitment and Selection _____

- Building a research-productive department begins with hiring faculty who possess the many individual characteristics—that is, the knowledge, skills, work ethic, socialization, orientation, and commitment—known to be predictive of research success. The most important criteria that departments look for in faculty recruits are a strong motivation or drive to conduct research, demonstrated research experience (seasoned researchers), an overall fit with the department, an ability to collaborate, and strong teaching skills.

- Many, though not all, research-productive departments elect to conduct focused faculty searches, that is, to hire candidates with expertise in a particular content area. In defining area(s) in which to recruit, departments adhere to long-range strategic plans, consider the fundability of candidates' research areas, and balance their research goals with their curriculum needs.

- Common strategies for identifying the best faculty candidates include using collegial networks and participating in national recruiting mechanisms. Some departments have adopted specific strategies such as regularly bringing desirable candidates to campus as visiting scholars, or hiring several faculty at once as a cohesive cohort. All emphasize being flexible, using multiple recruitment strategies, and spending extensive time and attention on recruitment.

- To attract the best candidates, research-productive departments play to their strengths. Some have earned a national reputation or otherwise project an image of quality. All emphasize the unique and attractive qualities of their department and their surrounding community, such as excellent technical resources or opportunities to collaborate within the larger university. Finally, these departments strive to offer competitive start-up packages, detailing these resources in the official letter of offer along with their professional expectations for new faculty.

- Research-productive departments don't shy away from retention offers. Rather, they view retention as a means of protecting their initial investment in faculty. Perhaps most important, they attempt to preempt the need for retention offers by creating an environment in which their faculty researchers can thrive. The many ways departments build and sustain such environments are described in the remaining chapters of this book.

3

Clear Goals That Coordinate Work and Emphasize Research

I think a department needs to identify itself as being expert in a few areas for research. You can't do it all.

(Donald Simone, Oral Sciences)

Literature Summary
Research-productive departments have clear organizational goals that place a high priority on research. This pervasive research emphasis is further refined into goals that serve to coordinate faculty work, as well as significantly influence other characteristics of the environment such as recruitment practices, resource allocation, and group climate.

Department Practices Covered in This Chapter
1) How do highly research-productive departments make use of and benefit from having an overall emphasis on research and, further, having specific research goals?
2) What undergirds a department's selection of specific goals that emphasize research?
3) How, in practical terms, are a department's research goals established?

What Does the Literature Say? _____

Research Emphasis
A research-conducive environment is one that makes research its top priority—or at least gives research equal priority to that of other missions (Baird, 1986; Blackburn, Behymer, & Hall, 1978; Bland & Ruffin, 1992; Clark & Lewis, 1985; Drew, 1985; Kapel & Wexler, 1970; Tschannen-Moran, Firestone, Hoy, & Johnson, 2000). Bean's (1982) causal model of faculty research productivity defines "research emphasis" as the weight given research criteria in promotion and tenure decisions.

Baird's (1986) study of 74 chemistry, history, and psychology departments found that those with clear, dominant, research-centered goals were the most productive. Psychology departments that emphasized training practitioners, for example, were less productive in research. Within research-oriented universities, Blackburn et al. (1978) found faculty productivity to be highest where the educational emphasis was on graduate students, followed by progressively less productivity as the institution increased its focus on undergraduate students. Research productivity also decreased when a unit focused on applied graduate training rather than academic graduate training.

This is not to say that training practitioners or providing quality education for undergraduate students does not occur in highly research-productive departments. Indeed, as will be seen in the sections below and in the chapters that follow, these are also very important and valued missions of the departments in our study. But, importantly, research does not take a backseat to these other missions.

Several studies highlight the importance of having a research emphasis by documenting the negative impact of not having one (Mainous, Hueston, Ye, & Bazell, 2000). Drew (1985) and Clark and Lewis (1985) report that a lack of institutional commitment to research—evidenced by lack of time, resources, finances, and facilities for research—is a significant barrier to research productivity. Commitment to research is very important, as Kapel and Wexler (1970) confirmed in their study of a university's transition from a primarily educational mission to a joint mission of education and research. This institution found it insufficient that faculty and administration recognize the need for and value of research. Rather, productive research environments have administrators and faculty who are highly committed to research and who allocate resources accordingly.

Occasionally a discipline or department can realize high research productivity, even when housed within a larger institution that does not emphasize research. Most often these are disciplines that are described as pure life science, with a highly developed paradigm (Biglan, 1973; Creswell & Bean, 1996; Smart & Elton, 1975). These disciplines have high levels of connectedness, strong collaborations in teaching and research, and a high commitment to research by individual faculty within the local group and across the nation. Collectively, these features provide an across-institutions environment that emphasizes research.

Coordinating Goals

Although having a research emphasis is vital, it is insufficient if it remains too generalized. This priority needs to be translated into clear, coordinating goals (Bland & Schmitz, 1986). This does not mean that faculty work is narrowly directed, for autonomy is an important individual characteristic of the productive researcher. Pelz and Andrews (1966), in their classic study of 10,000 scientists in 1,200 organizations in six countries, found individual autonomy to be compatible with group goals. For example, a leader in Bell Laboratories stated that everyone in the organization must know what the over-goal is, so that within each person's area he or she can look for those solutions that are most relevant to the goal. In other words, the organization points out the mountain to be climbed, but how each member climbs it is up to him or her (Morton, 1964).

The right mix of, and balance between, coordination and autonomy are important. Studies that have looked at this balance find that, in general, performance is low when either there is no coordination or, conversely, when there is an effort to completely control the direction of academics' work (Pineau & Levy-Leboyer, 1983). For example, Pelz and Andrews (1966) found that in the most loosely coordinated groups, only the most motivated researchers excelled. Clearly, a middle ground that balances coordination and autonomy is most conducive to research productivity. Organizational goals are clear and agreed upon, but for each individual there is significant autonomy in deciding how to contribute to achievement of these goals.

Department Practices

A key finding from our qualitative study is that highly research-productive departments place great value on having clear, coordinating goals that collectively emphasize research. In these departments, research is either the primary mission or, at a minimum, on an equal footing with other missions. Further, most departments have taken the additional step of establishing a set of specific research focus areas that help to motivate and coordinate faculty members' work.

The research-centered mission of the Institute of Child Development was described by Masten in this way:

> Our business is creating and disseminating knowledge
> about children in such a way that it will better the lives of
> children. The faculty are quite homogeneous in terms of

their commitment to that mission. And nobody would disagree about the centrality of research, although there are great differences in the nature of research people do. Some folks are doing more government, some more outreach, basic research, or applied research. There is a lot of respect for variations in people's activities, but there are also high expectations in this department for contribution.

These comments highlight another important theme from our study: These highly research-productive departments walk a fine line between setting research goals to coordinate faculty work and allowing faculty to pursue their own diverse interests and activities. Both practices, according to the literature, are required for organizations to maximize their research productivity.

This need to balance organizational goals with faculty autonomy was echoed by many leaders in our study, for example:

- "I have been pushing—and several colleagues have agreed—that we need to find some niches that we occupy centrally, because we are not such a large department. I welcome some concentration. Now, that being said, it's very important that the lone wolf persist. . . . We all adhere to strict principles of freedom of academic inquiry. I mean it more than just making the customary statement." (Industrial Relations)

- "If faculty are in it just for the university, they may not have that spark, creativity, or aggressiveness to really compete nationally for funding or for students; creativity comes from independence. But if faculty don't significantly contribute to the university, we get much less value from that faculty member." (Food Science and Nutrition)

How Do Highly Research Productive Departments Make Use of and Benefit From Having an Overall Emphasis on Research and, Further, Having Specific Research Goals?

In our study, we asked department heads/chairs to name the three most important factors contributing to their department's or school's overall productivity in research. Having a research emphasis and clear research goals was the second most frequently cited response. (The first was faculty recruitment, described in Chapter 2.) But why and how does research goal-setting at the department level have such a positive influence on their faculty's productivity? What we learned in our qualitative work is that these departments use their research goals in a number of very influential ways: in recruiting, evaluating, and rewarding faculty, in making budget decisions, in attracting outside funding, and in improving the overall climate for faculty.

Recruiting new faculty. The presence of well-defined and well-articulated research goals can be a boon to the recruitment process. Faculty candidates are likely to be attracted to departments that are deeply invested in the same or similar research areas as their own.

According to McMurry (Mechanical Engineering), his department has learned to grow by allowing individuals with strong reputations in their research area to take leadership. These individuals then serve as a magnet to draw in other excellent faculty with common interests. "What we have found over the years," he said, "is that this is a tremendous way to attract truly exceptional faculty, because the young people are aware of the work of this senior person, and they want to be associated with that individual."

Other leaders in our study pointed out that when there is a good alignment between a potential hire's research goals and the department's research goals, it is easier to overcome other barriers to recruitment, such as lower salaries or lack of space.

Evaluating and rewarding faculty. In highly research-productive departments, the research expectations for faculty are clearly defined in policy statements such as tenure requirements. Faculty understand these expectations, and are measured against these during annual merit reviews and promotion decisions. Consider these illustrative comments from our dataset:

- "We recently revised our tenure criteria, and it's clear that you have to be research productive. You don't necessarily have to have gotten a certain type of grant, but you do have to be research productive." (Nursing)

- "Published research is a driving force in terms of the [rewards] decisions our faculty make." (Public Affairs)

- "In evaluations, it is written down explicitly that peer-reviewed publications that are data based and in leading journals are the currency of the field.... With grants, it's pretty clear that, unless you are a statistician here, you won't get promoted without having an NIH R01 grant.... The currency is investigator-initiated grants, and people get that message early and frequently." (Epidemiology)

The many criteria and mechanisms that departments use to reward their faculty's research achievements are summarized more completely in Chapter 11.

Allocating resources. Another common use of a department's research goals is in making decisions about finances and resource allocation. In the

Department of Biology, for example, the choice of which faculty equipment needs are funded depends in part on whether these needs mesh with the department's overall research goals. In General College, their limited funds for professional development (e.g., conferences, meetings, semester leaves/sabbaticals) are awarded to faculty members whose work is focused on the research mission. This policy has broad support, even among faculty whose work is in areas outside of the research focus.

Acquiring funding. Departments can successfully leverage their research goals to attract external funding for research. A group of faculty members in Clinical and Population Sciences have become world leaders in managing information for large commercial dairies. "These large pharmaceutical companies that want to work in the dairy industry—they don't have any [other] place in the world where they could get that kind of research done," explained Ames. The lesson in this example is that departments can use their collective research goals as marketing tools to attract external dollars in particular areas, often beyond the level achievable by individual faculty.

> In the pre-interview survey, we asked study department chairs/heads to rate the extent to which their department matched the profile of high research productivity. The institutional characteristic with the highest mean at 4.14 was Research Emphasis—places priority on research or puts no less emphasis on research than on other goals. This emphasis on research mission serves to focus the climate, culture, resources, and faculty of high research potential as well as to guide the communication, collaboration, and service responsibilities.

Reinforcing culture and climate. Perhaps the most powerful outcome of having clear goals in research (and indeed, in all faculty work areas, including teaching and outreach) is the positive effect these goals can have on reinforcing a shared culture of research and contributing to a positive work climate. "We all share a common set of expectations that we will be productive researchers," said Feldman (Health Services Research and Policy). "All of the activities of the division—the teaching activities and the service activities—will flow from the research base."

Having common goals and values greatly increases the ease with which work is done. It also reduces conflict, as described by Collins:

> This faculty [in General College] is really committed to access, diversity, and social justice. There's no fight about that here. There's fight about the details—What does it mean to have a multicultural curriculum? But no one asks the question, "Why the hell would we want one?" We have fights about what kinds of research would promote greater

access to higher education among bypassed populations. But nobody argues about whether we ought to be doing it. So there is a culture with a common value set.

What Undergirds a Department's Selection of Specific Goals That Emphasize Research?

We found that most departments in our study are driven by a perceived need to narrow the number of research areas in which they try to excel. The criteria governing the selection of a department's research focus areas can vary by discipline, and might be based on a number of different factors—a desire to be at the top of one's field, an assessment of societal needs, the priorities of external funding agencies, and the research strengths and resources of the larger institution.

The Institute of Public Affairs has the goal of being the nation's top public policy school in a public institution. One important step toward meeting that goal, according to Archibald, is successfully banding their faculty together to maximize their strengths. She described her current faculty as "entrepreneurs" and "risk takers," which, while valuable, has also created some challenges for the Institute:

> This is a funny place. Faculty love it, they are passionately committed to it, but they are all operating in their own best interest. We have been very successful as individuals, but now we want to be more than the sum of our parts, so we are looking for a way to do that. . . . We don't have a common focus, and to be good you need to have a focus and a particular message to sell.

Many department leaders spoke of trying to align their goals with the identified needs of society, while simultaneously leading the advancement of their field. For example, the Department of Entomology has a mission to deal with the applied aspects of what the state and the region need. But, as Ascerno explained,

> We also have to be doing innovative, original research that keeps us grounded in new developments, the cutting edge. If you're in a particular area—potato, for example—we expect you to be doing work related to the industry, addressing the current problems, and looking forward to what is coming down the pike as the new problems to make sure that you're not caught blindsided. . . . Each person has,

I think, a clear set of goals for themselves, under the rubric of fitting together with this full-service mission.

Of course, this idealism of meeting the needs of society while advancing knowledge can be further constrained by the realities of funding. Ascerno pointed out that within identified priority areas, a department also needs to focus on areas that are appealing to external funding sources.

The Department of Medicine's research focus areas are, in addition to societal needs, determined largely by where there is a critical mass of faculty, nationally competitive recognized strengths, core resources, and the environment for new faculty hires to prosper. An important aspect of this department's approach is that their research priority areas also build on strengths across the Medical School.

How, in Practical Terms, Are a Department's Research Goals Established?

Getting consensus on research goals and keeping those of high priority in people's minds is a challenge at any level above the small work group. According to our qualitative data, these highly research-productive departments use a variety of strategies to facilitate their goal setting:

- Engage in strategic planning.

- Draw on the faculty's research strengths.

- Take direction from strong leadership.

- Respond to external and internal calls for change.

- Align department goals with university expectations.

Engage in strategic planning. The most common strategy used by these departments to, first, establish research as a departmental priority and, second, define their collective research goals is formal strategic planning. This planning typically takes place across a series of faculty meetings or at a faculty retreat. Moller (Pediatrics) admitted that while the strategic planning process can be difficult, his faculty do highly value the statements that emerge to guide their work efforts, such as the following:

> Each individual [faculty member] will pursue a unique brand of research, education, and clinical activities that fit in the overall program of the department. All faculty members are expected to be involved in scholarly activity, dissemination of knowledge, and publication. There is an

enduring expectation that scholarly education and clinical activities of all faculty members will progress throughout their careers.

Invariably, the leaders we interviewed talked about how crucial it is to get the entire faculty's input and ownership of the research focus. Ames (Clinical and Population Sciences) expressed this well:

> I think it is more important if they [the faculty] can decide the focus themselves than if you tell them. As soon as you start making external focus areas, everybody starts worrying whether they have been excluded. With strategic planning, I try to go along with the focusing process but be inclusive enough so that everyone can fit under the umbrella and nobody feels left out. . . . If they can all agree that this is a really important focus area, and we should work on this together, they will be more productive.

The value of this participative approach to major decision-making is more fully described in Chapter 7 and Chapter 14.

Draw on the faculty's research strengths. Some departments identify their research priorities by letting them emerge around significant faculty researchers. Mechanical Engineering is one example of this. Instead of trying to do everything well, they have focused on building areas of excellence in the department. "We have had tremendous success in hiring by following that strategy," said McMurry. "It means that we are not as broad of a department as we might otherwise be, but it also means that we are very deep, and we have a critical mass in selective areas." Historically, these areas were in the thermal sciences and heat transfer, though more recently the department has extended this model to other areas.

Take direction from strong leadership. Sometimes a department's goals are first put forth by the department head/chair and then "sold" to the faculty and the dean. Ravdin reported that when he first came to the university to lead the Department of Medicine, he pulled together a development plan which was the basis for getting resources from the Medical School. "The hypothesis was that we would invest in research only programmatically. We would invest in areas where there are resources and a critical strength, not just in a division or a department, but in the institution." This strategy, he explained, signaled a significant departure from the previous practice, whereby the chair was hired and then simply recruited whomever he or she wanted in the program. "I didn't believe that was the way to have a sustainable program that would grow," he said. Now, six years later after that first development plan, Ravdin finds he is able use a more participative approach to setting goals in a new round of planning, using input from the division heads, external reviewers, and partnering institutes and centers across the university.

A former chair of the Department of Chemistry (Lou Pignolet) also saw a need for a more cohesive, goal-oriented department. But, unlike Ravdin, he did not have the advantage of being newly hired from the outside. Instead, he used two external organizational consultants to facilitate the process. One consultant focused on the organizational structure of the department, the other on personal rewards and the psychological impact of change. Gladfelter, department chair at the time of our interviews, explained the value of this approach:

> We took a great deal of grief for having hired two shrinks, but the results justified the process. I would put Lou Pignolet, who organized all of this, at the equivalent level of Abe Lincoln for bringing the department together from what was an incredibly fragmented group. We now have a much tighter group of people who share common research goals and common teaching goals. It is a much better, less contentious group of faculty.

Respond to external and internal calls for change. General College has moved in the last 10 years from a less research-productive unit to one of the leading research units in developmental education. Collins credited this change in research productivity to a renewed focus on research in their mission, brought on by two external pressures:

> First, there was an externally imposed structural change by the university [Commitment to Focus] that led to a much more narrow range of appropriate activity for the college and that emphasized research. Then, six years ago, the administration wanted to close the college. All the markers of measures they used to ask whether we're doing our job were improving, but we really needed to focus down even more tightly. We were told, "Do this." And when the alternative to "doing this" was being put out of business, people took that seriously.

Their renewed commitment to research on under-prepared students has paid off, according to Collins. "In the last couple of years, we've gotten national awards for our research and academic programs," he said. These have included the National Association of Developmental Education's John Champaign Award for best access program in the country in 2001, and a ranking as one of the five best developmental programs in the nation from the American Productivity and Quality Center in 2000.

Nursing is another program that has dramatically increased its research productivity in response to calls for change. This came about when their faculty, particularly a few faculty champions, decided they wanted to achieve greater research productivity. They have since actualized this goal by creating two new centers of research excellence, by more strongly emphasizing research in their tenure requirements, and by hiring faculty with laudable research records; however, it was the single act of shifting the expectations and norms for research that drove these changes. Although this pressure for change came from the inside, it echoes the lessons from General College about the power of stating and expecting greater research productivity.

Align department goals with university expectations. Several department heads/chairs spoke of how the larger university's research mission influenced and assisted them in maintaining a research emphasis in their department. For example, above, we described how General College developed a more focused set of research goals in response to a university-based initiative, "Commitment to Focus." Ames, too, described some traditions at the university that "favor what goes on in the department," including a tradition of research and the importance of graduate education. Given this institutional emphasis, all of their veterinary residents are involved in the graduate program, in contrast to other veterinary colleges throughout the nation that do not do any graduate work.

This observation highlights a critical point: Although our study focused on the department-level features that result in high research productivity, these features are best viewed in the larger context of how the characteristics of one's school, college, and university reinforce research productivity at the department level.

Lastly, it is important to remember that a department's research goals are not static. Participants in our study talked about the need to revisit, update, and reaffirm their department's research goals. And often the department head is the one who keeps the department's vision in the minds of faculty. To quote Ek (Forest Resources), "I think the department head's role with respect to vision is to remind folks why we are into something."

Chapter 3 Review:
Clear Goals That Coordinate Work and
Emphasize Research _____

- To be highly research-productive, a department must place a strong and enduring emphasis on research. With this emphasis established, the challenge is for departments to translate this into a set of more specific research goals or areas that effectively coordinate faculty work—without stifling individual faculty autonomy, creativity, and innovation.

- Departments can make good use of their research goals. These goals come into play in recruiting, evaluating, and rewarding faculty, in making budget decisions, in attracting outside funding, and in improving the overall climate for faculty.

- The selection of a department's research priority areas might be based on an assessment of societal needs, a desire to be on the cutting edge or top of the field, the priorities of external funding agencies, and the research strengths of the current faculty base.

- Departments use an array of strategies for establishing their research goals. Many rely on formal strategic planning. Some follow the interests of their most productive faculty. Others respond to external forces, such as a need to align their goals with the aims of their larger host institution. Always, however, a department's goals must be revisited and reaffirmed by faculty and by administrators.

4

Shared Culture and Positive Group Climate

There is a sense of a cohesive theme in the education of our students and in the research we do. It makes the culture work. It contributes to the glue of the place and the process of staying vibrant.

(Ann Masten, Child Development)

LITERATURE SUMMARY
Research-productive departments are characterized by high morale and a positive climate. They also have a distinctive organizational culture that defines the group's shared values and collegially bonds its members.

DEPARTMENT PRACTICES COVERED IN THIS CHAPTER
1) On what might a department's culture or group identity be based?
2) How do highly research-productive departments describe their group climate?
3) What specific strategies are used by departments to maintain their shared culture and positive group climate?

What Does the Literature Say? _____

Shared Culture

The literature on research productivity finds that highly productive units have a distinctive organizational culture that bonds its members. Bland and Ruffin (1992) describe the culture as having a "... distinctiveness that sets an organization apart from other similar organizations, and it is a distinctiveness that everyone within the organization understands, shares, and values" (p. 388). In short, culture provides a group identity. It defines common values and practices, and creates a safe home in which group members can experiment with new ideas. In their study of the nation's colleges with the highest morale, Rice and Austin (1988) found that all possessed "distinctive organizational cultures that are carefully nurtured and built upon" (p. 52; see also Rice & Austin, 1990). Corporations, too, have long been aware of the positive impact that a strong culture can have on productivity (Collins & Porras, 1994).

Culture, however, is not self-sustaining. It requires attention to be preserved, both to maintain core values and to stop the intrusion of non-core values (Gething & Leelarthaepin, 2000). In the words of Tierney (1987), "Because new people join the institution every year and the institution changes constantly, a strong sense of identity must be cultivated, tended, and frequently revised" (p. 70). Senior faculty play a particularly pivotal role in maintaining a department's culture. With many faculty soon to be reaching retirement at the same time, or with senior faculty departing through early retirement packages, institutions risk losing their stories, legacies, and institutional wisdom—in short, their culture (Bergquist, 1992).

In addition, many campuses are seeing increases in management cultures (e.g., total quality management, responsibility-centered management), the collective bargaining culture, and a legalistic/adversarial culture (Staehnke, 1997). All of these forces have been present in some form for years, but their more recent increase in influence has spurred a concomitant weakening of the academic culture.

Positive Group Climate

Culture is often intertwined with group climate. Certainly, everyone wants to go to work each day to a place that is uplifting and reinforcing. But, does this really affect productivity? The answer is clearly yes (Baird, 1986; Birnbaum, 1983; Long & McGinnis, 1981; Schweitzer, 1988; Turney, 1974). Andrews (1979) assessed climate by looking at such things as the degree to which faculty feel free to offer their ideas, their opportunities to do so, the weight that is given to their ideas, and the sense of cooperation prevalent within the group. He found that when academics believed this accurately described their environment, productivity was greater. Birnbaum (1983) found similar results in his study of 84 randomly selected research projects in 15 universities (one in Canada, 14 in the U.S.). Productivity was higher in projects that reported low turnover, good leader-member relations, and open discussion of disagreements.

In a separate study, El-Khawas (1991) reported that faculty frequently said they were disillusioned with the declining sense of community in their college and with the deterioration of its intellectual climate and its quality of life. Writings on corporate downsizing illustrate the negative impact on productivity when the climate is not positive. A review of the research in this area finds that surviving members of downsized companies become less creative and more averse to risk. On average, three years after downsizing, these companies are less profitable than similar companies in the same environment that did not downsize (Cascio, 1993; Cascio & Morris, 1996). In short, in business and in education, strategies to support and nurture a positive climate are important to ensure the vitality of organization members.

Department Practices

In 2001 a survey was conducted of former University of Minnesota faculty who from 1997 to 2000 voluntarily left our institution for another academic position. The survey's objective was to assess information on the circumstances of faculty departures. One key finding was that respondents' greatest sources of dissatisfaction centered on their environment—specifically, their department's perceived social climate, management effectiveness, and sense of collegiality. (For the executive summary, see Appendix G. For the full report, see http://www1.umn.edu/usenate/scfa/exitsurveyreport.html.)

Congruent with these findings, culture and climate also emerged as a significant environmental feature in our qualitative study of highly research-productive departments. When we asked department heads/chairs, "What are the key factors that contribute to the research productivity of your faculty?" the third most frequently cited factor (after recruiting excellent faculty and having clear, coordinating research goals) was having a shared culture highly focused on research.

It was also striking how passionately many department heads/chairs spoke about the importance of culture and a positive climate in facilitating their faculty's research productivity. Consider these examples:

- "The strongest message I would like to deliver is how important our culture and group climate is to our department. . . . I think it's possible to build a highly ranked department where nobody likes each other, but I wouldn't want to work there." (Ecology, Evolution, and Behavior)

- "If you have faculty members who are working well together and who recognize each other's strengths, then everything is smoother. Research can be supported, and people support each other." (Biology)

Most of the culture and climate building strategies used by these departments are not new; their strategies include bringing faculty together through retreats, social events, or weekly research seminars. The critical element is not the specific type of mechanisms used, but rather that these departments are very proactive in ensuring that multiple strategies for cultivating their desired culture and climate are integrated into the everyday life of the department. These practices are so woven into the fabric of these departments that to the long-time faculty member they become like gravity—an ever-present, significant, but unnoticed force in their environment.

On What Might a Department's Culture or Group Identity Be Based?

A culture of research takes time to develop. It must be regularly cultivated by consistent, tangible practices until research becomes an inseparable part of the department's identity, activities, and reputation. Many of the departments in our study have long-held traditions of being highly research productive. A few, as noted in the previous chapter, have more recently, yet successfully, shifted toward a highly research-oriented culture through a set of carefully coordinated efforts (e.g., by redefining their mission and goals, changing tenure criteria, and hiring new faculty based on their research strengths).

Overall, in our interviews with the heads/chairs of these departments, we learned that their cultures are typically based on one or more of the following:

- A set of common, core values related to the department's research goals and mission (mission-based cultures)

- A commonly held image of the department that faculty actively work to maintain (image-based cultures)

- Traditions that faculty members value and want to pass on to future faculty (tradition-based cultures)

Mission-based cultures. Not surprisingly, we found that in departments with well-articulated research missions supported by commonly held goals, these same goals tended to undergird their shared culture. According to Collins, his college's overarching mission—to improve access and diversity in higher education among traditionally bypassed populations—is the basis of their identity as an academic unit. "Nobody within General College argues about whether we ought to be doing it," he said. "So there's a culture with a common value set. Nobody questions whether those values are the values we ought to have."

Ek (Forest Resources) described his department's culture in this way:

> There is a central thread among the faculty: They view themselves as helping society deal with issues and problems. That's fundamentally why they are diligent and productive.

It's more of a professional outreach culture than an academic culture. We have really looked at our unit's role (in the university and beyond). That's part of why we hang together.

Image-based cultures. Several heads and chairs described their department as having a commonly held image that their faculty actively work to maintain. The Institute of Child Development is one example. Masten said,

People who join the student body or faculty know that this is a high achievement place. One is expected to get grants from NIH and other top places—not just submit them, but get them; to publish in the top-notch journals; to be invited to give the keynote address at major society meetings or be elected president of a leading research organization. We don't talk about it. The expectation is part of the atmosphere.

The Industrial Relations Center is also built on a shared image of quality. "Basically, we aspire to excellence. That's clear, it's transparent," said Ben-Ner. There is a continued pressure to sustain this excellence, he added, which his faculty do by maintaining a collegial environment, readily exchanging information, and subsequently fostering new ideas.

> For most of the departments in our study, being highly productive in research is not a recent event. Rather, it is a carefully cultivated identity—one that has been a part of their cultures for a long time. When we asked leaders how long their departments had been research productive, 85% answered "for 10 or more years."

Tradition-based cultures. In some departments, a strong culture (e.g., of research, hard work, collaboration) is long-standing and deeply rooted in tradition, having been established by prior faculty and then passed down over the years. Bates (Chemical Engineering and Materials Science) explained, "We persist at behaving in a certain way, and we acquire that over time from our predecessors." Examples of his faculty's persistent behaviors are team teaching and a regular custom of interacting with one another. "We grow people up in this environment, and it works," he said. "They pick it up and they like it, so they pass it on. It's actually marvelous to see that. I've been here long enough now, twelve years, to see how that works."

Eidman (Applied Economics) spoke of the history of his department's culture as follows:

Well, the culture's been here a long time. I've been here since 1975, and it was here when I got here. . . . Faculty

> interact with each other when they think it's useful, they go
> to seminars together, they go to meetings together, they
> write papers together. It's a congenial working relationship,
> and yet it's not laid back. Faculty are working hard—lots of
> hours, lots of days. They're very intense while they're here.

Some departments can actually trace their culture as originating from one or more early leaders. For example, the Division of Epidemiology continues the traditions established by the department's founder, Ancel Keyes, and his successor, Henry Blackburn. The head of Pediatrics said he has consciously tried to maintain the guiding principles of his department's early founders by repeating stories about them and by regularly referring to the high standards they set.

How Do Highly Research-Productive Departments Describe Their Group Climate?

The literature has shown that research-productive organizations have, in addition to a shared culture of research, an overall group climate that is positive and enriching. By and large, the interviewed heads of highly research-productive departments concurred, for example:

- "The assistant professors that come here know that we want them to succeed, and that is a very powerful message." (Child Development)

- "I tell people with a straight face that I think we have the best combination of quality and humanity that you will find anywhere in the field. We work together on things." (Ecology, Evolution, and Behavior)

- "Overall, there is a congeniality here. People try to be civil and work things out in a productive way." (Public Affairs)

A positive group climate can manifest itself in many ways within a department. Here, we provide a few illustrations of how the department heads/chairs in our study described the climate in their work units.

- *High faculty morale:* "One of the rallying points for us is our graduate program. Everybody is really proud of it, and the success of our graduate students does a lot to make us all feel good about each other's work." (Ecology, Evolution, and Behavior)

- *Spirit of innovation:* "People are independent operators, and that's a culture that's been here for a while. . . . I try to stay out of the way and let people go after what they want. There isn't a lot of heavy-handed directions, saying 'Well that's not a good direction to go in.' I'm trusting the search process and saying, 'We've hired the best. You know better than I do where you should be going, so go for it.'" (Entomology)

- *High degree of cooperation:* "All of our keys open everybody's offices. The reason goes back to this interesting tradition: If a faculty member is here and working and knows that a colleague has a particular material or book in his or her office, they just go into their office and get it. On arriving, I thought this was the most bizarre thing. So early on, in my first semester, I sent out a memo asking faculty if they really wanted to continue this. Their response was 'What's with this guy? We want access to our colleagues' offices.'" (Law)

- *Low faculty turnover:* "We've had very few faculty leave the department. When they come, they tend to stay. This is illustrated by the tenures of our department heads, which have averaged 19.8 years over the 100-year history of the department. Stability is a characteristic of this department." (Mechanical Engineering)

- *Open discussion of disagreements:* "When trying to facilitate an issue, often there are other people in the department besides the chair who are known to be good negotiators and good peacemakers, and they will often be encouraged to step in and work something out.... On occasion we will have an explosion or something, but it's a pretty robust culture that keeps us on track. " (Child Development)

Additional examples of these features of a positive group climate are described in other chapters, particularly Chapter 7 and Chapter 14.

What Specific Strategies Are Used by Departments to Maintain Their Shared Culture and Positive Group Climate?

Most, if not all, of the environmental features discussed throughout this book can influence a department's culture and climate. For instance, cultural norms and values can be passed down from senior to junior faculty (Chapter 5). Faculty morale tends to be high when evaluations and salary decisions are conducted fairly and in accordance with established criteria (Chapter 11). And cultures of collaboration are more likely to emerge in departments whose faculty have diverse, yet complementary research skills and interests (Chapters 6 and 13).

From this perspective, culture and climate can seem rather intangible concepts—they are, largely, features that rise to the surface when all other elements of a research-productive organization are in place. Nonetheless, four specific strategies for attending to culture and climate did emerge in our interviews with the leaders of research-productive departments:

- Encourage peer modeling of desired behaviors.
- Provide opportunities for faculty development.
- Facilitate communication among faculty.
- Recruit faculty who match the culture and contribute positively to the climate.

Encourage peer modeling of desired behaviors. A clear contributor to a research-conducive culture and climate is a sense of "creative-supportive tension" that comes from one's peers (Pelz & Andrews, 1966). Leppert (Cultural Studies and Comparative Literature) put it this way: "There is a kind of encouragement that goes on automatically in a highly productive department. There's a real culture where people sense they've got to keep their nose to the grindstone. It's amazing how well that works."

Peer modeling is an important component of Mechanical Engineering's research culture as well, which McMurry described as follows:

> It's associating with people who are productive and aspiring to be equally productive. It's when new faculty want to be at least as good as if not better than the people who have come in the past.

The head of Entomology has observed a similar effect in his department, where seeing people working well beyond the 40 hours in a week translates, in an indirect way, to establishing their culture.

This type of positive peer pressure can be particularly effective in departments with strong researchers in their senior faculty base. The Department of Ecology, Evolution, and Behavior has benefited from "terrific senior leadership," according to Sterner:

> They were people who were well regarded by their peers as national academicians. But they were also central and established a sense for the department for how to conduct business, based on their own modeling of what they expected. I don't think you can necessarily legislate this sort of behavior, but when a couple of national academics speak up at a faculty meeting and carry themselves in a certain way, that has a lot of weight on how everybody acts.

Of course, Masten (Child Development) aptly noted that being surrounded by high-achieving peers does produce pressure. She said,

> I know that every one of the junior faculty I have ever
> talked to experiences the pressure of these expectations, just
> the way a child in a high-achieving family does. . . . The
> pressure does not arise from what people say or do; it is part
> of the atmosphere around a productive and generative
> group of people. Perceived pressure is a downside of such a
> place, but it is also an energizing environment.

Provide opportunities for faculty development. Ravdin (Medicine) thought that one of the best ways to keep people excited and working together (i.e., to maintain high morale) is to provide them with opportunities for growth and development. "Everyone wants to be part of a group that can grow," he explained. "If you can keep finding resources, you can keep growing, spinning off in different areas, and become better."

Closely tied to the theme of growth and development are two additional features of research-productive organizations, both discussed in separate chapters. These are mentoring (Chapter 5), whereby faculty receive assistance from established scholars; and brokered opportunities (Chapter 12), which can help faculty feeling stuck in their professional work to upgrade their knowledge and skills or otherwise provide them with avenues to advance in their careers.

Facilitate communication among faculty—substantive conversations as well as social interactions. Being able to have frequent, substantive interactions with one's peers within the department is an important predictor of research productivity (see Chapters 7 and 8). It is not surprising, therefore, that good communication is also a key feature of a positive group climate. Here, we provide a brief list of some of the strategies used by these departments to encourage socialization and information sharing among faculty:

- General College brings in new faculty recruits two weeks before the semester begins to allow them to learn about the campus, each other, and the research interests of other faculty.

- Veterinary Pathobiology provides small but frequent opportunities for faculty to gather to recognize an achievement, a holiday, and faculty or graduate student transitions.

- Marketing and Logistics Management has a weekly seminar for the presentation of faculty work.

- The Law School provides summer orientations and courses on teaching for new faculty. They also host a Thursday lunch series where faculty research is presented and discussed. These have a consistent attendance of about half the school, as well as faculty across the university interested in law or public policy. Occasionally, outside speakers present.

- Many departments hold retreats and traditional social events. For example, the Department of Cultural Studies and Comparative Literature has a retreat each fall, which includes social as well as professional activities. The Department of Biochemistry, Molecular Biology, and Biophysics hosts a party and reception for all new faculty after they arrive.

Recruit faculty who match the culture and contribute positively to the climate. A department's recruitment practices can greatly influence—positively or negatively—its culture and climate. Gengenbach (Agronomy and Plant Genetics) noted that good faculty are "the most important ingredient to start with" when creating an environment supportive of research. There is particular value, he added, in putting together a faculty group whose members have some degree of shared interest in one another's work. "When somebody is interested in what I'm doing, it makes me feel that my work is worth doing, and I might do it much better than I would have if I was out there by myself in isolation." Eidman (Applied Economics) echoed this, saying, "It's all about getting the right kind of people together—people who can work together and who are compatible with each other."

This attention to culture and climate of research can, in turn, have a beneficial impact on a department's ability to attract strong researchers in future hiring rounds. Consider these examples:

- "In terms of ethic and culture and values, I don't think we have hired anybody that doesn't value research—that didn't, in fact, come here because they perceived it was going to be a relatively supportive environment for doing research." (Geography)

- "There are cultural factors that make it attractive to work here. We had a very competitive hiring season last spring. We hired three new faculty and had to compete with Berkeley, MIT, Northwestern, and Johns Hopkins. Still, we got three for three, and part of the reason is the collegiality that's well recognized in this department." (Chemical Engineering and Materials Science)

- "We have been successful in recruiting highly sought-after faculty, in part because candidates sense that our faculty really like one another—and they tell us this in the recruitment process, as they are comparing us to other departments around the country." (Cultural Studies and Comparative Literature)

Departments also need to be conscious of faculty candidates who might disrupt their culture and climate. Boyd (Finance) called these people "externalities":

> There are certain people out there who are extremely good scholars, but are very divisive, not team players, not willing to help young faculty, etc. I don't want them in this department. I don't want them regardless of how good they are, because we look at a research group as a team. There is a lot of jointness, and one bad apple can just wreck the whole deal.

Ames (Clinical and Population Sciences) echoed this, saying, "I've placed a high priority in my hires on the ability to get along [with others] and fit into a team, because brilliant people can implode a department."

In conclusion, we found that in these highly research-productive departments, a research emphasis is imbued in nearly everything they do, from recruitment, to faculty review, to budgeting, to modes of communication, and to the distribution of faculty rewards and resources. These practices serve to ensure that both a shared culture and a positive group climate endure, even during periods marked by heavy change or conflict.

Chapter 4 Review:
Shared Culture and Positive Group Climate_____

- Research-productive departments have distinctive cultures that bond their members and provide a group identity. There are three typical bases for these shared cultures: 1) common research goals or mission; 2) a common image, such as being the top-ranked department in the field or being a place where everyone is high-achieving in research; and 3) tradition, in the sense that faculty persist in successful behaviors and maintain the high productivity standards set by a revered early leader or other predecessors in the department.

- The interviewed heads and chairs shared examples of how a positive group climate is manifested in their departments. Their responses reflected desirable climate features from the literature, including high faculty morale, a spirit of innovation, high degree of cooperation, low faculty turnover, and the open discussion of disagreements.

- These departments maintain their shared culture and positive group climate through common strategies such as mentoring, retreats, social events, weekly research seminars, and fair evaluation and salary systems. They try to recruit faculty who match the culture and strive to provide current faculty with opportunities for development. What is striking is that overall, these departments are very proactive in assuring that multiple climate-building strategies occur and are integrated into the everyday life and fabric of the department.

5

Mentoring

Each individual untenured faculty member is given a senior faculty mentor who is supposed to help him or her get acclimated to our academic ways. That includes not only teaching, but particularly the scholarship—the level, intensity, quality, and quantity that we would like to see.

(E. Thomas Sullivan, Law)

LITERATURE SUMMARY
Having had a formal mentor is highly correlated with research productivity. Highly research-productive departments provide their beginning and midlevel faculty with opportunities to receive assistance from more senior faculty. Mentors can advise mentees on their research activities, socialize them to the organization's culture, and connect them with the relevant research establishment.

DEPARTMENT PRACTICES COVERED IN THIS CHAPTER
1) What specific duties do mentors perform in highly research-productive departments?
2) Who takes on the mentoring role?
3) What kinds of formal mentoring structures do highly research-productive departments use? How are mentors selected or assigned?
4) How does mentoring occur informally in research-productive departments?
5) Which department features might determine the extent and type of mentoring that occurs?

What Does the Literature Say? _____

The term "mentoring" is attributed to Homer and his classic work, *The Odyssey*. (When Odysseus goes off to the Trojan War, he asks Mentor to serve as the tutor for his son, Telemachus.) Since then, a great deal has been written about mentoring and its use and benefits, not just for faculty careers but for careers of all kinds. Specifically with regard to faculty success, Rogers, Holloway, and Miller (1990) define mentorship as the "influence, guidance, or direction exerted by a close, trusted, and experienced counselor. A mentor is to be detached and disinterested to some degree, so that he or she can hold up a mirror for the protégé" (p. 186). Here, we briefly summarize those studies that relate to the impact of mentoring on research productivity.

Studies find that having had a formal mentor is highly correlated with research productivity (Blackburn, 1979; Bland & Schmitz, 1986; Cameron & Blackburn, 1981; Corcoran & Clark, 1984; Mills, 1995; Mundt, 2001). Individuals who associate early with distinguished scientists or who collaborate with them on research projects are more likely themselves to become productive researchers (Cameron & Blackburn, 1981; Paul, Stein, Ottenbacher, & Lui, 2002). Blackburn (1979) wrote, "Mentorship/sponsorship in the first years is critical for launching a productive career—learning the informal network that supports productivity—the inner workings of professional associations and who the productive people are, for example—is critical . . ." (pp. 25–26). Mentors can also provide emotional support and help inculcate new faculty into the academic culture. In Corcoran and Clark's study (1984), highly active faculty members reported learning how to behave from their advisers and having had many more research-related experiences during graduate school than did a representative group of faculty.

More recent studies confirm the importance of mentoring to research productivity (Curtis, Dickinson, Steiner, Lanphear, & Vu, 2003; Dohm & Cummings, 2002; Roberts, 1997; Tenenbaum, Crosby, & Gliner, 2001; Wilson, Valentine, & Pereira, 2002). For example, Byrne and Keefe (2002), who investigated the impact of mentoring on research competence in nursing, wrote, "in terms of scholarly productivity . . . there is no substitute for a sustained relationship grounded in research projects sponsored by one or more experts and supported by continuous resources . . . [p. 391]. When scholarly productivity with funded research is the desired outcome, intense involvement of a protégé with an expert researcher is essential" (p. 395). Melicher (2000), studying faculty in financial management, found that having a mentor "has a positive impact on salary levels, salary satisfaction, and promotion/tenure satisfaction" (p. 166).

Notably, not all mentoring programs are alike, nor are they equally successful. In a study of medical school faculty by Bland, Seaquist, Pacala, Center, and Finstad (2002), having or having had a formally assigned mentor was found to be the second-best predictor of high research productivity (having a passion for research was first); however, this association did not hold when the mentoring relationship was informal or nonstructured. Other studies echo the importance of being systematic in one's approach to mentoring. For example, Wilson et al. (2002), in their examination of social work faculty, report that mentoring programs must be "carefully developed and supported if protégés, mentors, and their organizations are to fully realize these benefits. Factors such as mentor-protégé matching, mentor characteristics, the roles of mentors, organizational support, and the mentoring process must be considered if a successful mentoring program is to be implemented" (p. 317). Drotar and Avner (2003) add, "prospective faculty mentors (and department chairs) need to recognize that mentoring is a rewarding privilege of academic life that demands protected time, energy, and extraordinary commitment, which cannot and should not be made by everyone" (p. 2).

A summative message that emerges from this body of literature is that mentoring, when done well, can have a wide-reaching, positive impact on the research productivity of faculty. Precisely how the mentoring role might be fulfilled, and by whom, was a key question that we sought to answer in our qualitative study. The many insights and examples offered up by the academic leaders we interviewed are presented next.

Department Practices

It is clear from the literature and from our qualitative study that research-productive departments can reap important benefits when their faculty are well mentored. In grooming faculty to value research and excel in scholarship, a department contributes to its long-term success and research reputation, creating a vital and scholarly culture that will continue to attract the best people and to build and maintain the department's national recognition. Perhaps one of the most convincing arguments in support of mentoring is that of the 37 departments in our study, those rated in the top 5% in their field (n = 9) all had formal mentoring programs.

Although not all of the departments in our study have concretized structures for facilitating mentoring among their faculty, each leader expressed a clear desire to have their untenured faculty succeed. Accordingly, they described ways—sometimes formal, sometimes less so—in which a variety of mentoring duties were fulfilled in their environments.

What Specific Duties Do Mentors Perform
in Highly Research-Productive Departments?

In discussing the mentoring activities that go on in their departments, the interviewed leaders identified diverse, sometimes interdependent ways in which mentors assist their faculty. For example, some noted how their more experienced faculty help junior faculty to network at conferences. A few described alerting their new faculty to start-up funding streams within the university or otherwise nominating them for awards that include discretionary funding. Providing critical feedback on teaching was also frequently cited. (This is discussed more fully in Chapter 9.) Most of their responses focused on ways to support junior faculty, but some provided examples of mentoring targeted to the unique needs of midcareer and senior faculty; these are addressed in Chapter 12.

Most frequently, the leaders of highly research-productive departments described the value of mentoring in the context of three specific mentoring duties, all of which have a direct bearing on a department's research productivity:

- Conveying the department's goals and culture

- Facilitating grant writing/acquisition

- Preparing faculty for promotion and tenure

Conveying the department's goals and culture. In Chapters 2 and 3, we noted the importance of research-productive departments having clear goals with an emphasis on research, a shared culture, and a positive group climate. Thus, orienting new faculty to these departmental characteristics is one important goal of the mentoring relationship.

"We do offer mentoring, usually across a couple of people, to help our junior faculty learn the norms and blend into the culture," said Ascerno (Entomology). On the Morris campus, junior faculty from all divisions and disciplines participate in an informal, "unofficial-official" group that meets every Friday. "It's a social introduction group," explained Garavaso (Philosophy). "The junior faculty get trained into the norms of the campus through that."

In the Department of Psychology (Twin Cities campus), a mentor is selected for each new faculty member to encourage the sharing of norms unique to that environment. Campbell explained, "They [mentors and mentees] typically have a lot of discussions about all the unwritten things one should know—how to get on in the department, what happens this year, what happens next year, what does it mean when the chair says I need this right away, things like that."

Facilitating grant writing/acquisition. Helping faculty succeed in their grant writing efforts was the most frequently cited mentoring task in our study. This was not surprising, given how important the acquisition of external funding is to a faculty member's research productivity. Funded grant proposals provide money and time for research-related activities. In addition, they are an important demonstration of faculty achievement, particularly for faculty in tenure-track positions. Garavaso (Philosophy) astutely pointed out that the grant writing process is also critical because "it forces you to think about your research plan and your research projects in advance. Thinking about a long-term plan is good, so you're not just working on your wonderful project; you also have several of them at different stages."

So how do departments provide mentoring in grant writing? This largely occurs through the provision of critical feedback to the faculty member via in-house peer review, with more experienced colleagues critiquing the proposal drafts of newer faculty. In some departments this task falls to mentoring committees. "They [the committee members] play a strong role in helping new faculty in grant development, reading grants—at least reading the first couple pages of grants and getting those things down," said Bernlohr (Biochemisty, Molecular Biology, and Biophysics).

In the Department of Pharmacology it is understood that a junior faculty member can approach anyone for input on their written work. "We [the senior faculty] always want to look at their first grant application. That is the most important," said Loh. "Junior faculty can ask me for advice; I look at many grants with them. While I may not know the details of the science, I can certainly ask, 'How come you don't ask a clear question?'"

Bates (Chemical Engineering and Materials Science) said new faculty tend to have their proposals looked at by another faculty member or two in the beginning as part of the learning curve. He pointed out, however, that faculty mentors must be cautious in delivering their critique, since proposals are often expressions of intense creativity.

> On the one hand, I would be pretty careful telling somebody, "This is not so good, you should change it." They really have to learn to do this themselves. On the other hand, it doesn't hurt to give them a little bit of advice, and usually our young faculty write better proposals than the older faculty do, so that's not a problem. They just don't know that yet.

It was also clear from our interview responses that mentoring occurs at all stages of the grant development process. These stages include acquiring basic grant writing knowledge and skills, getting feedback on study design, selecting a funding agency, organizing the proposal in a logical and compelling format, and responding to the criticisms of an agency's grant review panel. Consider the following examples:

- Some departments take active measures to teach junior faculty the basics of how to write a grant. For example, the School of Nursing offers a grant writing course, and the classes are always well attended. In contrast, Masten (Child Development) assumes that new faculty will come in with the knowledge of how to write a grant or learn by trial and error with the help of more experienced faculty.

- Help on the front end of proposal development (conceptualizing the central ideas, deciding on the study design) is sometimes facilitated by departments. A few years ago the Morris Department of Psychology began to hold once-a-month meetings, creating an opportunity for faculty to get together as a discipline and solicit feedback on their research results or, in some cases, their research design.

- Both the School of Nursing and the Department of Cultural Studies and Comparative Literature make copies of funded grants available to new faculty to use as a template.

- Senior faculty will advise newer colleagues on how to direct their proposals to the most appropriate institute or agency. Loh (Pharmacology) stressed how valuable this input can be:

    > In grantsmanship it is very important how you direct your grant to the right committee or right area. If you study nutritional epidemiology, but you direct your grant to the molecular biology area or the molecular study section, they would crucify you. So we teach our faculty about this.

- Leppert (Cultural Studies and Comparative Literature) noted that mentoring in grantsmanship does not end with the submission of the proposal: "If the proposal isn't funded, we do follow-up to try to find out as best we can how to improve the proposal the next time around. The net effect is that the success rate is very high within the department."

Preparing faculty for promotion and tenure. In many departments, mentoring is closely tied to the promotion and tenure process. Accordingly, there is a concomitant emphasis in their mentoring activities on helping junior faculty to attain the key markers of scholarly productivity necessary for promotion and tenure (e.g., establish strong research programs, acquire external funding, publish frequently in peer-reviewed journals). In these environments mentoring is usually, though not always, facilitated by some type of formal mechanism.

In Veterinary Pathobiology, every new faculty member is placed on tenure track and then assigned a mentor to help them achieve that goal. "These [mentors] are the successful people who have been very good at getting NIH grants, USDA grants, and have been very successful in research. And also successful teachers," said Maheswaran. Mentors spend a lot of time with their mentees talking about how to get grants and other professional issues. Their commitment to one another is put into writing, and the mentoring relationship continues until tenure has been secured.

Similarly, tenure-track faculty in Pediatrics are paired with a "scientific mentor"—someone they work with in a laboratory and with whom they can identify. In addition, the department's tenure track committee works with junior faculty to ensure they have enough space, time, and supervision to help them meet their research and other academic goals. Strengthening the relationship between this committee and their mentees is a goal of Moller's: "When you hire somebody, the expectation is that they'll succeed. And we have a responsibility to see they're going to succeed. These are our values, and we have to provide them with the opportunity to do that."

Keeping track of a faculty member's progress on the road to tenure is frequently formalized through a committee structure. The Department of Chemistry's approach is representative of this process. For each new faculty member, a three-member tenure committee is appointed. The committee performs ongoing mentoring duties such as reviewing grant proposals, then meets annually to discuss the candidate's progress. "Some of those meetings are very quick, because the junior faculty are doing great," said Gladfelter. "Others face more difficult evaluations, not only on their research progress, but also on their teaching. Committee members identify areas that need to be improved and often make specific recommendations."

Basham (English) explained how mentoring in the form of annual reviews can spur on her faculty's productivity: "Tenure-track faculty are given the tenure guidelines. This is followed up by reviews and annual evaluations which are like retrorockets if they don't do the right thing." These evaluations include comments from her as the department chair, as well as the dean and the chancellor.

Entomology does not have a formal mentoring program per se, but the department head described their practice of giving junior faculty a copy of a successful, experienced faculty member's dossier. This provides new faculty with specific examples of what resulted in tenure for others in the department (e.g., what balance of research and education). On the Morris campus, the Commission on Women facilitates mentoring among women faculty. Junior faculty are paired with senior faculty, in part to acclimate them to the university, but also to help them prepare their files for tenure.

Who Takes on the Mentoring Role?

The multitude of tasks that a mentor might be expected to take on—and in turn, the qualifications that a good mentor needs to succeed in these tasks— brings us to a central issue: Who do research-productive departments call on to serve as mentors for newer faculty? The academic leaders in our study identified the following groups as fertile ground for mentor candidates:

- Research-productive senior faculty

- The chair or head of the department

- Other experienced colleagues outside of the department, and sometimes outside of the institution

Research-productive senior faculty. New faculty are likely to come into a department with a strong foundation for their careers, having studied and acquired experience in research methods, statistics, writing, and in specialized content areas; however, they can still benefit from the extensive "real world" experience of their more senior colleagues. Productive senior faculty are some of the most valuable resources in research-productive departments. They were responsible for helping to build and/or maintain the department's current research stature; in turn, they are well equipped to ensure that this tradition of research excellence is nurtured and passed on to the next generation of faculty. The department heads/chairs in our study were consistent (and sometimes colorful) in describing the informed perspective that seasoned faculty can provide. Consider these examples:

- "Senior faculty have been around the block quite awhile. They've been kicked in the shins enough and gotten enough pink sheets that weren't positive, had enough grants funded that didn't deserve to be funded, so they've seen it all. That can help us in our development of new faculty." (Biochemistry, Molecular Biology, and Biophysics).

- "When new faculty come into the department, we try to give them a lot of resources and time to get going, but also a lot of resources in the form of more senior faculty who can give them advice and clues, who have a lot of savvy about how to get grants. They are in a position to offer really good advice. They know everybody, know lots of inside stuff about organizations, and how you should and shouldn't spend your time." (Child Development)

- "What has worked [for our junior faculty] is to talk to the group of full professors who are doing well with their work, doing well in their field—they're getting recognition, and they're getting all kinds of grants and support and the exhibition options that one would hope for.... We can be very important to the development of junior faculty by showing them the way." (Art)

Senior faculty may be some of the best mentors, but do they necessarily have the skills and/or the desire to "give back" to their departments in this way? Not always, noted Pharis (Art), who nonetheless stressed the importance of their doing so. Even the department's most productive faculty (the research stars) need to give of their time and to share their knowledge with new faculty. In being research productive, they are "doing what they're supposed to do," said Pharis, "but they also need to recognize that this is not a gifting situation where they're always the recipients. They need to participate and feed it back into the organization and to the department.... Part of their service needs to be to lead and show the way, to be enthusiastic and gain accolades, but also to help faculty in a mentorship role."

Bates (Chemical Engineering and Materials Science) said that in his department's culture, no faculty member would consider it an imposition to review article and grant proposal drafts for their colleagues. "No, nobody would, absolutely not. It makes good sense. And it doesn't take much effort." The Institute of Child Development has "a history of great researchers who were very generative," said Masten. "They were research advocates, and they nurtured young researchers in the department." As such, there is a long-standing, ingrained expectation among faculty that research mentoring will occur at all levels—from the most senior faculty and graduate students on down to the least experienced faculty and students. Moreover, the director has a special responsibility to ensure that this happens among the faculty.

Department heads/chairs. Several of the interviewed department heads/chairs (being senior faculty themselves) reported playing very active, hands-on roles in helping to mentor their faculty. In Oral Sciences, either the chair or another senior faculty member is assigned to look after assistant professors just coming out of postdoctoral positions. The chair of Cultural Studies and Comparative Literature reviews drafts of grant proposals written by both junior faculty and senior faculty new to the department, drawing on his experience as a reviewer for fellowship and grant programs (e.g., for the National Endowment for the Humanities, the American Council of Learning Societies). The discipline coordinator for Psychology (Morris campus) sees himself as the coordinator of support for new faculty, asking them what the department can do to help them with their research with respect to space, equipment, funding, and so on.

Masten (Institute of Child Development) expressed a very broad view of mentoring in her capacity as a faculty leader, one that is focused on both junior and midcareer faculty: "The job of the chair that was conveyed to me includes very much a nurturing of the faculty's development along many different points in their careers." McEvoy (Educational Psychology) echoed this, saying, "I see the department chair as playing an important role.... It's serving as a professional mentor. It's taking the information and experience in seeing the broad picture, and helping young faculty with what they need to know to be successful."

Mentors from outside of the department. Up to now, we have focused our discussion on the mentoring capacity that exists within departments. This is congruent with our study's goal of identifying specific research-facilitating strategies enacted at the departmental level. It is well-recognized, however, that sometimes the best mentors—particularly content mentors with a close connection to one's specific area(s) of research interest—are found outside of one's department or even one's home institution.

A few department heads/chairs commented on the need to look externally for mentors, sometimes dictated by the inherent diversity in their faculty's research interests. On the one hand, a very diverse department can present mentoring challenges. Consider these statements by Vayda (Diagnostic and Surgical Science):

> Mentoring for a specific area of science, when we bring people in that are not automatically hooked up to someone in the building, has been somewhat of an issue. There's enough people in the building who are successful at grantsmanship. They are good resources, but you can certainly start to feel you're operating in a vacuum if your area of science isn't in sync with anybody else in this school.

On the other hand, diversity within departments and the larger institution can be a boon to mentoring. This is particularly true for faculty preparing for

tenure review and seeking supportive evaluations from scholars outside of
their discipline. Hogan described how this is facilitated for faculty in Family
Social Science:

> All faculty, within the first year, select a mentor committee.
> We have three members on each committee, usually two in
> the department and one from outside. It's really a good idea
> to have somebody from the outside, because when our fac-
> ulty go up for tenure, there really is going to be somebody
> from the outside judging them. . . . I'm on a mentoring
> committee for an assistant professor who is in graphic
> design. What do I know about graphic design? But she
> wants to be certain her credentials show that she is going
> into things respectable to social scientists, because there are
> a couple of them who will be on the college promotion and
> tenure committee. We can offer her that.

Within Liberal Arts on the Duluth Campus, there is a mentoring program specifically developed to prepare faculty for promotion and tenure. Part
of its purpose, explained Knopp (Geography), is "to connect people with faculty outside their home department, so they can have a little bit of breathing
room, share their concerns, and speak more candidly with somebody who
isn't going to be voting on their promotion and tenure eventually but who is
nonetheless tenured." He noted an important caveat: If the relationship goes
well, this same external mentor might be an ideal outsider to serve on one's
tenure review committee.

Mentoring across different departments also occurs on the Duluth campus. Basham (English) shared this example:

> Some scholars have done papers which have been read on
> the campus by other readers. I was a reader (with four other
> people) of a sociology person's paper which was published.
> . . . People with too few supports in their immediate envi-
> ronment can find that support [in both teaching and
> research] at the university level.

Basham went on to describe how on her campus, departments oftentimes
lack the more extensive cross-pollination of different disciplines that can
occur in larger Ph.D.-granting departments. Consequently, many of their faculty acquire mentors by visiting the Twin Cities campus and by going to professional meetings.

What Kinds of Formal Mentoring Structures Do Highly Research-Productive Departments Use? How Are Mentors Selected or Assigned?

As noted above, some departments foster mentoring relationships by officially assigning one or more mentors to each junior faculty member. Some specific examples of mentoring structures and activities were presented above in the section on promotion and tenure. Here are a few more:

- In the Department of Medicine, every faculty member establishes their own academic development plan. They discuss this plan with their mentor, and then get feedback from the promotion and tenure committee on their progress.

- Mechanical Engineering assigns two senior faculty mentors to each new faculty member. "We try to have one of them in the area and another one from outside the area to get cross pollination," said McMurry. "They seriously review the candidate's activities every year and provide feedback about what they think he/she needs to do. I also meet with that committee, and I get recommendations from them, and ensure that junior colleagues hear their important messages."

- On the Morris campus, a formal mentoring program (initially funded by the Bush Foundation, but now supported by university funds) pairs junior faculty with senior faculty. They discuss topics such as teaching, campus politics, how to make and stick to a research plan, and how to prepare a tenure file.

Among departments which actively pair up faculty with one or more mentors, some do so in similar ways. Oral Sciences is among several departments which select a mentor for people based on how well their research meshes with that of another. "Of course, they don't address the same questions or the same techniques," clarified Simone, "but their research is just close enough that they can speak the same language and have an understanding of what each other do."

In the Law School, Sullivan has "casual conversations" with his new faculty

---

Studies Consistently Emphasize the Importance of Mentors

- A 1999 study found that faculty members who are highly productive researchers were twice as likely to report having had a formal mentor. (Bland et al., 2002, 2004)

- The most influential variable in predicting research productivity of junior faculty is the presence of a mentor. In addition, senior faculty feel mentoring actually enhances their research productivity. (Paul, Stein, Ottenbacher, & Liu, 2002) to decide on an appropriate mentor, one with the potential to connect with mentees both socially and intellectually. "Typically it falls around academic or teaching interests for some obvious reasons," he said. But once the assignment takes place, he adopts a largely hands-off approach, letting the mentoring relationship develop on its own.

> I try to work out with the new faculty member who would be the ideal mentor and then vice versa with the senior colleague. I check in once or twice a year to see how is it going. But in terms of that relationship and how it gets built, it's completely dependent upon the chemistry and personality of the individuals.

In Epidemiology, Luepker lets new faculty select their own mentors, but does give them some guidance.

> Every new faculty member is sent around to meet everyone (which gets a little harder, the bigger we get). Then I sit down with them and ask them, who do they want to choose for a mentor? I say, "You would be wise to choose someone you're not going to work with, someone different from those in your area who will regularly talk to you and give you advice." I try to pair men with women and vice versa. I think there's something to be learned in both directions.

How Does Mentoring Occur Informally in Research-Productive Departments?

Just as there isn't only one area (e.g., research, teaching, culture, and norms) in which faculty should be mentored, there isn't only one way in which faculty should be mentored. Despite our emphasis thus far on more structured mentoring programs, it is essential to note that in highly research-productive departments successful mentoring also occurs through informal faculty interactions. Consider the following illustrative quotes:

- "There is a fair amount of coaching or mentoring happening indirectly. Two or three senior faculty are pretty good at it. We usually don't assign formal mentors. Most (but not all) people want to pick their own mentors. And typically, people seek understanding of what is really expected from them." (Forest Resources)

- "We haven't made it a departmental function to teach grant preparation, and I don't think it has been necessary. What typically happens is that a new faculty member teams up on a collaborative proposal with someone who is more senior. Through that process they'll learn how to make it work. Sometimes they might team up with someone outside the department. I think probably each individual finds a different path that is most suited to their area and personality." (Mechanical Engineering)

- "We do have a mentoring process, but it isn't so much related to an individual. Our senior faculty mentor some; they're responsible for the annual evaluation of the faculty member. But besides that, if you ask, how often do they function as a mentor, formally, I'd say probably never. Conversely, you'll find ten of us who eat lunch together every day, so the amount of contact a young faculty member has with the faculty as a whole is enormous." (Chemical Engineering and Materials Science)

Notably, these types of informal mentoring interactions, while not explicitly structured, are proactively encouraged, even expected, and at some level have become an integral part of the department's culture. Knopp (Geography) expressed this well when he said,

> We don't have a formal mentoring program in the department, but we try to collaborate in a way that sends the message to each other that we're going to support each other in our endeavors, to develop reputations in our disciplines, to network, to present at conferences, to organize sessions at conferences (to chair, to be a discussant, that sort of thing). It's clear that the culture in our department values this.

Which Department Features Might Determine the Extent and Type of Mentoring That Occurs?

The size of a department can have an impact on how structured or unstructured a mentoring program should be. For example, in smaller-sized departments such as Geography, the collaborating, nurturing, and supporting of faculty tends to happen naturally. Larger departments, particularly those in which faculty members are housed in multiple locations, typically need more formal mechanisms to ensure that mentoring occurs.

Houston (Marketing and Logistics Management) has observed that due to the diversity within their field, junior faculty will "informally gravitate toward other faculty based on a natural merging of interest." The same thing happens in the Industrial Relations Center, according to Ben-Ner: "Economists will talk to economists, in the department or elsewhere. It's a natural process. It does not, in my view, require a lot of formal intervention, unless you have somebody who has a peculiar disposition. And we haven't had that problem in the past."

Hicks (Biology) pointed out a potential stumbling block to formally assigning research mentors:

> I think some people would take it well if we set it up in a formal way, yet other people might think it was a slap in the face. They may feel that we were treating them like a kindergartner, because most people come into a new position at the university having been in a position (such as a postdoctoral appointment) just focusing on research.

Consequently, this department places greater emphasis on mentoring in the area of teaching, while supporting research in other ways such as giving faculty adequate time and other resources to do research.

The Department of Ecology, Evolution, and Behavior has had no formal mentoring program for a number of years, largely because almost all of their most recent hires have been senior faculty. "In the time span of eight years or so, we've had maybe one person come in who hadn't been a faculty member somewhere else. So it's maybe not a big surprise that mentoring hasn't been a big departmental issue," said Sterner. That, however, has changed recently in response to an influx of younger faculty.

Some departments, such as Pharmacology, will assign mentors to faculty who ask for one, but don't do this routinely as an across-the-board practice. In Agronomy and Plant Genetics, Gengenbach asked some of his junior faculty if they would like to have a mentor. "'No,' they said. They think they can get what they need without it. It's not a question we are avoiding, but at the current time the junior faculty, as a cohort, serve somewhat as their own mentors, and they are often engaged in meaningful projects or activities with other senior faculty."

McEvoy (Educational Psychology) has taken a middle-ground approach to mentoring. She reviews junior faculty every year using synopsis committees of three tenured faculty members, keeping the same chair year to year for continuity. In addition, she asks the chairs to be available if the junior faculty member wants assistance.

> Some of the junior faculty members seek it out. Others find their own colleagues within their own program area. So I'm pretty confident, in fact I know, that no one is out there just free floating. They're all connected with someone.

In conclusion, though mentoring is crucial, there is no gold standard for how to facilitate it. Highly research-productive departments use a multitude of diverse mentoring strategies in accordance with their size, diversity, geographic proximity, and so on. But always, mentoring is valued, expected, and facilitated in one or more ways. In short, it is tailored to best fit the department. Given this reality, this chapter is best viewed not as a "how to" primer on mentoring, but rather an important source of potential mentoring strategies that departments can turn to when considering how best to facilitate research productivity.

Chapter 5 Review: Mentoring

- Mentors can perform any number of tasks, but in these research-productive departments, mentoring was most valued as a mechanism for conveying the culture and norms of the department, for facilitating grant writing, and for keeping tenure-track faculty on track.

- Research-productive senior faculty are the heart and soul of a department's mentoring capacity. They are uniquely poised to share their lived experience and their skills, serving as role models for younger faculty on whom the department's future research productivity rests.

- Department heads and chairs can assign mentors to junior faculty, but many also serve as active mentors themselves. A department's mentoring capacity can be extended by calling upon faculty in other departments or institutions. This might occur when departments lack cohorts of faculty with similar research interests, or alternatively when faculty are actively seeking mentors with interests or experiences markedly different from their own.

- Although mentoring is crucial, there is no gold standard for how to facilitate it. Research-productive departments use both formal and informal mechanisms, in accordance with their size, diversity, geographic proximity, and so on. But mentoring is always valued, expected, and facilitated in one or more ways. In these departments, mentoring is an essential part of the research culture.

6

Interdisciplinary Collaboration

To be effective, departments need to recognize that they are part
of a team. Not only is the department a team, but also the
department among its equivalent departments, and the college.
If we take the attitude that we're competitive with everybody
else, it doesn't work.

(Mark Ascerno, Entomology)

LITERATURE SUMMARY

Increasingly, scholars are working collaboratively within or across the
boundaries of their disciplines. There is growing evidence for an association between an individual's productivity in research and the extent
of his or her collaborations. Academic institutions are called to facilitate their faculty's research partnerships by actively working to mini-
mize barriers and providing structures to promote and support collaborative work.

DEPARTMENT PRACTICES COVERED IN THIS CHAPTER
  1) Why is collaboration so highly valued in research-productive
     departments?
  2) By what means can departments and colleges/universities stimu-
     late collaborative research?
  3) What challenges inherent to collaborative research do faculty
     and administrators need to be aware of and respond to?

What Does the Literature Say?

"Interdisciplinary collaboration" was a frequent response to the first question
we asked in our interviews: "In your assessment of your department, what are
the key factors that contribute to the research productivity of your faculty?"
This finding was initially a surprise to us, because collaboration had not
emerged as a discrete research-facilitating feature in our earlier literature
reviews. However, there is evidence that faculty collaboration in research is a
potentially powerful driving force for productivity, particularly in disciplines

with robust paradigms. Below we provide a brief overview of prior literature on this topic. Particular attention is paid to the relationship between collaboration and measures of research productivity (e.g., published articles), as well as the benefits and challenges inherent to collaborative work.

Are Productive Scholars More Inclined to Collaborate Than Less Productive Scholars?

We went back to the literature to investigate this key question and found reports that high scholarly productivity (e.g., publishing output) is indeed correlated with high levels of collaboration (Balog, 1979; Beaver & Rosen, 1978, 1979a, 1979b; Hodder, 1979; Lawani, 1986; Pao, 1980, 1981; Price de Solla, 1963; Price de Solla & Beaver, 1966). In regression analyses of data from 437 academic scientists and engineers, Bozeman and Lee (2003) found that the number of collaborators was the strongest predictor of research productivity, measured by both fractional and normal publication count. Moreover, the explanatory power of collaboration was not diminished by factors such as job satisfaction, rank and age, gender, or nationality. When Pravdic and Oluicvukovic (1986) examined collaborative patterns in chemistry at both the group and the individual level, they found scientific output " . . . is highly dependent on the frequency of collaboration among the same authors" (p. 259). The effect hinged on the nature of the associations; collaboration with highly productive scientists tended to enhance personal productivity, whereas collaboration with less productive scientists tended to decrease personal productivity. The most productive authors appeared to collaborate most frequently. Furthermore, authors at all levels of productivity collaborated more with highly productive authors than with less productive authors.

Why Are Faculty Drawn to Collaborate With Other Academic Scholars? With Industry Partners?

The concept of interdisciplinary collaboration in academia is not new, and more and more scholars are working collaboratively within or across the boundaries of their disciplines. In a survey of science and engineering faculty at major U.S. research centers, respondents reported spending 84% of their time collaborating with others versus working alone and having an average of 13.8 (median = 12) collaborations per year (Bozeman & Lee, 2003). This included work conducted with graduate students and others in the faculty member's immediate research group.

Katz and Martin (1997) found that

> among the factors which motivate collaboration are funding
> agencies' need to save money, the growing availability and
> falling (real) cost of transport and communication, the
> desire for intellectual interactions with other scientists, the
> need for a division of labour in more specialised or capital-
> intensive areas of science, the requirements of interdiscipli-
> nary research, and government encouragement of interna-
> tional and cross-sectoral collaboration. (p. 16)

Collaborations between academic and industrial partners have their own
unique benefits. They allow scientists to move forward their own research
while facilitating companies' ability to get their products into the market-
place. Such partnerships also help fulfill societal needs and encourage economic growth by successfully leveraging more broad state and federal support
of fundamental research being conducted on academic campuses across the
U.S. (Business–Higher Education Forum, 2001).

A natural outcome of collaborative work is coauthored publications. Several studies have identified rewards to multiple authorship. Nudelman and
Landers (1972) suggest that the total recognition given by the scientific community to every one of the authors of a multiple-authored paper is larger on
average than the recognition given to the author of a single-authored paper.
There are reports that research conducted by bigger groups tends to be more
prestigious (Crane, 1972; Goffman & Warren, 1980). In his study of cancer
research literature, Lawani (1986) found a highly positive correlation between
multiple authorship and the production of high-quality papers (defined as
papers cited repeatedly by others). Moed, de Bruin, and Straathof (1992)
found that internationally coauthored papers are cited significantly more frequently than single-country papers. Finally, Diamond (1985) found that citations to multiple-authored papers enhance the authors' earning capacity or
salary more than do citations to single-authored papers.

What Are the Challenges of Collaboration?
How Might They Be Overcome?

Collaboration can be an enriching experience for those involved, but it can
also be a "personally challenging relationship complicated by a large number
of potential difficulties" (Snyder, 1992, p. 197). Collaboration between faculty members can provoke issues of influence, power, integrity, and professional
identity. Moreover, the traditional academic environment is rife with barriers

to collaborative work. Many academics are not trained to work routinely with others; most administrative structures are not designed to promote or support collaborations, especially across disciplines and departments; and the academic reward structure is not easily adapted to group work, but is focused instead on rewarding the work of the individual (Bohen & Stiles, 1998). When an industrial partner is involved, collaborators might also wrestle with issues surrounding intellectual property, confidentiality, indirect costs, conflicts of interest, and background rights. (For more on these challenges and recommendations for addressing them, see *Working Together, Creating Knowledge: The University–Industry Research Collaboration Initiative* [Business–Higher Education Forum, 2001] and current issues of the journal *Industry and Higher Education* [IP Publishing Ltd., Turpin Distribution Services Ltd., Blackhorse Road, Letchworth, Herts SG6 1HN, UK].)

There is no one way to achieve an effective collaboration. Numerous case reports on collaborations have been published, all of which conclude with differing recommendations for success (Engebretson & Wardell, 1997; Gibbons, 1998; Hutchens, 1998; Kellett, 1999; McWilliam, Desai, & Greig, 1997; Nyiendo, Lloyd, & Haas, 2001; Reynolds, Giardino, Onady, & Siegler, 1994; Rovegno & Bandhauer, 1998; Scherger, Rucker, Morrison, Cygan, & Hubbell, 2000; Walker, 1988). Yet across the many different types of collaboration, four key (albeit basic) steps consistently occur: Colleagues or team members are selected, the labor is split among team members, work guidelines are set up, and the collaboration is ended (Austin & Baldwin, 1991/2000). Administration can play a pivotal role in the development of effective collaborations. This might occur through resource distribution, the development of accommodating policies that reward collaborative work, and the elimination of organizational barriers (Austin & Baldwin, 1991/2000). Many universities have formalized their efforts to collaborate with industrial partners by establishing an industry–university research center to help facilitate these relationships (Meagher & Gray, 2002).

Department Practices

The qualitative findings from our interview study mirror many elements of the existing literature on collaboration. The heads/chairs of highly research-productive departments clearly perceive significant benefits to collaboration. And they use specific strategies to both promote collaboration and address the inherent challenges that come with this practice. Notably, the frequency with which collaboration was cited as an important facilitator of research productivity varied across disciplines; this occurred more frequently in data disciplines (e.g., chemistry, engineering), and less frequently in word disciplines such as English. Others similarly report that collaboration is rare in disciplines such as literature or philosophy (Bayer & Smart, 1988; Berelson, 1960; Fox & Faver, 1984).

Why Is Collaboration so Highly Valued in Research-Productive Departments?

The academic leaders in our study offered up a variety of ways in which interdisciplinary collaborations can (and routinely do) positively influence their departments' research productivity. From their responses, the following emerged as dominant themes:

- Collaborations can stimulate new avenues for research, help with answering complex research questions, and advance faculty careers.

- Interdisciplinary projects are appealing to many funding sources.

- A collaborative work environment can attract outstanding faculty researchers.

Collaborations can stimulate new avenues for research, help with answering complex research questions, and advance faculty careers. In some areas of scholarly inquiry, a faculty member's research objectives cannot be achieved alone. Rather, a multidisciplinary approach is required to successfully address the question or problem of interest. "We can do so much more together than we can independently," said Gengenbach (Agronomy and Plant Genetics). In his department, he reported,

> Every researcher has some sort of ongoing, meaningful collaboration with at least one other person. In many cases, it will be half a dozen people trying to look at bigger issues. Most of our research grants go in with two or three PIs [principal investigators].

Many researchers welcome opportunities to collaborate because they know that such partnerships can yield ground-breaking new knowledge. These advancements in scholarship can, in turn, advance a faculty member's career.

For example, a faculty member in the Department of English has developed a very strong publishing record by writing collaboratively on the topic of education with Native Americans and other tribal people. "There's a network of people all over the world who are involved in this kind of research,"

Basham said. "They do primary interviewing research, as well as summary books. They keep generating interesting projects, and they're rewarded for that in the system—with grants, with dominance at conferences, and with interview possibilities."

Vayda has observed several midlevel faculty in her dental school department (Diagnostic/Surgical Science) succeed by developing the clinical component to a project and then collaborating with faculty from the basic sciences. "That really was the key to these individuals' success," she said. "The collaboration drove the project which, by themselves, neither of them could have initiated."

Hogan spoke of a faculty member in her department (Family Social Science) who is finishing a book on ambiguous loss—an endeavor that began when a colleague in the Medical School called her up, looking to involve a family researcher in a project on Alzheimer's disease. "Sometimes principal investigators will need a 'family person,' because they are required to look at these variables in a study they want to conduct," explained Hogan. This can lead to productive forays by her faculty into new areas of research. For example, the aforementioned family social scientist has since extended her work on ambiguous loss to Native American populations.

Again and again, the department heads/chairs in our study acknowledged that a good share of their faculty members' productivity is an outcome of their active collaboration with others. "Our field really requires you to cooperate on big projects or make interdisciplinary connections of one sort or another," summarized Sterner (Ecology, Evolution, and Behavior). "It's a rare person in our field who can achieve national/international reputations working on his or her own."

Interdisciplinary projects are appealing to many funding sources. More and more, funding agencies are looking to support research projects whose objectives call for interdisciplinary activities. Funders are attracted to the high potential for research breakthroughs, as well as the cost sharing that can result when collaborating investigators pool their resources. It is clear from the responses gathered in our study that the faculty in these highly research-productive departments recognize, and indeed, have capitalized on, this important funding trend. Consider these examples:

- A reproduction specialist in Clinical and Population Sciences is currently working with researchers in the Medical School on freezing semen, using the horse as a model for humans. The funds for this project came from an internal university funding initiative that specifically supports research crossing disciplinary lines.

- The Minnesota Materials Research Science and Engineering Center, originally launched under the leadership of two faculty in Chemical Engineering and Materials Science (Drs. Bates and Ward), has since expanded to include over seven departments across the university. "Funding agencies are pushing a lot more of that," said Bates.

- In Family Social Science, faculty members are collaborating with investigators from the University of Georgia to conduct a federally funded project on fatherhood. Another major grant on adolescents involves a co-investigator from Utah.

A collaborative work environment can attract outstanding faculty researchers. Given the potential benefits to collaboration, it is perhaps not surprising that many faculty candidates are searching for work settings in which collaboration is prevalent, encouraged, and strongly supported. The departments in our study are aware of this and, as described in depth in Chapter 2, they take great care to highlight local opportunities for collaborative research when wooing promising faculty candidates.

Simone (Oral Sciences) said he considers himself to be "a big promoter of cross-disciplinary activities." His expectation is that incoming faculty will establish the collaborative links they need to succeed, and he encourages this through an awareness of what is going on in other departments and schools. For example, a tissue engineering researcher coming into his department might collaborate with other faculty through the university's Stem Cell Institute. The head of Pediatrics explained that collaborative opportunities are attractive to many new faculty, who view them as opportunities for their careers to advance and grow.

Some departments will actually frame a faculty position and post it with specific opportunities for collaboration in mind. When the Twin Cities Department of Psychology is writing up a job description and evaluating candidates, "We are constantly thinking about how an individual will be interconnected with other parts of the department, and with other departments, because psychology itself spans a huge variety of work," said Campbell. "There are very few people in our department who are not working with or otherwise connected with somebody from another discipline."

By What Means Can Departments and Colleges/Universities Stimulate Collaborative Research?

Clearly, the leaders of highly research-productive departments value collaboration, both as a route to new knowledge and as a means of attracting valuable fiscal and human resources to support the research enterprise. But how, specifically, do these departments foster productive collaborations? What strategies or practices do they apply to make this important environmental feature a reality? Recall that in our structured interview protocol, we did not specifically ask department leaders about collaboration; nonetheless, their unsolicited comments did reveal a set of common practices which they use to stimulate collaborations.

Some of these practices are discussed in other chapters. For example, in Chapter 7 we describe the many ways that these departments facilitate their faculty's communication with both local and more distant colleagues—an essential precursor to collaboration. In Chapter 2, we describe their efforts to hire faculty candidates who already possess a willingness and ability to collaborate. Here, we focus our discussion on four additional strategies for stimulating collaborations which emerged from our study:

- Physically group researchers together.

- Establish strong linkages with other departments.

- Encourage faculty participation in interdisciplinary research centers or institutes.

- Promote an overall culture of collaboration.

Physically group researchers together. Within a department, it can be advantageous to house likely collaborators together. For example, in Chemical Engineering and Materials Science, faculty members with common research interests (for example, theory and computations) are loosely grouped together into research subgroups. Similarly, in the polymer area there is an open style of research in which colleagues work together, share lab space, and buy equipment together. "This is not new that faculty work together, but it's a little more structured than it used to be," explained Bates. "The atmosphere and environment should be conducive for shared equipment, shared proposals, and so forth."

Similar advantages can be realized in departments whose faculty members have very diverse areas of interest and expertise. General College is one example of this, with faculty in writing, mathematics, the social sciences, the humanities, and the biological and physical sciences all housed in close proximity. As Collins explained,

> You're not next to another English teacher for another 18 doors down the hallway; you're next to people whose training and thinking and reading methods are different from

yours. That leads to some pretty interesting opportunities
for collaboration, and more and more we're seeing that
break through.

Besides sparking collaborations, one's ability to interact frequently and
substantively with productive local colleagues can bear fruit in other ways.
For instance, it can increase opportunities for informal mentoring, contribute
to a shared culture of research, and encourage faculty to share new ideas and
take risks with a safe, readily accessible group of colleagues. These and other
benefits to having a strong local peer network are addressed in Chapter 7 and
Chapter 8.

Establish strong linkages with other departments. Although productive collaborations can, and frequently do, occur in-house, it is also commonplace for
faculty members in these departments to develop research ties with faculty in
other departments or research centers. Numerous specific examples of this
were expressed in our interviews. Pediatricians and internists routinely work
with researchers in the university's Cancer Center; Biology faculty in Duluth
collaborate with ecologists in the Natural Resources Research Institute and
with cell biologists in the School of Medicine; faculty in Food Science and
Nutrition work with chemists, microbiologists, and geneticists across campus.

"Most of our faculty [in Ecology, Evolution, and Behavior] have very
active research connections with other departments or other colleges—geolo-
gy, agriculture, biochemistry, physiology, and forest resources," said Sterner.
"This culture we have in Minnesota—of people not being too worried if it's
in the department or not—is really important to us." Other departments play
a "big factor" in the success of Applied Economics, according to Eidman:

> The fact that the econ department is here and is a quality
> department, makes a lot of difference. . . . They're extremely
> good colleagues and very knowledgeable. We benefit a lot
> from having them here. Our Ph.D. students take their the-
> ory there, and that is good interaction. The statistics depart-
> ment is also very valuable to us. Public Health is another
> one that we frequently work with.

Some departments have strengthened their relationships with one another by working together on faculty recruitment. They collectively interview
candidates and pool their resources to offer a joint appointment (for example,
in both the Law School and the Department of Philosophy, or in the Cancer
Center and the Department of Medicine). "It turns out, we had a wonderful

relationship with Philosophy, and we grew closer by reason of these candidates coming in," said Sullivan (Law).

Encourage faculty participation in interdisciplinary research centers or institutes. A more formal mechanism by which faculty can develop productive collaborations is by participating in the activities of research institutes, centers, or other such entities at their institution. Regardless of their membership scope or unifying subject area, these research centers typically share a common goal: to bring together researchers from diverse disciplines but with overlapping interests, and to provide a forum for these scholars to productively interact. The interviewed department heads/chairs offered up several examples of the center mechanism in action at the University of Minnesota.

Bearinger (Nursing) explained that her school's research centers "play a huge role" in drawing their faculty into collaborations, particularly new faculty. "We now know what each other are interested in, and we didn't used to know that. We are saying, 'Would you work with me on this? How can I help you move this another step forward?'"

Collins called General College's Center for Developmental Education and Urban Literacy "a catalyst for faculty research." The center hosts a seminar series and invited meetings. These events bring in leaders from around the country, including the editors of the key disciplinary journals, to discuss future directions in the field. These interactions have resulted in a nationally circulated monograph series.

Faculty in the Industrial Relations Center started a research institute two years ago with the objective of facilitating collaborative research across and within disciplines. "The institute has helped us to establish ourselves in a particular niche," explained Ben-Ner. In addition, the research emphasis of the center provides a useful complement to their faculty's more practice-oriented and applied work.

In the Department of Clinical and Population Sciences, faculty have successfully partnered with industry to develop the Center for Swine Disease Eradication. The center bridges faculty members' research interests in infectious diseases with the private sector's concerns about food safety and environmental issues. "Now, everyone wants to be at the table," said Ames. The center's advisory board (with a $25,000/year membership fee) includes representatives from genetics companies, large hog production chains, and pharmaceutical companies. "Our researchers reinvented themselves," Ames said. "They figured out how to work as a team on something that's important. And they've generated a revenue stream that they can at least use as seed grants. It's fantastic."

Seeing the success of their colleagues, other faculty in Clinical and Population Sciences have adopted a similar strategy for researching bovine diseases that is more appropriate to meeting both the needs of today's larger agribusinesses and their teaching needs. This new partnership involves a large existing dairy in Wisconsin and a new dairy that will be built to handle clinical trials, with laboratory facilities, restraint and treatment facilities, dorm rooms, and classrooms. This particular collaboration began with $150,000 in funding from the university; the faculty have since raised an additional $450,000 from industry, with an additional commitment for $400,000 in operating expenses over the next three years.

Promote an overall culture of collaboration. Creating interdisciplinary research centers, providing grants for stimulating collaborative research, emphasizing collaborative opportunities during recruitment and hiring—all of these practices have resulted in the University of Minnesota being perceived as having a shared culture of collaboration. Indeed, numerous statements expressed during our interviews reflect the existence of an organizational culture in which collaboration is valued and supported:

- "It's really important that all faculty integrate their work with the rest of the university." (Food Science and Nutrition)

- "We talk about collaboration, and we encourage it through grant programs that give preference to collaborative researchers." (Clinical and Population Sciences)

- "We have benefited from the university putting up money for interdisciplinary collaboration to start new areas of research. Those initiatives really do help." (Child Development)

- "One place that Minnesota really shines is in the interdisciplinary work, and that is largely because of the graduate school. The way the university is configured, with the graduate school and its support for interdisciplinary programs and research, helps us." (Ecology, Evolution, and Behavior)

As explained in Chapter 3, culture is a powerful environmental characteristic in research-productive organizations; it provides a set of common core values, an identity understood and shared by all group members. The fact that collaboration is

> "The guiding principle for taking the first step toward any collaborative research endeavor is simplistic but crucial to success: The partnership must bring together people who have the right mix of talents, an identifiable common goal, and a vested interest in the practice and/or policy issues to be investigated." (McWilliam, Desai, & Greig, 1997)

integrated into the culture at our university might explain, at least in part, why collaboration emerged as a dominant theme in our study, despite its absence from our interview protocol and from the original literature-based model of research-productive organizations.

What Challenges Inherent to Collaborative Research Do Faculty and Administrators Need to Be Aware of and Respond to?

Up to now, we have focused our discussion on the many benefits that inter-disciplinary collaborations offer. However, as mentioned earlier in the litera-ture review for this chapter, collaborations also present some interesting chal-lenges. The leaders in our study seemed acutely aware of these complexities. They were candid in pointing out potential problems with, and barriers to, collaboration. And they stressed the importance of attending to these issues if the many advantages to collaborative work are to be realized.

Finding the right collaborator. In spite of the University of Minnesota's collab-orative culture and the existence of specific mechanisms for facilitating research partnerships, it remains a very large institution. On the one hand, this is helpful; the depth and breadth of scholarship that extend across its many campuses and colleges can be conducive to collaborative research. On the other hand, the uni-versity's sheer size does complicate the task of finding a suitable collaborator, par-ticularly for faculty who are new to campus or who have a specialty that isn't log-ically tied to anyone else's research agenda in their home department.

"It's very difficult to come in here and figure out who you should be talk-ing to, especially if there is no one else in your building that can provide that link for you," said Vayda (Diagnostic/Surgical Science). "The Academic Health Center should play a more active role in linking the units together and in helping to establish some of those collaborations. . . . There should be a mechanism for connecting junior faculty when they walk through the door with the appropriate group." Although the university does have a database for sharing information about the faculty's research expertise, many faculty mem-bers are not taking full advantage of this resource.

On the Morris campus, similar disciplines are grouped into divisions; how-ever, this does not necessarily lead to interdisciplinary work. According to Gar-avaso (whose discipline, philosophy, is part of the Humanities Division), it is important for faculty to look beyond division lines. "I'm not saying we should abolish divisions, but we need to have more connections. . . . We really haven't evolved inside our division as much as we should have, and we still need to work more with others, for example, in the Division of Social Sciences."

Finding space to work together. A particularly sensitive issue at many institutions, the University of Minnesota included, is the allocation of research space. Space is a precious environmental resource, and lack of sufficient space with reasonable proximity to one's collaborators can impact the growth of collaborative work.

Several department heads/chairs in the Medical School noted that competition for laboratory space can make it difficult for their faculty to collaborate, particularly for clinical scientists seeking to work with basic scientists. Moller in Pediatrics offered this example:

> We have this grant, a very competitive grant, to develop
> pediatric scientists and to have them trained in basic science
> laboratories. So they go over there, work for two or three
> years, but then when they get to the point of paying their
> own independent support, they can't keep a lab in the Cen-
> ter for Immunology. It's all right as long as they're training,
> working with somebody and developing a collaborative
> relationship with somebody in one of the basic science
> departments. But then they can't get an adjacent lab.

Masten (Child Development) also commented on the challenges of collaborative research related to space and distance. "Requiring extra time to get somewhere is a deterrent to collaboration," she said. One problem for her faculty is that the Center for Neurobehavioral Development, though ripe with opportunities for collaboration, is located on the other side of campus.

Further complicating the space issue is that as much as faculty want to have physical space near other researchers in diverse areas, they also want to stay connected to their home departments—the main office, the graduate student offices, and the space shared by local colleagues within their discipline. These desires are not always reconcilable. These and other issues related to space and its impact on research productivity are discussed further in Chapter 8.

Keeping ties to one's home discipline or department. Too much collaboration outside of one's home department, institute, or college can, at the extreme end, lead faculty so far astray that their professional relationships with local colleagues are weakened. "Our faculty do a lot of interdisciplinary work, in my opinion almost too much," said Archibald (Public Affairs). "All of us have interdisciplinary ties which draw us apart and make less time for us to come together here. The university has been encouraging this cross-disciplinary work, but it makes it hard to find time to work with your colleagues."

As interdisciplinary connections increase and the lines between disciplines blur, the issue of "Where do I belong?" becomes increasingly complex. As McMurry (Mechanical Engineering) explained,

> Many of us could be equally at home in the mechanical engineering department or the chemical engineering or electrical engineering departments. Mechanical engineering provides a home (and I think everybody needs that), but sometimes it's not always the most effective grouping for people working in different areas. I don't see any obvious solution to that. It's an organizational challenge.

Determining project ownership and authorship. Deciding who gets first authorship on a journal article or who serves as the principal investigator on a grant proposal can be a delicate issue for any research team. This is further complicated when the team members are collaborators from different disciplines.

Finances are one potential problem. Different departments and colleges may have different fiscal policies, and thus struggle with how to fairly distribute indirect dollars when the funds are brought in on collaborative grants. Promotion and tenure codes can also contribute to the tension. Consider these comments by Sullivan (Law) on judging multiple-author publications fairly:

> We have always talked in our tenure and promotion process about how we judge and weigh joint publications. We as a faculty have come to believe that it is important not to prejudice it, that it's something to be celebrated and encouraged. . . . It becomes difficult, though, when one person is going up for promotion, to try to figure out whose work it is.

Issues such as this can also arise during discussions of merit-based faculty raises.

Given these complexities of collaborative work, finding the right mesh of personalities is important to consider. Collaborations are more likely to thrive when the team members share common ideas and aspirations, communicate well, and have trust in one another. Two of the interviewed department leaders shared specific examples of a give-and-take approach to collaborative grant writing that has helped them to develop successful, highly collegial research programs with colleagues in other disciplines:

- "Sometimes we write the grants, occasionally the other department will write the grants; sometimes we're the main person, sometimes we're the secondary. It means more grant participation that way." (Food Science and Nutrition)

- "I've had an ongoing research project to study the Buyer's Healthcare Action Group, where a faculty member in the Business School was the PI [principal investigator]. We just flipped into the second round of that, and now I'm the PI. I have other projects with a sociologist on our faculty, where we just flip back and forth, so our research is both collegial and collaborative." (Health Services Research and Policy)

Striking a balance between collaborative and independent scholarship. Finally, and perhaps most important, the benefits of collaboration must be appropriately balanced with an individual faculty member's need to develop into a skilled independent researcher. To be productive over the long term, faculty must have a well-rounded set of research skills as well as the liberty to set their own path and develop their own theories. This is particularly important for new and/or junior faculty. "There's a distinction between working collegially in an area with others and really working so closely that a young faculty member might feel threatened," said Bates (Chemical Engineering and Materials Science). "They've got to establish their own research program. We have to be very careful not to infringe on their independence."

With their independence established, faculty have greater freedom to work with, and be challenged by, some of the finest researchers worldwide. Warthesen (Food Science and Nutrition) described the balance this way:

> "More faculty collaboration will not eliminate the work faculty do independently; rather, it will diversify and enrich professors' work lives." (Austin & Baldwin, 1991/2000)

> It's important for faculty to understand that they need to be an independent researcher and a collaborative researcher. That sounds like you are telling them two different things, and you are. They need to be both. Almost all successful researchers are collaborative and independent as well.

Chapter 6 Review: Interdisciplinary Collaboration _____

- Interdisciplinary collaboration is both encouraged and proactively facilitated in highly research-productive departments. This is in part due to a growing realization that many of today's toughest research questions are best addressed through the joint efforts of top researchers from diverse disciplines.

- Collaborations can be encouraged through purposeful efforts: housing faculty in common interest areas in close proximity, establishing interdisciplinary research centers or seminar series, hiring faculty on joint appointments, and offering financial incentives (grant or seed money) to new collaborative initiatives. Having a pervasive institutional culture of collaboration is a particularly powerful way to increase interdisciplinary work.

- Interdisciplinary collaboration comes with some inherent challenges. These include finding appropriate research partners, negotiating the power within a collaborative relationship, finding space to work together, and maintaining one's disciplinary identity.

7

Communication With Colleagues: Professional Networks

Our faculty members do a good job of maintaining their professional network. They are leaders, presidents in their respective associations. The joke is that nobody is ever here, because they are all on an airplane somewhere.

(Sandra Archibald, Public Affairs)

LITERATURE SUMMARY
Research-productive faculty members have frequent, substantive (i.e., not merely social) conversations with research peers located inside and outside of their institution. These networks of colleagues enable faculty to build their knowledge base, to critique and replicate work, and to ensure the quality of work in the field. These networks also provide faculty with knowledgeable colleagues for recognition and celebration. Highly research-productive departments actively employ strategies to facilitate their faculty's communication with local, national, and international colleagues.

DEPARTMENT PRACTICES COVERED IN THIS CHAPTER
1) How do highly research-productive departments promote open, substantive internal communication among their faculty, that is, within their local work environments?
2) How do departments facilitate their faculty's substantive communication with external colleagues, that is, their professional networks?

What Does the Literature Say? _____

Numerous studies have found a positive correlation between communication among researchers and their productivity (Aran & Ben-David, 1968; Bland

& Ruffin, 1992; Blau, 1976; Fox, 1991; Kelly, 1986; Pelz & Andrews, 1966; Sindermann, 1985; Tschannen-Moran, Firestone, Hoy, & Johnson, 2000). In a cross-national study by Teodorescu (2000), "membership in professional societies and attendance of professional conferences was a significant correlate of article productivity in all the countries in the sample" (p. 216). Also, in a study of the published products of research groups in six countries, Visart (1979) found that 31% of the variance in productivity was explained by communication (both within and between groups).

In their study of 10,000 scientists in 1,200 different research groups in six countries, Pelz and Andrews (1966) found that the most productive researchers had the most frequent conversations with colleagues (e.g., 15 hours a week) and spent the most time doing such things as reviewing drafts of colleagues' papers, visiting each others' labs, and exchanging reprints. In their review of professional academic networks, Hitchcock, Bland, Hekelman, and Blumenthal (1995) concluded that faculty who communicate more with colleagues produce more and better research and are promoted more quickly, are more likely to receive an increase in income and to be the recipients of distinguished awards, and also evince a higher satisfaction with the work itself.

A vital network of colleagues is so important that it is consistently found to be a major predictor of research productivity (Blackburn, 1979; Bland & Schmitz, 1986; Corcoran & Clark, 1984; Pelz & Andrews, 1966; Visart, 1979). In establishing these networks, it helps to have colleagues both physically and conceptually close. A classic MIT study looked at the correlation between communication and distance of faculty members' office space and found that the probability of communicating with each other was 25% if offices were 5 meters apart, but only 8% to 9% if 10 meters apart (Peters & Waterman, 1982).

Clearly, it is essential to productivity to provide mechanisms for faculty to communicate with each other in person, on the phone, and by email. In times of financial constraints, it is tempting to curtail support for long distance calls and travel. Such strategies are likely to decrease productivity in both the classroom and laboratory, especially among those faculty who are most inclined to become isolated and, as a result, potentially less productive (Bergquist, Greenburg, & Klaum, 1993).

Department Practices

Faculty members in highly research-productive departments have extensive professional networks, the vitality of which is sustained through frequent communication with colleagues. Consider these illustrative quotes from our qualitative study:

- "Almost all our faculty are members of regional research groups." (Entomology)

- "Most of our faculty members are getting elected to office within the professional organizations that they work in. . . . Many of them are working for the Department of Children, Families and Learning or helping with Human Services or something within the state, so that they are highly visible in those organizations. We also have a significant presence at the legislature." (Educational Psychology)

- I remember sending a note to the faculty about connections. I asked faculty to give me the names of their top three, four, or five contacts— those they had around the state and the region, people they were in touch with regularly about professional practice, research, or extension. I figured I'd get a few contacts from most folks. Instead I was buried by replies. Everyone had 15 or more contacts they saw regularly, and I learned who they were. I was amazed at how connected people were." (Forest Resources)

Although frequent communication with colleagues is in part self-driven, there are a number of ways in which departments can actively help their faculty to develop, and maintain, productive professional relationships with peers. In this chapter we report on these departments' most commonly cited strategies for facilitating substantive communication among faculty. Methods for fostering internal communication (i.e., with local peers) are presented first, followed by methods for facilitating faculty's communication with their research colleagues who are located outside of a department's halls and walls.

How Do Highly Research-Productive Departments Promote Open, Substantive Internal Communication Among Their Faculty, That Is, Within Their Local Work Environments?

Good communication within a department can have numerous benefits. It can help spark collaborations, ease conflict resolution, facilitate goal-setting and decision-making, and foster a positive group climate. All of these outcomes, in turn, can positively influence faculty productivity. Thus, it was not surprising to find that the department leaders in our study typically use multiple strategies to keep their faculty talking to one another. These strategies include the following:

- Hire faculty who fit the culture and who demonstrate an interest in collaborating.

- Routinely inform faculty of one another's work.

- Create opportunities for frequent, impromptu conversations.

Hire faculty who fit the culture and who demonstrate an interest in collaborating. A culture of good communication is nurtured when faculty are hired who match that type of environment. Recall that when recruiting new faculty members, these highly research-productive departments specifically look for candidates who value a spirit of collaboration. They seek candidates who will be a catalyst for one another's work and who appreciate the value of their local colleagues (Chapter 2). It is this type of faculty member who typically goes on to be highly productive in research. Hicks (Biology) summarized this well:

> The people [new hires] who come and are productive are the ones who recognize there's more than just this department in their research interaction. But we have also found that although they will be collaborating with researchers from across the United States, these are the ones who turn out to be the most successful in our local environment. . . . It's important for people to have others they can talk to locally and interact with. So, we strive to look for people who might fit in that way.

Routinely inform faculty of one another's work. Communication is enhanced when faculty are brought out of their isolation and alerted to one another's activities. "You try to get people into the network as soon as possible," explained Ek (Forest Resources). "That's part of why I circulate everyone's annual report. I want everybody to see who all is doing what, who they are connected with, and what kind of resources they are able to find." In Clinical and Population Sciences, division heads will occasionally take time during faculty meetings to describe what is going on in their unit—what classes are being taught, what research is being worked on and by whom—as an attempt to say, "let's find out what everybody is doing and understand each other's behavior," said Ames.

Most research-productive departments hold seminars or workshops, sometimes over lunch, where faculty members can present their latest research. New faculty on the Morris campus are encouraged to give seminars for the faculty. In the Law School, faculty workshops are held every Thursday during the academic year. "The presenter gets 20 minutes to present his or her thesis, and then we go at him or her for the balance of the hour of so," said Sullivan.

It's a very collegial, intellectual, fairly high-plane discussion. Everybody benefits. We have a broad spectrum from feminism to intellectual property—we don't have it set or specialized in one subject matter area. These workshops have been so successful that many of our colleagues, while they are here in the summer, continue with a more informal lunch off campus where a paper or an article or a book is assigned, and we read it and discuss it over lunch.

Create opportunities for frequent, impromptu conversations. Often superceding the value of more formal communication strategies are ample opportunities for informal, face-to-face interactions—group lunches, hallway chats, or bumping into each other in the break room. Such opportunities tend to be integrated into the faculty's everyday routine. The Department of Agronomy and Plant Genetics, for example, has a specific place for faculty to get coffee and where they tend to congregate at around 9:30 in the morning and 3 o'clock in the afternoon. "If I'm available I'll stick my head in there for five or ten minutes," said Gengenbach. "Some of the more interesting conversations will happen in that setting."

Faculty in Eidman's department (Applied Economics) operate with an open-door policy. "If I want to see somebody, I'll call them and say, 'I'd like to talk to you,' and they say, 'Well, why don't you wait 30 minutes and then come up.' That's the way things work here." He also has observed his faculty interact informally with one another over lunch around an issue such as resource economics or farm management. "We don't force that kind of thing very much; it just happens."

Of course, the physical layout of a department can affect how often and how substantially its faculty members communicate. Faculty with offices close to each other have the advantage of increasing their informal communication through proximity alone. In Forest Resources, "almost anyone can run into almost anybody else on a given day," said Ek. Similarly, in General College, a lot of

> One of the most basic needs for good communication is for offices to be located close enough that the faculty can interact with each other. At many universities, however, this can be difficult to achieve as departments outgrow their original space and then are dispersed randomly across the campus. Departments in our study do keep their faculty together with some success. When asked, "Where are the offices of the majority of your faculty located?" their responses were:
>
> - 8: all in one building on one floor
> - 13: all in one building on different floors
> - 8: in different closely located buildings
> - 3: in different buildings far apart from each other

business is done face to face. But Collins also had high praise for their email communication, which is enhanced by having address lists for faculty, as well as staff and graduate students. "People know how to be in touch with each other, even in the summer. People with research questions can quickly be in touch with people about methods. We can develop proposals over the week-end pretty easily."

Distance can be a significant barrier to communication. Garavaso (Philosophy) on the Morris campus expressed a need for greater communication with scholars from the Twin Cities campus:

> I really don't understand why that doesn't work. We are far away, but it would be so simple for some of them [faculty] to come here and give talks during the year. There are a lot of good scholars that could be hosted by us . . . in particular the junior ones who need the experience of going into graduate departments and giving talks.

As the faculty and staff in the Institute of Public Affairs have grown more numerous, communication has become more challenging. "People are starting to complain that they don't have the same sense of being informed of things," said Archibald. "We are trying to improve the way we communicate, which means we are a little more formal (for example, weekly meetings with midlevel staff)." In addition, they recently hired a director of communications and set up an intranet for internal communication.

Issues of size and distance need special attention to overcome. Particularly in these situations, departments must be persistent in facilitating peer interactions. Email, the Internet, faxes, and other technological tools are particularly useful for departments whose faculty are geographically dispersed. Many heads and chairs routinely share information in written form such as internal newsletters (weekly, monthly, quarterly) or regular email blasts.

How Do Departments Facilitate Their Faculty's Substantive Communication With External Colleagues, That Is, Their Professional Networks?

"Your best research colleagues may be in another department, on another campus, or in another state," acknowledged Hicks (Biology). Popular means by which the departments in our study facilitate the growth of their faculty's external networks include the following:

- Provide technological tools for electronic communication.

- Link faculty to appropriate organizations and people within the discipline.

- Encourage and provide financial support for travel to professional meetings.

- Host conferences or lecture series.

Provide technological tools for electronic communication. Communication tools such as email and the Internet can provide faculty with entrée into larger peer networks. Garavaso commented that technology has really improved her faculty's ability to connect with a broader group of scholars in their field. "That used to be a handicap for a place like Morris, because we are small and isolated," she said. Some faculty members, like those in the Industrial Relations Center, have their own web pages where they can post their curriculum vitae. This helps them to network and initiate collaborations.

Link faculty to appropriate organizations and people within the discipline. All faculty benefit from communicating with key researchers and becoming active in organizations within their discipline. Senior faculty can help facilitate these linkages for more junior faculty in a variety of ways. Consider these examples:

- Ascerno (Entomology) sees part of his job as identifying federally supported regional research groups that match the expertise and interests of his faculty. "I'd say, 'Well, there's this group that's being formed in agriculture. You should be part of that.' It's an opportunity for scientists to come together around a common topic and to exchange information, so that opens up networks."

- The chair of Clinical and Population Sciences considers it the division heads' responsibility (as they are the most familiar with their particular subdiscipline) to link their faculty with the right professional organizations and the prominent funding agencies, as well as to encourage people to write grants, collaborate on projects, and share authorship.

- In Forest Resources, new faculty are given particular attention to help them build their networks. Explained Ek, "We help them in the first or second year, especially if they have never been in this region, to make a lot of contacts. . . . Senior faculty are pretty helpful with this. We take them along to meetings, conferences, workshops, special events, and our various agency offices and research centers."

Encourage and provide financial support for travel to professional meetings. Attending and, more ideally, presenting at scholarly conferences is one of the most important means by which faculty develop their research networks. As Bearinger (Nursing) aptly stated, "The only way to get national recognition is to pump out research and publish and then present it at national meetings. It's very hard to have a national reputation if you don't show up at meetings, meet people, and get involved." Ascerno (Entomology) encourages his faculty to participate both on their own and with their students at regional and national meetings. "In fact, I give points for giving peer presentations at a national meeting. That's to encourage people to take their information out, and also provide a networking opportunity." Similarly, in Food Science and Nutrition, "Doing national meetings and accepting invitations to other places is encouraged," said Warthesen. "To do that, we might have to find a substitute teacher for a day or a guest lecturer or have somebody fill in, but it is important that our faculty get outside the building and get some national exposure with some senior faculty outside our own unit." Knopp (Geography) added, "We encourage networking and getting involved in special groups within the discipline, and taking a leading role and organizing sessions at conferences."

Unfortunately, even in these highly research-productive departments, travel funds can be hard to come by. "What we can do for faculty in terms of travel is limited," said Campbell (Psychology, Twin Cities campus). "We essentially only provide one airline ticket a year for faculty. That's a sore point, since most of them use a lot more than that. A lot of them pay their own way with their research funds." Many other academic leaders in our study shared similar laments.

On the contrary, some heads/chairs described their units as being very well equipped to support faculty travel. In Education Psychology, for example, "We give each faculty member financial support in professional development funds that he or she can spend on travel, journal subscriptions, professional organization dues, etc.," said McEvoy. The Psychology department on the Morris campus enjoys "a vigorous program for funding conference trips," according to Klinger. Run by the dean's office, this program pays up to 50% of faculty's travel expenses to professional meetings. In Philosophy, "One paid trip a year is what we have, and it seems to be adequate," said Garavaso.

Host conferences or lecture series. Another way of facilitating faculty communication with a wider set of peers is to bring outside scholars to campus. In the Department of Cultural and Comparative Literature, "We do things like mount ambitious conferences that create a lot of publicity," said Leppert. "We invest money in speakers, and over the years we have brought in a number of people who are not just important people in their discipline, but also as public intellectuals." Events such as these can be especially advantageous for junior faculty, who get to rub shoulders with big names in the field. As Simone (Oral Sciences) said, "I think it's important to have your seminar series, bringing in folks and making sure that particularly younger faculty are going out to dinner with these people and interacting, sharing ideas."

In summary, frequent interactions with productive peers can drive faculty's research productivity. Colleagues might, for example, provide constructive feedback on project design and written work, advise one another on how to best maximize their limited work time, or become active collaborators in research projects. These and other benefits to sustaining vital peer networks are described in Chapter 6 and in the beginning section of Chapter 8.

Chapter 7 Review: Communication With Colleagues _____

- There is a documented association between faculty having frequent, substantive communication with professional colleagues and being highly research productive. Accordingly, departments in this study use multiple strategies for getting, and keeping, their faculty connected to peers within their discipline.

- Intradepartmental lines of communication are kept open in a variety of ways. Faculty are kept abreast of one another's work by sharing their written work and presenting their research-in-progress at faculty seminars. Substantive conversations can also occur in the context of other routine faculty gatherings (e.g., faculty meetings, impromptu hallway chats).

- Presenting at professional meetings is the primary means by which faculty in these departments connect with other scholars in their field. Some departments host onsite conferences or lecture series. Department heads and chairs and other senior faculty can, through active mentoring, successfully link their junior colleagues to high-profile, well-connected researchers.

- Overcoming the distance separating colleagues—whether they are across the street or across the globe—can be difficult, particularly if travel funds or support for electronic forms of communication are scarce.

8

Resources

There are three things I would say are absolutely critical to the success of any program. The first is outstanding faculty; these are the people you are going to be working with. The second is staff; nobody in a department can succeed without sufficiently well paid and good quality people who buy into the program's mission. The third, of course, is the location where both of these two groups of people work; you have to build and maintain state-of-the-art facilities.

(Wayne Gladfelter, Chemistry)

LITERATURE SUMMARY

The tasks of the research-productive faculty member require resources in the form of time, space, equipment, supplies, and facilities. Some of the most crucial resources, however, are people. These include excellent students and highly capable staff, but especially productive local colleagues with whom faculty members regularly communicate.

DEPARTMENT PRACTICES COVERED IN THIS CHAPTER

1) How do strong local peer networks facilitate faculty productivity?
2) In what ways do high-quality students (research and teaching assistants) contribute to the research enterprise? How do departments allocate this important, sometimes scarce human resource?
3) What types of support staff are considered essential human resources in these highly research-productive departments?
4) How do departments attend to their faculty's research space needs?
5) What are the major sources of money to support research? What strategies do departments use to help their faculty secure research funding?
6) How does money affect research productivity?

What Does the Literature Say?

In a study by Andrews (1979) in which resources were classified into library, equipment, colleagues, and workspace, it was the human resources that accounted for the greatest variance in research productivity. National colleagues are important, but local colleagues are particularly valuable for both the specific assistance they provide and their role in maintaining the department's shared research culture and positive climate.

Peers stimulate vitality by being available to listen to new ideas, critique writings, serve as guinea pigs for innovative teaching strategies, or provide access to recent research findings (Bland & Ruffin, 1992; Dundar & Lewis, 1998; Tschannen-Moran, Firestone, Hoy, & Johnson, 2000). In their survey of 42 Lilly fellows at a large public research institution, Kalivoda and Sorrell (1994) found that ". . . the most common method of handling both teaching and research problems, at all faculty levels, was to discuss the matter with one's colleagues" (p. 265). Additional information about the importance of communication and peer networks can be found in Chapter 7.

Beyond providing specific help, productive local colleagues can provide meaningful praise, recognition, and support for all facets of academic work. Indeed, the many ways in which colleagues maintain a culture of high achievement in research and a positive group climate is, suggests Reskin (1977), the most important role colleagues play—and the way in which they most positively impact productivity. This interpretation is supported by research that finds that the absence of research-oriented colleagues destroys the research interest and energy of even the most research-productive faculty member (Blackburn, 1979; Creswell, 1985; Meltzer, 1956).

Notably, the availability of other quality human resources (e.g., support staff, research assistants) is also positively associated with research productivity (Andrews, 1979; Kotrlik, Bartlett, Higgins, & Williams, 2001). Studies by Pineau and Levy-Leboyer (1983) and Sindermann (1985) report that the presence of able secretarial staff and technicians is highly associated with research productivity. Blackburn, Behymer, and Hall (1978) found that faculty working with graduate students were much more likely to publish than those working only with undergraduate students. Similarly, Mervis (1999) reported that "post docs' expertise and commitment are crucial to the research enterprise" (p. 1,519).

The importance of adequate resources seems obvious. Yet today, faculty in many institutions are finding themselves not just without highly regarded local colleagues and support staff, but also responsible for emptying their own wastebaskets and cleaning their desks, floors, and windows. These personnel shortages undoubtedly have a negative impact not only on research productivity, but also on the enormous efforts faculty are being asked to make in meeting the pressing challenges of new technology, diverse students bodies, and interdisciplinary research and coursework.

Department Practices

Resources is an expansive topic; it touches on issues related to faculty and funding, students and staff, and of course, salaries and space. In the pages which follow, we summarize the interviewed department leaders' collective insight about the types of resources that faculty need most to be highly productive in research, as well as the ways in which these resources might be acquired and allocated.

How Do Strong Local Peer Networks Facilitate Faculty Productivity?

Productive local peers are perhaps the most valuable resource a researcher can have. Consider the many ways in which faculty support one another's scholarly work: They mentor (Chapter 5); they exchange knowledge through local, national, and international peer networks (Chapter 7); they celebrate one another's research achievements (Chapter 11); and they direct each other to promising opportunities for career growth and development (Chapter 12). The importance of local colleagues was a recurring theme in our qualitative data set. Here, we provide just a few additional examples that vividly illustrate how the presence of a vital, local network of research-minded colleagues can positively influence a faculty member's research productivity:

- Peers model a culture of high achievement, particularly in research.

- They provide constructive feedback on research.

- They share work strategies (e.g., on time management, teaching).

Model a culture of high achievement. One very powerful influence of productive local peers is the degree to which they catalyze one another's energy and interest in research. Simply being surrounded by productive colleagues can be inspiring. As Hogan (Family Social Science) explained,

> I've been here for 25 years. I walked into a department with productive faculty, and my expectations for myself just went way up. I can't imagine anybody coming in here who wouldn't feel guilty about not producing manuscripts,

> moving the science forward, conducting outreach, etc. I
> think the peer group makes a huge difference.

The head of Epidemiology uses the collective achievements of his faculty to help motivate individual faculty members during annual evaluations. Every year Luepker hands out a summary of the faculty members' average productivity, by rank. "When I do an evaluation, I'll say, 'Your productivity has been less than average for your rank. This is what your colleagues did.' And I think that pushes people."

In departments with a culture that highly values research, faculty will push one another to improve and excel in their scholarship, if given the opportunity (e.g., via seminars). This occurs in the Department of Applied Economics: "We do have people who will certainly call another faculty member to task if they think that what they've done is not up to what it should be (in terms of conceptual background, quantitative analysis, or whatever it may be)," said Eidman. "Believe me, you won't get out of the room without knowing it; but it will be done in a reasonably tasteful way. It is the culture we have."

Provide constructive feedback on research. In highly research-productive departments, faculty habitually critique one another's research-in-progress. In Marketing and Logistics Management, for example, faculty pass around their manuscripts to get reactions from their colleagues. The chair also assists by sharing his experience as an editor for a key journal in the discipline. In Applied Economics it is up to individual faculty members to decide whether to seek out internal review of their writing. But the practice is highly encouraged. "I think you'd be foolish not to take advantage of your peers," said Eidman. "Why be embarrassed in front of outside people if you don't need to be?"

Faculty members coming up for promotion in the Law School are encouraged to give a workshop on their current projects, at which time all faculty can comment on the work. Sullivan recalled one such workshop that propelled forward—to a significant degree—both the quality and quantity of the faculty presenter's work:

> It may have been the best workshop I have seen in six years.
> Virtually everybody in the room, the senior faculty, jumped
> in and thought "I have got to help here," recognizing the
> importance of pieces that hadn't been thought about yet. I
> know that they followed up with this particular person,
> because I heard along the way that there were many conver-
> sations after the workshop. I thought this was an example of
> some of the very best cooperative, supportive work going on.

Share work strategies. In addition to supporting one another's research-in-progress, local colleagues can act as a safe sounding board for a host of other work-related issues. Geography faculty have successfully assisted one another in writing grant proposals to the graduate school and the university. This type of shared strategizing also occurs in the Law School. Their faculty with high success rates in acquiring grants will participate in collegial brown bag lunches, presenting their strategies for securing external funding.

In Philosophy, the older faculty advise the new associate professors "to keep to their own plans" and give up some of their administrative responsibilities to prevent getting stuck in their careers, said Garavaso. "We do a lot of therapy with each other, just talking about what we do and why things are happening," she said. This type of informal mentoring is invaluable, in that it can help prevent or overcome faculty disillusionment and help faculty deal with the challenge of managing diverse, oftentimes competing responsibilities.

A strong sense of esprit de corps among faculty does not necessarily occur on its own; it can require attention to cultivate. The head of Health Services Research and Policy said he thought his faculty would benefit from having a stronger internal seminar series and more established mechanisms for teaching junior faculty how to write proposals. Archibald (Public Affairs) observed that in her environment, "the junior faculty help each other a lot, whereas the senior faculty are more reluctant to share what they are doing." Finding ways to replace some of that individualism with a greater spirit of collaboration within the institute is one of her priorities as associate dean.

In What Ways Do High-Quality Students (Research and Teaching Assistants) Contribute to the Research Enterprise? How Do Departments Allocate This Important, Sometimes Scarce Human Resource?

It was apparent from our interviews that well-trained and highly motivated students, especially at the graduate level, are considered an extremely valuable human resource. Striking to us was that several of the interviewed department leaders ranked the importance of attracting excellent graduate students just below the importance of recruiting excellent faculty:

- "Certainly high-caliber graduate students are high on the list, and of course, high-caliber faculty, in inverse order. You choose the right faculty, and then you attract good graduate students. You don't have to do almost anything else. You give them enough space and they produce, and I'm not being facetious. I think it's that simple." (Chemical Engineering and Materials Science)

- "The biggest thing that the department does for faculty research is to support graduate students. . . . Graduate research is the engine of research, as far as I'm concerned. If you get good grad students, faculty have a hope of achieving their potential." (Ecology, Evolution, and Behavior)

- "In the culture of this department, graduate education is the heart of research." (Food Science and Nutrition)

As teaching assistants (TAs), students provide faculty with more time for research-related pursuits. As research assistants (RAs), they help to advance their faculty mentors' research agendas. And as productive researchers themselves—completing dissertations, presenting at meetings, copublishing with faculty—students attract the attention of similarly driven students and faculty. Such is the case in the Department of Health Services Research and Policy. This is entirely a graduate program, and largely a Ph.D. program. Consequently, its 40 or so graduate students are very important to the faculty. "The students are the source of our research assistance," said Feldman. "They are our collaborators, and when they go out on the job market, they also spread the reputation of our department."

> In 2001, a study was conducted on all agricultural education faculty in colleges and universities to determine which factors were the greatest predictors of their research productivity as measured by publications in refereed journals. The following items predicted 50% of the variance.
>
> - Number of doctoral students advised to completion in the last five years ($R^2 = .37$)
> - Faculty members' research confidence scale mean ($R^2 = .09$)
> - Number of graduate assistant hours allocated to the faculty members ($R^2 = .04$)
> (Kotrlik, Bartlett, Higgins, & Williams, 2001)

In Clinical and Population Sciences, faculty "use graduate students more than we use technicians," said Ames. "Placing the emphasis on graduate education ties into the desire to do research." Knopp (Geography) agreed, noting that "graduate students are intellectual stimulators for faculty." Accordingly, his department, which currently serves only undergraduates, has plans to submit a proposal for a master's program:

> I think we all feel it's going to serve our individual as well as collective interests to have the resources, the numbers, the students, the status, and the prestige—everything that comes with having a graduate program. We think our department could prosper as a result.

Undergraduates, too, can help support the research enterprise. On the university's Morris campus, for example, undergraduates in their junior year can participate in what is called the Academic Partners Program. The students are provided with a stipend corresponding to the highest amount of work-study funds for which they are eligible; they then use their time to work on a project with faculty. "Many [students] have worked on books— reviewing, editing, and helping faculty to get them finished," said Garavaso (Philosophy). "We tell new faculty, you will have to be productive and you will be able to do that, because we have very good students." Similarly, the Department of Biology's large undergraduate research program is a strong stimulus for faculty research. When students come to faculty members to ask about research projects, faculty are often led into topic areas that they might not otherwise have pursued.

Meeting the demand for research/teaching assistants can be difficult. Thus, these departments strive to maximize their student enrollment by making their programs attractive to potential students. They build strong reputations, they hire faculty with whom students will want to work, and they seek out training grants, fellowships, and endowments to support their students' early years of graduate training. Still, the degree to which RAs and TAs are available to faculty can vary considerably by discipline.

Limited-time RA support is a common component of new faculty start-up packages. This is true, for example, in the Institute of Public Affairs, though the level of support given to junior faculty is disparate with that achievable by their more senior faculty who hold endowed chairs. This led the associate dean to recommend that the institute's next campaign fund focus on creating more generous start-up systems for their junior faculty.

Most departments, of course, assume that their junior faculty will successfully bring in grant money to support their research programs, including stipends for research assistants:

- "Our department only supports the first-year graduate student. . . . If faculty don't have a grant, maybe their research program is not approved by their peers and they should not have a graduate student at this time. Right or wrong, that's what our practice is." (Pharmacology)

- "I do allocate a small amount of money to our faculty per year, but it's not enough to support a technician. That helps set the culture of going after additional funds." (Entomology)

- "Faculty take great care and great measure of their resource needs. If they need additional RAs, they get grants." (Industrial Relations)

In Ecology, Evolution, and Behavior, faculty benefit from having access to a pool of TAs paid for through departmental resources. Their students are also successful in getting fellowships and other types of external support. In the Industrial Relations Center, each faculty member is assigned one RA who is centrally appointed. Law School faculty are given a standard allocation of funds each year to help support research assistants, typically second- or third-year students. The funds can be increased if the need is well justified, and carried over to the next year if unused.

In some departments, the demand for research and teaching assistants routinely exceeds the supply. Knopp (Geography) noted that although his faculty could use RAs and TAs, they typically have to do without: "We do get TAs for one big undergraduate class, but we have typically at least three big undergraduate classes, and two of those don't get TAs. This means more time spent on grading and much less time spent on research."

The Institute of Child Development has teaching assistantships available, but often struggles with filling them, particularly for their larger, writing-intensive undergraduate courses. Ironically, this problem is exacerbated by their graduate students' high degree of success in acquiring research fellowships (e.g., from the National Institutes of Health and the National Science Foundation, as well as college and university fellowships). To solve this dilemma, they have turned to hiring recently graduated bachelor's-level students as course coordinators to aid instructors. Often, these coordinators are former undergraduate honor students from their own program. "We have found that a lot of them want to work for a year or two before they go to graduate school," said Masten. "The advantage of hiring from among our own graduates is that they have taken the courses and know the material."

What Types of Support Staff Are Considered Essential Human Resources in These Highly Research-Productive Departments?

In querying department heads/chairs about their staff-related resources, we identified a wide range of personnel who contribute, in direct and indirect ways, to the research productivity of the faculty. The most frequently mentioned staff in these departments were people who perform the following types of roles:

- Technical support (for computers, instrumentation, facilities)

- Grants development and management

- Administrative assistance

Of course, not every department head/chair reported having adequate staff in each of these key support areas. In their interviews, the academic leaders were quite candid in pointing out deficits in their staffing, while at the same time extolling the many virtues of the staff they did have employed (much as they did above in their comments about the value and availability of student RAs/TAs). Given their financial limitations, the departments in our study appear to have adopted a highly tailored approach to staffing. Who they hire to perform what tasks is driven by the most demanding needs of the faculty at the time. This includes a need to support key research facilities and instrumentation housed in the department.

With this context in mind, we encourage readers to reflect on the staffing examples presented below and to consider potential advantages to investing in these types of human resources as their fiscal resources allow.

Technical support staff. Technical equipment and facilities, be they computer hardware/software, wet labs, libraries, clinical research centers, or survey centers, are essential for faculty research productivity. In turn, it is essential that departments have on board the personnel with the know-how to develop, use, modify, and maintain these resources over the long term.

Computer-savvy staff are one such type of personnel. Ascerno (Entomology) commented, "Computers are like cars. I used to be able to work on a car, lift up the hood, and know what to do. With computers, I can't do that anymore, and that's the way most faculty are. So where we really need support is in software support, hardware support, troubleshooting, web page design and construction, those sorts of things."

Computer support is important for all disciplines, even those with fewer technology needs. This is not surprising, given the fast rate at which technology is changing and the growing dependence of faculty work on computers (e.g., for project design, data management and analysis, web-based teaching, and the electronic submission of grant proposals, abstracts, and journal articles).

Several department leaders described the value of having in-house computer support. The Twin Cities Department of Psychology has a small technical services group (one manager, plus the equivalent of 2.5 full-time staff) to support technological aids to instruction and computing systems in the research laboratories. The Department of Health Services Research and Policy has a full-time computer hardware person and a full-time software person. Forest Resources employs undergraduate students as part-time computer technicians to keep its hardware and software hooked up and running.

In General College, five full-time technology staff support 34 faculty, 29 teaching staff, and 22 advisors. A major role of the technology center is to attend to their classroom infrastructure. This is a critical service, since General

College faculty use the classroom as not only a teaching venue, but also as the laboratory for their research in education. Collins provided these examples:

> In a classroom that's designed to work with refugees in improving oral communication skills, we wired that room with all of the videotaping and audiotaping equipment we could get in there, so that the people doing that teaching then have a trace of that teaching to use in research. In our writing classrooms, which are all networked computer class-rooms, we can do keystroke capturing. We can learn about students' writing processes retrospectively by looking at what they've done. The basic psychology course that we offer is all done in a network environment where we've modified WebCT so that every act a student performs is recoverable against time and interval.

Another highly desired technical resource is staff responsible for the upkeep of specialized research instruments and the activities of in-house research facilities (e.g., large-scale survey centers, nuclear magnetic resonance instruments, other equipment). The participants in our study shared many examples of the more specialized research and instructional needs of their faculty which are met by skilled personnel:

- The Department of Art has a technical staff of approximately three full-time people to take care of the studios and related equipment in photography, ceramics, sculpture, and electronic media.

- The Department of Psychology (Twin Cities campus) houses a technical shop with two full-time technical employees and one half-time student employee. "They support all the mechanical, electrical, and related construction repair support needs of the researchers, so they have a long history of fabricating equipment," said Campbell. "Now they are getting more into the business of using established computer platforms for laboratory management and that sort of thing."

- Forest Resources has limited support (a half-time lab position) to look after safety, training, equipment, laboratories, and the greenhouse. It also has what Ek called "modest support" for its remote sensing and geospacial analysis lab. "That's a pretty dedicated facility," he said. "It is slim support. Of course, grants can and do augment this support on a project basis."

- A staff member in Family Social Science performs a wide range of technology-related tasks. She maintains multiple research databases and ensures file compatibility for faculty receiving data from research collaborators. She also trains graduate students in statistical software packages and answers their technical questions when their faculty advisors are unavailable. Of particular value, said the chair, is that this person was trained as a research scientist. As such, she understands not only the technology issues, but also the scientific issues that come along with it, such as data confidentiality.

- The Morris Psychology Discipline employs a part-time technician who provides a host of electrical and carpentry services. As their equipment has become more computerized, they are gradually evolving to having this person be on call, with the understanding that they could use up to 50% of his time.

Although technical support personnel are widely recognized as a key resource, many of these departments struggle with how to fund such positions. This issue is addressed uniquely by different departments. The Department of Biochemistry, Molecular Biology, and Biophysics has traditionally devoted some of its flexible dollars to fund its technical people. Grant funding is also applied in many departments, sometimes in innovative ways. Luepker (Epidemiology) offered up this example: "Since we're very highly computer dependent, we all take out of our grants $150 per person per month, and we get everything kind of taken care of, from helping choose equipment to immediate technical support when something breaks down."

The technical shop in the Twin Cities Department of Psychology has a "multisource budget," explained Campbell. "That is financed jointly with the Institute of Child Development, because they use the shop as well . . . Right now, the College of Liberal Arts provides the majority of our funds. We still must fill in the gaps with funds from indirect cost return on grants or other kinds of funds." For some technical support facilities, such as the soil analysis and cartographic labs in the Department of Geography, the facility itself is expected to become a cost-recovery vehicle. As an example, Epidemiology runs its own survey center, largely serving the university community, with a budget of over $1 million per year. Chemical Engineering and Materials Science houses a four-person machine shop that is financially independent. "That is something that I absolutely drove them to do," said Bates. "We have to pay to use them, but it's still a resource, and we don't subsidize them."

Although technical staffing can be costly, these departments widely endorsed these personnel as well worth the investment. Warthesen (Food Science and Nutrition) commented, "It would be great to have more technical laboratory support. Faculty have said that would provide a lot of continuity for their research programs." In his department, 26 faculty have access to one full-time technician. Ascerno (Entomology) is working toward having a technician for each faculty member: "If one key person had a technician that they could count on, and didn't have to chase dollars to support that person, the productivity would not just be the sum of the two people. It would be a lot more than that. You would return that easily in extramural funding."

Gladfelter (Chemistry) commented that although the university has done a good job of providing matching funds for equipment (e.g., $250,000 to match funds from the National Science Foundation for a half-million dollar spectrometer), there must be follow-through on that initial investment. "That gets the equipment in the door, but ten years down the line you are going to still need people to run it, and that's where sufficient support and staffing is critical."

Staff for grants development and management. In most academic departments, the acquisition of external research funds—"grant getting," in more colloquial terms—is both a prerequisite for and an important indicator of faculty research productivity. Well-trained support staff can greatly facilitate many of the essential pre- and post-award tasks that would otherwise take up critical faculty time. The need for grant support staff is particularly great when faculty members are engaged in multiple projects (and all of the accounting that goes with it) and when departments experience an unexpected, albeit welcome, increase in the number of submitted and awarded grants.

The department leaders in our study clearly valued the knowledge and skills that experienced grants personnel can provide:

- "I think the faculty desperately need to know that they can depend on someone with grant experience to guide them. Especially if you work on a grant for the first time or if you write a grant only once a year, you're not going to be efficient at it. So what you want to do is work with someone who has got it like this [in a snap]." (Nursing)

- "We have decided it's worth spending money to have people who are experts in grants management. . . . They do a budget for you, and they follow the rules (things that faculty do poorly), and understand what you can and can't do. So it's taken care of for us." (Epidemiology)

- "We have a grant coordinator position. It's a soft money position, and it is a person who is hired not to write grants, but rather to enhance the faculty's creativity by providing technical support. The grant coordinator has been a big boost to our productivity." (Food Science and Nutrition)

Department heads/chairs also shared examples of the many specific tasks that well-trained grants staff can perform. Their responses touched on two major types of activities: pre-award and post-award.

Pre-award activities. On the front end of grant getting, commonly known as the pre-award stage, support staff in these highly research-productive departments assist with any number of tasks. These might include searching databases for suitable funding sources, developing budgets, entering information into the university's electronic grants management system (EGMS), working on biosketches and boilerplate sections of proposals, serving as liaison with the university's Office of Sponsored Projects, and pulling together the final proposal package prior to submission.

In some departments, these tasks are distributed among administrative assistants or accounting personnel. A few departments benefit from having a single, highly skilled staff member capable of handling all, or nearly all, of these areas.

General College supports a full-time grant writer, but her duties clearly extend beyond her job title, as Collins explained:

> Her involvement with faculty at all stages of grant development is diverse. She walks the halls. She meets with each of them twice a year. She has a pretty elaborate web site that she maintains with funding opportunities. She targets faculty and notifies them. She coaches them through the writing process, and just does some writing that they might be reluctant to do or don't know how to do. She's responsible for making sure that the budget gets all the eyes on it that it needs and helps people who aren't used to the IRB [Institutional Review Board] process. When we have grants that we're writing across units (for example, with Disability Services), she does a lot of the point work in getting both groups on task.

The Department of Biochemistry, Molecular Biology, and Biophysics restructured an administrative staff position so as to dedicate all of that individual's time to pre-award work. Bernlohr said, "This person sits down with all new faculty, goes through search engines, lets them know when common grant deadlines are, things of that nature. But that is a modest component compared to the actual development of grants, actually putting the pages together." Those pages might include biosketches, budget pages, and other sections of a standard PHS 398 grant application that supports the actual project description. This model of pre-award staff support has been so successful that Bernlohr is striving to move another person out of their financial accounting (post-award) sector and into grants development.

Hogan (Family Social Science) spoke highly of her department's grant coordinator, whose position arose out of an identified faculty need and who has since developed a sophisticated set of skills:

> She really reinvented herself from a department administrative secretary into just being so savvy that faculty would hang me from a tree if she was not here. . . . Everybody knows that she's not writing the grant, but from moment one she walks the faculty through—she sets up deadlines, sets up timetables, and makes them stick to it. She refuses to do last-minute stuff. I tell you, it's brought sanity from an administrator's point of view, but I think from the faculty's too.

This same individual is also on a first-name basis with project officers at funding agencies that support the social sciences. "When the grant reviews come in, she's able to make telephone calls to the agency for clarification and asks to see what does this score really mean. She is just meticulous," said Hogan.

Among the departments in our study, some of the most common and highly valued personnel with respect to grants development are the finance/accounting staff. Again and again, department heads/chairs described how invaluable it was to their faculty to be able to prepare a rough budget for their proposals and then have the edges smoothed out by experienced and savvy accounting staff.

Feldman's (Health Services Research and Policy) high praise for the division's finance staff, who can "put together a grant proposal overnight," is illustrative of the importance these persons play in research-productive environments. Perhaps even more compelling is Feldman's observation that when a few years back the financial staff started to thin out due to turnover, "the whole place started grinding to a halt. . . . The research infrastructure is critical."

Post-award activities. The roles of support staff do not end once a grant proposal is submitted. Rather, for research-productive departments with high grant hit rates, the resulting influx of funds presents another challenge: that of providing oversight and accountability on how grant dollars are spent.

Clearly, having adequate support staff for post-award financial tasks is critical, as was noted by many department leaders in our study. Consider these comments from Hicks (Biology):

> The most critical thing is having someone who can help with purchasing and accounting. We were fortunate to find someone to fill that role: an account supervisor who had never been involved in research accounting before, but who had worked as an accountant for many years for a state government and was just the right person—always well-organized, on top of things, could immediately tell you what you'd spent and what you hadn't. . . . Researchers could come and get instant information. They love that, and that's still the way it is. We have been very fortunate.

In the Department of Art, two administrative staff members have proven themselves to be "extremely valuable," said Pharis. They are particularly so because of the many small ways that they help, rather than hinder, faculty researchers. Faculty want to have easy access to their money; they don't want to have to "jump through hoops," he explained. When the accounting is easy and transparent, the faculty's research gets done and in turn, these staff are incredibly valued and respected.

Administrative support staff. A third, very critical human resource found in these highly research-productive departments is talented, well-trained administrative support staff. Although the need for traditional clerical skills still exists (typing or word processing, phone triage, writing correspondence, setting up meetings, etc.), the desired skill set for administrative support staff is becoming increasingly diversified. Consider these examples drawn from our study participants' responses:

- "The clerical type of activities that were common in the pre-computer age don't occur anymore. People are doing their own typing and putting it directly on letterhead; you can do all sorts of things, so that . . . what we really need is more support on the computer end." (Entomology)

- "In the old days, staff did all of the typing for you. Now, everybody uses their own word processor. So, our staff members don't type the grant anymore, but they will work on the final formatting. From then on, they take over everything: the accounting, the purchasing, and many other things. . . . If you have a problem with anything other than the science, the staff will help." (Pharmacology)

Recognizing the changing support needs of faculty, many departments have taken to hiring staff into new, hybridized positions or into very specialized roles. For example, Health Services Research and Policy is trying to hire a full-time communications person to help communicate their faculty's research results to the field, the state legislature, and local employers. Epidemiology has created its own personnel department—above and beyond the human resources assistance provided by the university—to help its faculty more efficiently bridge the gaps during staff turnover (for example, when old research projects end and new projects begin). Additional examples of unique staffing arrangements were provided above in the section on grants personnel.

Another staffing strategy used by many departments is that of hiring nonfaculty coordinators for key programmatic areas such as graduate and undergraduate education. Positions such as these can positively influence faculty productivity, as Eidman (Applied Economics) described:

> We hired an undergraduate coordinator to, number one, help market our undergraduate degree and, number two, to help with the routine advising on issues such as what course substitutes for what, and all of these questions that come up and just drive faculty members up the wall, because they haven't heard the question before, or because they only hear it once every third year. That person has taken quite a load off the faculty, and they seem to be very appreciative. My feeling is help of this type frees up their time and makes them more productive.

Department heads/chairs can also directly benefit from having excellent support staff to assist them with their many day-to-day management tasks. Two staff in the Institute of Child Development help the director with a variety of tasks that are either business related (grants, budgets, human resources) or related to academic affairs (e.g., tracking when graduate students are ready to instruct, providing information about teaching apprenticeships, summer school, and technology evolvement issues). Bates, upon becoming head of Chemical Engineering and Materials Science, created a new executive officer position. "Jeff has done a very good job of slowly acquiring certain responsibilities," said Bates. "For example, computers, he takes care of that. He's acquiring responsibilities for the staff, certain internal operational issues."

Under this new management system for the department, Bates has had more time for external fundraising and other responsibilities.

Recruiting, rewarding, and retaining exceptional staff. Among the departments in our study, there were wide-ranging differences in the availability of key staff positions, with clear haves and have-nots. Departments that lack adequate administrative support staff can quickly find themselves struggling to support essential services or otherwise using up valuable faculty time on tasks that readily could have been delegated to (and perhaps more efficiently accomplished by) a skilled staff person.

The have-nots in particular, but all departments to some degree, are challenged to find ways to carefully husband their valuable staff resources and to creatively elicit the highest levels of productivity from their staff. Below, we present a few such strategies—both fiscal and managerial—as voiced by the department leaders in our study:

- *Judiciously allocate staff time.* In Mechanical Engineering, the clerical staff are distributed around the department, with each staff person assigned to a faculty group. "We allocate several hours per week per faculty member to provide them with copying assistance and other reasonable requests," said McMurry.

- *Diversify existing staff.* The Department of Applied Economics recently shifted to a more cooperative, team approach to staffing, with people shifting roles and filling in as needed. In this way, they are better able to accommodate the flux that typically occurs in faculty support needs, both during the course of a year and from year to year as new faculty are hired. To encourage cross training, as well as keep staff morale high, the department pays for staff training (e.g., in Dreamweaver or other software programs), which the staff are free to attend on company time (during their regular workdays).

- *Recognize and reward staff performance.* Finding ways to celebrate outstanding work is another way in which these departments maintain a highly productive staff. According to Bernlohr (Biochemistry, Molecular Biology, and Biophysics), "We need to do things for staff each third of the year or every quarter [lunches out, an evening at the theater or a major league baseball game] to make sure that those people recognize that they are just not nameless cogs, they are really important. The faculty can't get their work done unless the office is happy and running efficiently and productively." Eidman (Applied Economics) added, "You can't send the staff overseas . . . but you try to do little things." In his department, staff are given a small yearly gift of appreciation—a plant, for instance, or a half-day off work to be taken during light workload periods.

- *Promote a culture of teamwork between faculty and staff.* In Forest Resources, "we try to avoid an elitist culture [between faculty and staff]," explained Ek. Instead, "the focus is on support and getting the job done." In the Department of Art, the relationship between faculty and staff is also one of shared responsibility. Their accounting staff, for example, has demonstrated their value to faculty, in large part by making things less cumbersome for faculty. In turn, "the structure is not 'We're up here as faculty and you're down here as help,'" said Pharis. "Things have leveled out a lot, so we don't have this distinction of the faculty lording over the help. Instead, we have the relationship where the faculty has a role, the staff has a role, and these roles are valued by the faculty, because it makes their work easier. It's just more fluid."

- *Recruit exceptional staff.* As with faculty, hiring excellent staff to begin with—and supporting their professional growth over the long term—is an important and effective strategy for creating a successful work environment that facilitates faculty research. Ek (Forest Resources) described his office staff as "probably the best, in this type of position, in the university. The administrators and staff have exceptional work and people skills. They hire extremely well, and together these people maintain a very organized, functional, and supportive office." A few years ago, the Department of Art performed a staff assessment ("which was kind of a smoke screen for actually making changes that needed to be made," explained Pharis). The end result was overwhelmingly positive for the department, "We have been able to recruit some really terrific staff— folks who perform as a team and who really provide the faculty with a willingness to help, a willingness to be available, and a willingness to listen that wasn't here in quite the same way before."

- *Retain valued staff.* The Department of Chemistry has offered competitive retention packages to valued staff members who were being recruited by other departments or universities. Gladfelter described one such instance: "The consensus to retain her was not difficult to reach. The question of where to get the money was a little bit more of a problem." To make the retention offer financially appealing, they successfully tapped into user fees for their instrumentation facilities.

How Do Departments Attend to Their
Faculty's Research Space Needs?

Up to now, we have focused our discussion on the many types of human resources that can positively influence faculty research productivity—productive local peers, research-oriented students, and a variety of skilled support staff. In this section, we begin to address resources of a different type, specifically, the space and facilities in which faculty (and their students and staff) actually conduct their inquiry work.

Ek (Forest Resources) shared what he called his "philosophy about facilities":

> When you buy people equipment and things that have bright lights (new computers) you are really telling people you are investing in them, and they take that to heart. . . . New equipment also tells people they are valuable and allows them to be more creative. . . . There are some very subtle ways of trying to keep the place semi-attractive and welcoming to students and employees. If the place looks friendly, it works better for you.

Space—both its quality and its quantity—is an important resource issue that came up in almost every interview. In some of the departments in our study, such as the Industrial Relations Center or the Department of Cultural Studies and Comparative Literature, the faculty's space needs are not heavy. For others, the research laboratory or work studio is the foundation of their faculty's research programs. In these settings, department heads, chairs, and deans find that space negotiation is an ever-present, time-consuming management task.

In our interviews with the heads/chairs of highly research-productive departments, they shared some of their challenges and strategies for addressing both their current and anticipated space needs.

Department leaders plan ahead for the space needs of new faculty. In space-conscious departments in space-limited institutions, the question of who gets what office or laboratory is a serious, sometimes contentious issue—particularly when it comes time to secure space commitments for new faculty hires. Bates (Chemical Engineering and Materials Science) commented, "I think the space issue is one area that young faculty are extremely sensitive to now . . . so your space should be in order. You should be clear how you're going to manage this when they [new faculty] come."

Lack of adequate space can be a serious barrier to faculty recruitment. Masten (Child Development) said, "We have a faculty search this year, and we are worried about space for this person. We don't have enough space for people in the department; we are having to double people up." Moller (Pediatrics) offered up an additional example of space as a barrier to recruitment:

> I've been trying to recruit somebody for a chair who's an immunologist. The immunology group liked him. I said, "This person wants five benches in the immunology center." But I couldn't get them . . . we just don't have space. We need people in the dean's office who are willing to help and make some of these harder decisions, because I think this person could have brought a lot. He had several three-year NIH grants, is a leader in developmental immunology, and would have added to the program. Maybe that's just a general issue: There's not enough space for clinical departments.

Ravdin (Medicine) concurred, stating, "Our biggest problem in recruitment is not money, it's space." To combat this issue, he has adopted a plan for proactively attending to their future space needs. One strategy is recruiting new faculty together with the Cancer Center and other units that have more space. In addition, the department maintains an ongoing summary of all the planned recruitments.

> We have a process we've refined. My administrator may complain, because I end up being too aggressive in hiring faculty before we have an office or resources. But my position is one of a very aggressive growth approach—then making sure we get the resources. We've kept every commitment we've ever made.

Bates (Chemical Engineering and Materials Science) has observed that once people acquire space, they never want to let it go, despite the fact that nobody really owns university space. He also acknowledged that it can be awkward to try to recover space and then use it for something else. Consequently, he is always thinking ahead ("I know about every square inch of space in this building, I mean literally every square inch in this building, and in my head I know exactly where the space is going for the next two or three years.") He has also worked diligently to set a standard for how space is negotiated within the department:

I know where the hires are going to go, and I know how we're going to do it. When the appropriate times arise, I share this information with people. We talk about it; there's no single formula for how this is done, but as long as it's planned well enough ahead of time, the opportunities do arise when you can move a lab or move an office. . . . This space is the department's space, so when people come here, we flex, we have to, and the people that interview here should see it.

Some departments are benefiting from new construction. Bates was able to set his space-flexing standard in motion very shortly after first becoming department head. With a new addition to their building having just opened, he moved 15 faculty offices. "They didn't have to move, but I wanted to make the department more efficient, so everybody did it. Because we had the addition, we could do it and everybody felt good about it," he said.

The Department of Mechanical Engineering had just recently moved into a new building when we spoke to McMurry. "That has been a huge boon for us," he said. "In the past we were very cramped. We have a new wing for Mechanical Engineering now. Some of the labs are still very crowded, but the space situation is far more positive now than it was a year ago."

Getting to that desirable endpoint does require careful long-term planning. The Department of Art's new building "has been in the pipeline for years," said Pharis. The process leading up to its construction was carefully thought through. It began with a vital faculty need, followed by advocacy on the part of faculty and the presentation of their case by a former department chair to the higher administration. Throughout the planning, the faculty took time to collectively assess their resource needs for the future, including anticipated student enrollment in specific subject areas, faculty growth, and emerging technologies. And of course, there was the fundraising.

Soliciting funds for their new instrumentation facility is a high priority for the Department of Chemistry, where "perhaps our limiting resource right now is space," according to Gladfelter. "We are going to build the facility, raising the money from donations." By turning to donations and endowments ($1.8 million) solicited from their thousands of alumni, they are facilitating a major capital improvement which, Gladfelter says, "would not have been possible in the next decade if we had to wait for the funding from the state."

The Department of Geography is enjoying several newer labs and equipment (geographic information systems, a cartographic analysis lab, and a soil analysis lab). Their windfall is the result of significant investments on the part of campus administration. According to Knopp, "We've been treated well because the dean and the administration see us as a highly productive unit, because we've hired people who've needed those facilities, and because they see those facilities as ultimately being cost-recovery vehicles."

What Are the Major Sources of Money (External and Internal) to Support Research? What Strategies Do Departments Use to Help Their Faculty Secure Research Funding?

The cost of doing research, and the sources of funds to support that research, vary widely across disciplines and departments. Typically, research is supported by external grants and contracts, but in some disciplines extramural funding for research is rare. "In the business school, we kind of fall between the cracks when it comes to grants," said Houston (Marketing and Logistics Management). "We're either too theoretical for business companies or we're too applied for government agencies. We don't have a lot of extramural grants."

Even in disciplines with promising sources for external research support, external dollars are never sufficient to completely fund all of the research that faculty do. Fortunately, in general, most of the other major sources of revenues in academic departments (i.e., tuition, state funding, patents, endowments/private sources, and fees for services or products provided) can also be used to support any academic department activity, including research.

At this macro level, the major money sources for academic departments are similar. At the level of individual schools and departments, however, significant differences are observed in the amount of money that is generated in each of these categories and in the purposes for which these funds are used. Take tuition as an example. At the University of Minnesota, not only does the amount of tuition charged to students differ by academic level (undergraduate/graduate), but also the fees charged are very different in the School of Business, compared to the Medical School, compared to the College of Liberal Arts (CLA), and so on. In addition, the proportion of a department's budget that comes from tuition is disparate. In the Medical School, for instance, tuition accounts for a very small portion of the revenue and does not cover teaching costs, much less provide a means to support research. In CLA, however, tuition dollars are a major revenue source to support faculty teaching as well as other faculty activities. Another example is fees for services, which are a significant portion of the revenue for many clinical departments that can sometimes be used to support research, but which play no role in the funding of most other departments.

For the departments in our study, differences in their funding sources are summarized in the demographic table in Appendix E. Revenue from the state and tuition (called "central" in the table) varies from 8% to 100% of the total department budget; revenue from external sources varies from 0% to 90%; and revenue from other sources (e.g., patient care, equipment rental) varies from 0% to 50%.

These differences notwithstanding, each of the department leaders we interviewed described specific strategies they use to help their faculty acquire the funds they need for their research activities. Below, we outline several such strategies as offered up by our study participants. Both internal and external revenue streams are discussed, with examples provided from departments, schools, and colleges with widely disparate practices for how their many revenues sources are allocated for research.

Acquiring external and internal (university-sponsored) research grants and contracts. In these highly research-productive departments, external funding for faculty research comes from every conceivable source. These include federal agencies (the National Institutes of Health, National Science Foundation, Defense Department), state agencies (Departments of Health, Natural Resources), industry (pharmaceuticals, agribusiness, aerospace), and foundations (W. K. Kellogg, Bush, McKnight).

Where common ground is found is not so much in the particular funding sources, but rather in the major strategies these departments use to help faculty acquire external research dollars. Each of these strategies is discussed in depth as the main subjects of other chapters in this book. They include mentoring (see Chapters 5 and 12), providing support staff for grant writing (see the staff section above), and facilitating collaboration with other productive researchers (Chapter 6).

The leaders of these departments also spoke highly of the many internal research grant programs offered by the university. Many described how their faculty were very proactive in tapping into these programs for research support. Here are some examples:

- "The Graduate School Grants-in-Aid and summer research fellowships are terrific for people who compete for them and use them. We have people who apply every year. And, even if they don't get it, it gives them a chance to put together a narrative that the grant writer then takes and shops out to places." (General College)

- "We have had several faculty members who have been getting money ($150,000–$200,000) from the Academic Health Center's grant program." (Veterinary Pathobiology)

- "In the College of Liberal Arts, we rely a lot on small internal seed money opportunities. Some of them are university-wide like the Grants-in-Aid program, the McKnight Fellowships, and some research fellowships, but there are a lot just within the College of Liberal Arts and on the Duluth campus that are designed to facilitate research. The chancellor has a small fund that she uses on a competitive basis to award people around $750. There are small funds from various committees in the college that go through the dean's office, the research committee, and the teaching committee. And there are campus-wide sources which are sometimes earmarked for research and sometimes earmarked for teaching." (Geography)

Departments associated with agriculture have a unique source of state funding through the university's Agricultural Experiment Station. All Family Social Science faculty have Experiment Station money, "which means they teach one less class and so their teaching load is automatically reduced, and they all have an RA," explained Hogan. Experiment Station funds can also be used to jumpstart faculty research, thereby assisting them in getting other, more substantial levels of external funding. As Gengenbach (Agronomy and Plant Genetics) described, "It [Experiment Station money] doesn't make anybody's research program independent of other funding, but it does provide a good foundation to begin new projects that may or may not pay off. Then, if they start to pay off, you can go out and get competitive grants to really bolster the program."

Facilitating research productivity with funds from sources other than grants or contracts. The highly research-productive departments in our study also rely on funds from nongrant sources to support research. The major funding sources are indirect cost recovery, gifts, services provided, state allocations, tuition, and miscellaneous charges such as from use of equipment.

Indirect cost-recovery dollars. For departments that acquire a large number of external research grants, a major source of discretionary funds to support research comes from indirect cost-recovery (ICR) dollars. Here are some examples of how these departments use these funds in unique ways to facilitate research productivity:

- Maheswaran (Veterinary Pathobiology) uses ICR to support office staff, as many agencies don't allow staff to be included in direct costs. Also,10% of the ICR goes for faculty professional development.

- Loh (Pharmacology) described using grant funds to provide faculty bonuses: "In my department, one-third of the people got a bonus last year. I love that. The amount is not significant, but it is still a good gesture. . . . There are two criteria. One is that you bring in the money, so you have the money to pay that bonus. The second is to be in the top third in the department in terms of grant dollars generated. . . . So I will see it work eventually as a good reward, a good carrot for people. I think it will work."

- Ravdin (Medicine) uses the ICR as a research incentive. "We have a research incentive plan that is indexed to percentage of effort and total direct funding. There's also an incentive for getting a program project or a training grant. The incentive kicks in at about 60% of your salary funded, and then it's indexed to per $100,000 of direct funding, and it's capped at $12,500. The faculty get it and can take it as compensation, they can use it for their lab without it being taxable, it's up to them. It really has worked. It is particularly good for junior and midlevel faculty. However, as they become full professors, it becomes more difficult for them to meet the criteria, because their salaries get higher."

- Luepker (Epidemiology) uses ICR in several ways. "Depending on how many grants you have that generate ICR, you get secretary support in a proportional basis to that. . . . Also, if you make over 100% of your salary (and that characterizes over half of the faculty here between their teaching and their grants), you get to bank. You get to bank 5% as a fund which you can use during the year for whatever you want to buy: new furniture, memberships, professional meetings, research assistants, software, whatever. It's called the 5% fund."

Other discretionary dollars. Besides ICR, these departments have other sources of discretionary funding which they can opt to apply toward their research mission. Our interview transcripts were filled with many rich and diverse illustrations of how these funds are used to good effect—that is, in ways that foster a research-productive environment.

Several departments talked about raising money for endowed chairs and how greatly that can contribute to research productivity. Consider these comments from Archibald (Public Affairs): "The people who have the endowed chair money can be very productive; they can have eight RAs. More money gets money." The Law School has about 30 endowed chairs, typically funded though contributions. These are awarded to senior faculty who have performed at a distinguished national level. There is a built-in productivity incentive, since these chairs are not awarded in perpetuity, but rather are on a seven-year appointment and subject to a re-review process.

McMurry (Mechanical Engineering) described the importance of having monies available for matching funds for research proposals:

> Our department has been very aggressive in terms of trying to keep a pot of money available that we can use for matching purposes. Oftentimes funding agencies don't want to provide equipment. If the university can find some way to provide that equipment, it can improve the chances that a proposal will be funded. Our research budgets have gone up by 70% or a little less over the last three years. One of the reasons for that is being very aggressive with matches. I'm convinced it has helped. I know the university is always struggling with where to get that matching money, as do departments and colleges, but I think it makes a difference.

Many departments with faculty on nine-month appointments (and whose salaries are funded by state/tuition dollars) use department funds to support their faculty's research over the summer. In Biochemistry, Molecular Biology, and Biophysics, faculty on nine-month appointments who are successful in covering part of their academic salary on external dollars will get 75% of the amount they cover back from the department. This money is put into an individual research account that can be used to pay themselves summer salary dollars. The Law School has a competitive summer research grant program for faculty members engaged in research that will presumably result in a publication. At the time of our interviews, the awarded amount was $14,000 per grant.

Finally, a good portion of the departments in our study provided some level of professional development money to be used for scholarly activities of the researcher's choosing:

- The Department of Biology provides their faculty with "mad money"— usually a small amount ($500) to be used by the faculty member for their teaching or research programs. "Very often people use it for travel or to buy some supplies or to help support a graduate student's research," said Hicks.

- Cultural Studies and Comparative Literature uses department funds to set up a research budget of $1,500–$3,000 for each faculty member, which they use for books or other expenses.

- Ascerno (Entomology) said, "I allocate a small amount of money, about $15,000 per person per year, based on a proposal. . . . It's on a three- to five-year running basis, as long as faculty are productive and producing. They can buy software off of that, those sorts of things. It's not enough money to support a graduate student or a technician, so faculty know that they have to have money beyond that to run their programs. This helps set the culture of going after additional funds."

- Ravdin described the Department of Medicine's allowances for academic business expenses: "For assistant professors it's about $4,000, which they can use to go to meetings, buy journals, or join societies. The faculty members love it, they don't want to lose it, they think it's so valuable. . . . I think it's very good that faculty have some flexible resources to attend a meeting. When I think back on my career, the key formative events in my career occurred at meetings."

- In the Law School, each faculty member gets a professional development account ($3,500 for unchaired faculty, $4,000 for chaired faculty). "They can use it at their discretion for anything they want that will promote their own professional and academic development," explained Sullivan. "I don't second-guess that. If they want a specialized PC that goes well beyond our standard, or they want to buy some books for their own library, that's what they use it for. If they go over that, they can come to the dean and ask for more; if it's a reasonable request, they get it."

How Does Money Affect Research Productivity?

Pure and simple, money does have an impact on research, but perhaps not in the way many might think. The most powerful way money facilitates a researcher's productivity is by providing a research-oriented support structure (i.e., in the form of research space, facilities, staff) and productive local colleagues. Accordingly, we devoted the majority of this chapter to describing these types of resources.

Still, we would be remiss if we did not address the question, "Does money in the form of salary directly influence research productivity?" The research on what motivates researchers finds that money in the form of salary is not a highly valued reward, unless salaries are much lower than comparison groups or are seen as being distributed unfairly. In the departments we studied, care is taken to fairly distribute merit increases and rewards (see Chapter 11). Unfortunately, in many of these departments, salary levels are indeed low compared to their counterparts in other comparable institutions.

What we learned from our findings, however, is that lower salaries, coupled with a department's lack of ability to give major salary increases, are seen not so much as a hindrance to the productivity of current faculty, but rather as a barrier to recruiting the best-of-the-best among future, highly research-productive recruits. As Boyd in the Department of Finance said,

> The very best people are going to demand more money. Whether it's a dean or a school or another administrative unit, you have to have somebody give you the money. If the market clearing price for assistant professors at the top schools is $100,000, and your dean is only going to pay $80,000, you have no chance. You're going to get third-tier people.

Of course, recurring salary increases that come to faculty based on their individual research productivity are meant to motivate high research performance. Money can also be used to increase research productivity when it takes the form of salary bonuses or accounts that can be spent on professional development, summer salary, or other research-related expenses.

There is one exception whereby salary money associated with research is a major force in facilitating current faculty's research productivity: Faculty who are passionate about conducting research will be driven to acquire external grants and contracts if that is the only way they can acquire protected time to conduct research. Feldman (Health Services Research and Policy) said, "We have a performance expectation that every person funds half of his or her salary with external dollars." He went on to say that one of the key factors to his department's research productivity was "the wolf was always at our door. We're essentially a soft money shop, and in order to make the place go, we need to be productive [in grant getting and research]."

Ravdin described a similar scenario in the Department of Medicine:

> We essentially don't do unfunded research except for people in the development phase: All research time needs to be funded. We do distribute some state support to fund unfunded research efforts (this amounts to about four FTE distributed across the department). But that's because even in the very best of departments of medicine nationally, you can never completely fund extramurally 100% of the

research effort for everybody all the time. Recognizing there's that piece that will always be unfunded, everybody else knows that if they're going to be a physician-scientist, or they're going to spend time doing research, they need to generate the funding in order to do so, and that's a tremendous stimulus.

In summary, highly research-productive departments put significant effort into helping their faculty acquire external funds for research by providing grant preparation staff, matching funds, and internal peer review. In addition, these departments use dollars from other sources to recognize and provide incentives for research productivity (for example, by selectively providing highly research-productive faculty with endowed chair status, salary bonuses, contributions to development accounts, or monies to be used in their research). Some departments provide all of their faculty with some level of discretionary professional development funds. How dependent a department is on external research grants varies greatly by discipline. But, for those departments where the majority of the budget is not from state or tuition sources, a faculty member's ability to spend time on research is significantly determined by the amount of his or her salary covered by external research grants or contracts.

Chapter 8 Review:
Resources _____

- Faculty researchers thrive when surrounded by other research-driven peers. They become motivated to perform at a level that equals or exceeds that of their colleagues; they seek to sharpen their skills by soliciting feedback on their research-in-progress; and they act as a support network for one another, sharing survival strategies and other timely career tips.

- Students, particularly at the graduate level, are a catalyst for faculty research. However, securing funding to support students' time as research or teaching assistants can be a significant challenge. Faculty are typically called to meet this need by acquiring external grants. In some cases, student stipends are provided as part of new faculty start-up packages or paid for through a central pool of funds managed by the department chair or dean.

- Skilled and diversified staff are a highly valued resource. In particular demand are people with the know-how to maintain computers or other technical facilities and the ability to smoothly shepherd faculty through a grant proposal's development and subsequent fiscal management. Departments with productive, proven staff take care to appropriately reward and retain them.

- Among the departments in our study, research space is highly coveted and often in short supply. Leaders emphasized a need to be flexible and to plan ahead, especially during heavy faculty hiring periods.

- Research simply cannot happen without the funds to support it. In highly research-productive departments, faculty are actively supported in their efforts to secure research grants (e.g., through the allocation of grant preparation staff, seed money for pilot projects, travel funds). Some departments provide faculty with incentives for going after external dollars. These range from endowed chairs and salary bonuses to administrative support and discretionary dollars.

9

Teaching

*Another thing that I am particularly proud of in this depart-
ment is the extent to which our faculty are committed to excellent classroom instruction. Sometimes we say that excellent
teaching and excellent research go hand-in-hand. Maybe it's
true. There does seem to be a connection. People here seem to be
committed to both at a very high level.*

(Peter McMurry, Mechanical Engineering)

LITERATURE SUMMARY

Effective teaching is positively correlated with high levels of research
productivity among faculty. Further, spending moderate amounts of
time on nonresearch activities, such as teaching, is positively associated with high research productivity.

DEPARTMENT PRACTICES COVERED IN THIS CHAPTER
   1) What strategies do highly research-productive departments use to
      support their faculty's teaching responsibilities?
   2) How can departments facilitate an appropriate balance between
      teaching and research?

What Does the Literature Say? _____

Contrary to what some have hypothesized, there is no indication in the
empirical literature of a negative relationship between being a productive
researcher and being an effective teacher. Similarly, studies have found that
productive researchers are no less likely than other faculty to use creative
teaching strategies or to be strongly committed to teaching.

The relationship between effective teaching and research productivity has
been studied extensively (Braxton, 1983; Feldman, 1987; Michalak &
Friedrich, 1981; Norbeck, 1998; Noser, Manakyan, & Tanner, 1996; Stack,
2003; Terenzini & Pascarella, 1994). Allen's (1995) meta-analysis of this body
of literature, which included over 40 quantitative studies, revealed "a small,
heterogeneous, positive correlation between teaching effectiveness and

increased research productivity. Positive teaching evaluations correlate with increased research productivity" (p. 2). Braxton (1996) too, in his meta-analysis of the literature on the relationship between teaching and research, came to the conclusion that ". . . research does not interfere with teaching effectiveness" (p. 8). Rather, his appraisal suggests that in some institutions, particularly research universities, the teaching and research roles are independent of one another and do not detract from one another. In other colleges and universities, a complementary relationship appears to exist between teaching and research in that both of these faculty roles require the same general ability, manifest a similar value pattern, and/or are mutually reinforcing.

Olsen and Simmons (1996) looked for differences in the teaching behaviors of highly research-productive faculty versus others by studying 114 faculty in the College of Arts and Science and the School of Business at a large public Research 1 institution. Their

> . . . findings failed to support the current view that many positive teaching behaviors are inversely related to research productivity. Faculty with strong research profiles did not avoid teaching lower-level undergraduate classes, did not rely more on lecture and less on active learning techniques, and did not use more multiple-choice tests in their classes than other faculty. (p. 36)

Wanner, Lewis, and Gregorio (1981), in a national cross-sectional study of 17,399 faculty members in universities and four-year colleges, found a positive correlation between research productivity and commitment to teaching. Kuh and Hu (2001) looked at the relation of teaching and research at the institutional level, examining multiple indicators of undergraduates' learning productivity (e.g., active learning, peer cooperation, student-faculty contact, amount of required reading and writing, and time spent on school work, both attending class and studying). They found that the learning productivity of students at research universities was "on a par with other types of colleges and universities with the exception of selective liberal arts colleges" (p. 22).

As with all cross-sectional work, these findings should not be thought of as direct evidence of any causality between teaching and research; however, they do put to rest the myth that highly productive researchers are less likely than other faculty to be effective teachers overall, to use effective teaching strategies, or to be committed to the teaching mission.

A related issue, addressed in prior studies, is how the actual amount of time spent on teaching affects a faculty member's research productivity. As is discussed in the literature review for Chapter 10, committing significant amounts of time to nonresearch activities, such as teaching, is associated with lower research productivity. For example, Fox and Milbourne (1999) report that "a 10% increase in the number of teaching hours may reduce research output by as much as 20%, whereas a 10% increase in the number of grants held per year may raise output per year by as much as 15%" (p. 256).

That said, it also appears that the teaching-to-research relationship is not a completely zero-sum relationship. For example, significant gains in research productivity are not realized when faculty members spend more than 80% of their time on research. In fact, a study by Mitchell and Rebne (1995) found that spending moderate amounts of time in the nonresearch roles of teaching and consulting—up to four hours per week of consulting and up to eight hours per week of teaching—actually increases faculty's productivity in research.

Along with other authors (e.g., Brand, 2000; Linsky & Straus, 1975), Fairweather (2002) has suggested that "the key to increasing research productivity and teaching effectiveness may lie in looking for group solutions rather than relying on each faculty member to increase productivity levels in teaching and research" (p. 44). The expectation is that faculty members who are more effective at teaching than research would increase the department's overall teaching effectiveness, whereas faculty who excel in publishing or producing other scholarly products would contribute to the department's collective research productivity. The effect of such faculty role differentiation is an emerging area of research in higher education, as will be discussed in Chapter 10.

Department Practices

Although our study focused exclusively on how institutions facilitate faculty research, it was nonetheless quite clear from our participants' responses that these highly research-productive departments also expect excellence in teaching. As Sullivan (Law School) said, "This is not a place where one can be a great scholar and a mediocre or poor teacher, or vice versa. The value here is that you have to do both well."

From our interviews with academic leaders, we found that their expectations for high-quality teaching were supported by two interrelated sets of strategies: 1) practices for facilitating their faculty's teaching, and 2) practices for helping faculty members balance their dual teaching and research roles. We present these strategies below, but with two important caveats.

First, since we did not specifically ask any questions in our interviews about teaching, the description which follows is undoubtedly incomplete and in no way representative of the information we would have collected if we had asked all departments questions in this area. Still, we were struck by the information that emerged in spite of that constraint, and share it here, along with this caveat.

Second, since the University of Minnesota is both a land grant and a research institution, it is a major provider of education to its over 60,000 students. The importance of excellence in teaching is visible and reinforced from the highest administrative levels and in all official documents. In light of this backdrop, we acknowledge that the emphasis on teaching that emerged from our interview responses may not be representative of highly research-productive departments in other institutions whose missions are different from ours and whose faculty have different responsibilities for student instruction.

What Strategies Do Highly Research-Productive Departments Use to Support Their Faculty's Teaching Responsibilities?

The department leaders we interviewed offered up multiple strategies for facilitating effective teaching:

- Communicate clear teaching expectations when hiring and evaluating faculty.
- Model a commitment to teaching.
- Block out discrete faculty teaching time.
- Provide opportunities for teaching development.

Communicate clear teaching expectations when hiring and evaluating faculty. In these highly research-productive departments, the message that good teaching is expected and valued is communicated in multiple ways. First and foremost, these departments place considerable emphasis on hiring candidates who possess strong teaching skills (see Chapter 2). The chair of Marketing and Logistics Management was explicit in saying that although the dominant focus in their hiring considerations is on the candidates' research qualifications, this is not at the expense of teaching. Garavaso (Philosophy) echoed this, saying that "teaching and scholarship are of equal importance" and that division chairs have a responsibility to make this point very clear to faculty candidates during the recruitment process. She continued, "We make a big deal of being a part of the University of Minnesota, which is a research institution. . . . But excellence in teaching, accomplishments in publications, good service, and good citizenship are all part of a discipline's tenure considerations."

Garavaso's mention of tenure considerations highlights another major way in which teaching expectations are communicated and reinforced: the manner in which teaching is recognized and rewarded. (For information on how faculty accomplishments in research are evaluated, see Chapter 11.) Promotion and tenure are some of the most valued rewards in academia. Accordingly, if teaching is truly valued by an institution, then the promotion and tenure requirements should give weight to teaching accomplishments.

"Nobody here would get tenure who did not have a good teaching record," said Hogan (Family Social Science). All departments review teaching, along with research and service, when assessing a faculty member's performance. Ascerno provided an example of how this is done is his department (Entomology): "When I evaluate teaching I look at not only the student evaluations, but also student credit hours and the number of courses the person teaches, so that I can weigh that against their appointment to see whether or not they are teaching above or below their expected output."

Some departments have adopted different faculty appointment types, for which the expectations for teaching (and other faculty roles) vary. For example, in the Department of Biochemistry, Molecular Biology, and Biophysics, there are two major appointment tracks for faculty: a traditional research, teaching, and service track (with time allocations of 55/30/15, respectively); and a teaching-and-service-only track (70/30, respectively). The two tracks differ in their evaluation criteria, but, as Bernlohr explained, "The average teaching track raise is the same as the average research track raise. We don't devalue teaching. It is evaluated and monetarily compensated at the same value."

The practice of hiring faculty on teaching-track appointments is revisited later in this chapter. We also provide a deeper discussion of this practice—sometimes called faculty differentiation or the unbundling of faculty roles—in Chapter 10.

Model a commitment to teaching. Some departments in our study allow faculty with externally generated research funds to occasionally buy out of their semester teaching obligations. This strategy can help faculty acquire the time they need to conduct their research. Other departments, however, either prohibit or severely limit this practice. Having such a policy is one way of demonstrating their commitment to undergraduate and graduate education. Hogan (Family Social Science) expressed this well, saying, "Our faculty are committed to teaching. They really believe the quality of our program is dependent on teaching, so they won't allow anybody to buy out all of their teaching. We all need to teach two courses [per year]."

Allowances for reduced teaching loads are sometimes made for faculty with heavy administrative responsibilities. Yet, even the department heads/chairs in some of these highly research-productive departments continue to teach as a way of tangibly demonstrating their commitment to the overall educational mission. As Bates (Chemical Engineering and Materials Science) put it, "It's the only way to keep any respect. So, heads in this department teach a full load, period. There's no buyout. . . . I think that's important."

"I teach two courses a year," said Luepker (Epidemiology). "I expect all of my faculty members to teach, and I tell them that, even when they have 100% external research funding. I used to teach the intro course, because I needed to set an example for people." The role of the department leader as a peer model in research and teaching is discussed further in Chapter 14.

Block out discrete faculty teaching time. Some departments provide teaching assignments that allow faculty to devote larger, uninterrupted blocks of time to their teaching and research activities. For example, in Marketing and Logistics Management, "the way it turns out is, one semester faculty dedicate almost exclusively to teaching, another semester they dedicate almost exclusively to research," said Houston. This appears to be a strategy that can benefit both missions. The practice of stacking courses is also discussed in Chapter 10 as a means of directly supporting research productivity.

Provide opportunities for teaching development. Lastly, our study participants described a range of professional development and mentoring practices they use to facilitate quality teaching. Here are some examples:

- In the Department of Biology, new faculty members are mentored by having a more experienced faculty member sit in on their lectures and provide a peer evaluation. Hicks said, "Most of the faculty recognize this as a nurturing thing, that it isn't somebody spying on them. Rather, it provides them with positive, constructive feedback on their teaching."

- In the Department of Family Social Science, faculty with a strong interest in teaching have been encouraged to apply to the Bush Enrichment Program.

- The Law School summer seminar series for new faculty includes a session on teaching. During this session, "We talk about our values of teaching, share our war stories, discuss what we think our students' expectations are; we talk seriously about the value and importance of teaching," said Sullivan.

- All of the larger courses in Chemical Engineering and Materials Science are team-taught by two or three professors. Bates explained the advantage of this practice: "They [new faculty, or senior faculty who move into a new course] are able to learn the course and the teaching style from somebody who's already teaching, while they are actively involved . . . When I first got here, having a senior expert who knows more about the field out in the audience while I was giving lectures in a big course was the best way to keep the quality of the lectures up."

How Can Departments Facilitate an Appropriate Balance Between Teaching and Research?

"Of the things department chairs have control over, one of the most difficult is trying to create a balance between faculty members' research and teaching loads," said Masten (Child Development). This challenge was clearly evident from our interviews. It seemed impossible for most department heads and chairs to talk about the time needed for research productivity (the focus of our questioning) without also talking about the importance of—and subsequently the amount of time needed—for effective teaching.

Most of the department heads/chairs we interviewed described the intended time distribution of their faculty to be 40% research, 40% teaching, and 20% service and other activities; or 50% research and 50% teaching and service (with the exception of clinical departments, where more time is devoted to service in the form of patient care activities). Nonetheless, it is well acknowledged by faculty that, even under the best of circumstances, these time distributions can be hard to achieve. And when the pressure is on, research time is often the first to suffer given the high, oftentimes more immediate demands that teaching requires of them. For instance:

- "Research is one thing that you don't have specific deadlines for. You don't have specific evaluations by your students in the same way as teaching; so it tends to get squeezed out." (Psychology, Morris)

- "Faculty members are not thinking research, not when you have a class to teach, because you don't want to walk into the classroom and embarrass yourself." (Nursing)

- "Our teaching loads in CLA [College of Liberal Arts] are no longer competitive with our chief competitors. We are asked to teach more here. It is a serious problem if you want to compete with Michigan or Illinois or

Cornell or Stanford or even some of the California universities. We are at a disadvantage." (Psychology, Twin Cities)

In light of these pressures, highly research-productive departments have adopted strategies to try to maximize both the quality of instruction and the quality of research. Two such strategies that emerged in our interviews were 1) linking teaching and research responsibilities, and 2) using differentiated staffing.

Link teaching and research responsibilities. Ideally, the teaching and research roles of faculty are highly complementary, rather than competing. Houston (Marketing and Logistics Management) said that his department encourages this by attempting to link what people teach, in at least a general way, to their research interests:

> A recent study looking at the relationship between research faculty and student evaluations of teaching found a significant positive relationship between more highly research-productive instructors and positive (high) evaluations from students in regard to their teaching ability. (Stack, 2003)

> For example, if we have someone who draws a lot on economics in their research, they will teach in areas that draw a lot on economics. . . . We try to create some synergy between teaching and research, and actually try to put on the backshelf the idea that there's a tension between them.

Garavaso (Philosophy) noted that teaching can lead faculty into new, productive avenues of research that they might not otherwise have explored:

> When I first came here, I had my own [research] plans, and I was pursuing that plan. But it was almost totally detached from my teaching. . . . Now, after 15 years, I [have] learned to enjoy a lot of other research topics that I didn't work on before and that can be more easily connected with my teaching.

Adopt a differentiated staffing approach. Increasingly, to provide sufficient time for researchers to be productive while at the same time providing quality education, departments at our university are taking advantage of our menu of academic appointment types to hire faculty whose primary role is teaching or teaching and service.

General College, for example, hires full-time personnel on Professional and Academic appointments to teach in multisection courses. These staff have teaching loads double that of faculty who are hired with the more traditional expectation of having both research and teaching responsibilities.

Hicks's department (Biology) also hires some faculty to serve solely as instructors, without an expectation of doing research.

> They are excellent instructors; they provide a vital role in the department. They are particularly good with introductory students. So these instructors teach in some of our introductory courses, which has released some of the faculty who are more research oriented to develop upper division specialty courses which are more research oriented.

Their department has taken measures to prevent the creation of a faculty class system or hierarchy by appointment type. They conduct peer reviews of teaching performance, secure multiyear contracts for their excellent teaching faculty, and regularly recognize the contributions of nonresearch faculty at meetings. Again, Hicks:

> The department head sees teaching evaluations of all faculty members, and I have been able to convey to all the faculty how good certain instructors are who are only doing instruction, and how well they were received by students. They have been able to convey it, too, in other ways, because often in department meetings or other times when they are talking about teaching, they have ideas that no other people had thought about. . . . It was obvious they had researched the area, or they had actually tried something in class that worked real well and were sharing it with other people. So, the entire faculty has come to recognize how valuable these instructors are.

In the next chapter, we provide additional examples of the use of differentiated staffing and summarize the rather limited literature on this practice. There, readers will be alerted to the benefits and potential problems that come with unbundling faculty roles.

Chapter 9 Review: Teaching

- Faculty members are not only researchers; they also have interests and responsibilities in teaching, outreach, and service. The literature finds that highly research-productive faculty are as effective in their teaching— slightly more effective in fact—than faculty who are not highly research productive. Also, spending a limited amount of time on teaching (or other nonresearch activities) is compatible with high research productivity. Indeed, it may actually be conducive to research productivity.

- Highly research-productive departments expect their faculty to also be high-quality teachers. Most departments have specific strategies for supporting this part of their mission. They set clear teaching expectations from the outset (at hiring) and reinforce this through recognition and rewards; they model a commitment to student instruction; and they optimize their faculty's teaching performance through strategies such as mentoring and professional development seminars.

- Helping faculty best manage their time in research and teaching so that both roles are done well is a significant challenge for all departments. Helpful strategies might include closely linking teaching and research responsibilities and using some degree of differentiated staffing.

10

Sufficient Time for Research

Faculty need more time, and I'm not sure how to solve that problem. It would be a major step if I could clear off everybody's calendars somehow and give them more time for scholarship.

(Robert Sterner, Ecology, Evolution, and Behavior)

LITERATURE SUMMARY
Productive researchers devote significant periods of uninterrupted time to research. Research-productive departments recognize and respond in creative ways to their faculty members' need for protected research time. Nonetheless, carving out enough time to succeed in all facets of the faculty role (i.e., research, teaching, service) remains challenging, as does adapting faculty members' research-to-teaching time ratio in response to their changing professional interests.

DEPARTMENT PRACTICES COVERED IN THIS CHAPTER
1) What proportion of research time to teaching and service time is typical among faculty in these highly research-productive departments?
2) How are faculty members' time commitments determined?
3) How do faculty in these departments maximize their research time?
4) In today's academic climate, do faculty have enough time for their scholarly pursuits?

What Does the Literature Say? _____

Faculty have always put in more time than the standard 40-hour work week. For example, in a 1996 study at the University of Michigan, faculty across colleges reported working an average of 57 hours per week, and the medical school faculty reported working an average of 62 hours (Center for the Study of Higher and Postsecondary Education & Center for the Education of Women, 1999). Similarly, in 2001, faculty respondents to the Minnesota

Medical School Survey reported working an average of 58 hours each week (mode = 60) (Bland, Seaquist, Pacala, Center, & Finstad, 2002). These figures are typical for faculty at research-oriented institutions.

The question then becomes, what distribution of time across tasks is necessary to be productive in the areas of importance to oneself and to the institution? In the area of research productivity, Knorr, Mittermeir, Aichholzer, and Waller (1979)—who studied the publication rates of scientists in university and industry settings—found that research is unlikely when the time allotted to research falls under 10%, whereas 40% is probably ideal. Others advise that at least a 50% time commitment is necessary to be successful in research (Bland & Ruffin, 1992; Culpepper & Franks, 1984; Knorr et al., 1979; Reif-Lehrer, 1982). Nearly all studies of research productivity find that higher levels of research output are associated with lower levels of time commitment to teaching and service (Bellas & Toutkoushian, 1999; Fox, 1992). Interestingly, however, the full-time researcher (100%) is not necessarily the most productive one; the right mix of scholarly pursuits can actually be more advantageous. Mitchell and Rebne (1995) found that up to four hours per week of consulting and up to eight hours per week of teaching are indeed facilitative of research productivity.

The optimal time commitment needed for effective teaching is less clear, but there is no doubt that the necessary time investment can be substantial. El-Khawas (1991) summarized national surveys of faculty and discovered that both senior and nonsenior faculty at four-year institutions typically teach nine hours or more each week, and nearly a quarter of these teach for 13 hours or more. If one estimates two to three hours of outside class time (for preparation, grading, and advising) for each hour spent in class, the total time investment is considerable. Of course, faculty also spend time on institutional and professional service, outreach, and patient care. It is no wonder that El-Khawas also found that half of the faculty are not satisfied with their teaching load, nor with their opportunities for scholarly pursuits.

Unfortunately, it is becoming increasingly difficult for faculty to devote sufficient time to the primary tasks of research, teaching, and service. Faced with realities such as diminished state dollars for faculty work, increasing competitiveness for federal research dollars, legislation such as the federal balanced budget act, and enormous changes in the health care system, many faculty are spending more time on activities aimed at generating income (for example, writing grants, caring for patients) than on those associated directly with teaching and conducting research (Bland & Holloway, 1995).

Several recent articles in higher education have discussed formalizing the prevalent informal practice of adjusting faculty members' distribution of time to various roles over a career to accommodate changing interests. A caveat is that research universities are advised to use this adaptive mechanism only after a faculty member has been tenured—that is, has demonstrated the ability to excel in both research and teaching (Brand, 2000).

Fairweather (2002), a researcher in higher education, describes this practice as differentiating faculty. He writes:

> For most academic departments, the key to increasing teaching and research productivity may lie in looking for group solutions rather than on relying on each faculty member to increase productivity levels in teaching and research. Viewing faculty productivity as an aggregate across faculty members permits department chairs and departmental committees to combine the efforts of their individual members to achieve acceptable levels of productivity. Faculty who are less productive in research can increase the departmental average teaching productivity, whereas faculty who publish extensively can contribute to aggregate research productivity goals. In any case, the departmental or aggregate view of faculty productivity implies far more interdependence than is currently accepted as the norm for faculty behavior. (p. 44)

Differentiating faculty also addresses the concerns of some faculty, especially in the health sciences, that one can no longer be simultaneously competent at research, teaching, and service (i.e., patient care) (Schrier, 1997).

Some authors have expressed concern about the use of differentiated faculty (Hearn & Anderson, 2001). Finkelstein and Schuster (2001) analyzed national studies and found that faculty on nontenure-track appointments, compared to tenure-track faculty, published fewer articles, worked five fewer hours per week (up to 10 fewer at research universities), spent less time out of class with students, were less committed to their institutions, but were more satisfied with their work. Further, it is unclear if departments composed of differentiated faculty, on various appointments, working varying percentages of time, are able to provide the supportive culture and research emphasis needed to facilitate high productivity among faculty with research (see Chapters 3 and 4). In sum, although faculty differentiation has been increasing, the effect of these changes on higher education outcomes has yet to be fully understood; indeed, this is becoming an active area of scholarly inquiry among higher education researchers.

Department Practices _____

Recognizing the importance of protected time for research, the highly research-productive departments in our study use multiple strategies to help their faculty spend sufficient time on research. They also reported angst over meeting their dual commitments to high-quality teaching and high-quality research. Trying to meet both these goals resulted in an unfortunate, though consistent, observation that there just isn't enough time.

What Proportion of Research Time to Teaching and Service Time Is Typical Among Faculty in These Highly Research-Productive Departments?

Department heads in our study were asked, in a short written survey, to estimate the average time their faculty members spend on research. The modal response was 50% (mean = 45%, range = 10%–85%). This figure was reflected in many of their qualitative responses as well. Forest Resources faculty are generally hired on appointments that are 50/50 or 40/60 teaching/research. Similarly, in Applied Economics, typically 50% of a faculty member's time is protected for research, the other 50% for teaching and service. "I think faculty need to spend half their time on research if they're going to really stay up with their area," said Eidman. "Fifty/fifty seems to be a good target," echoed Warthesen (Food Science and Nutrition). "Fifty percent allows them to be fully engaged in the research process."

Other departments don't necessarily expect each faculty member to contribute equally to teaching and service and research at all times. Consider these comments from Hicks (Biology):

> For faculty on appointment types where research is expected, department chairs/heads estimated the time faculty spent on research. When compared to responses from full-time faculty participating in the 1998 NSOPF, it's clear that our highly research-productive department faculty were given more time for research.
>
> • Our 37 research-productive departments spent 46% of their work week on research activities.
>
> • Full-time faculty from the NSOPF spent 26% of their work week on research activities.

> We have people in this department with different talents. Some are very talented in research, some are not. Sometimes

that changes over a career. So what we try and do is find the best way to use people's talents and have them do things that they are interested in.

Hicks said he prefers this strategy over trying to force everybody into one mold, because faculty are more apt to excel in their chosen areas of emphasis.

In our study, the practice of faculty role differentiation (also called the unbundling of faculty roles) was clearest in two types of settings: the agricultural sciences, where faculty have separate extension or Experiment Station funding and outreach responsibilities; and the health sciences, where a formal clinical scholar track has been developed with its own career ladder and the potential for a multiyear contract upon promotion. According to Vayda, the use of both faculty tracks in her dentistry department (Diagnostic/Surgical Science) has been favorable: "There's a culture in our department of a sense of team. The tenure-track faculty, particularly junior faculty, are very appreciative of their clinical-track colleagues, because they know that's what allows them to be freed up to do research."

In Pediatrics, clinical-track faculty are 30% research and 70% clinical/ teaching, whereas tenure-track faculty are just the opposite (70% research and 30% clinical/teaching). When asked how the department supported the 30% research time for clinical scholars, Moller explained,

> We are a socialistic system, and although we have a so-called "productivity model," we recognize that some of our divisions are high earners and bring in a lot of money, like the intensive care unit, and certain ones can't. So for those who can't, we rob from the rich to help develop the poor, and with that provide research time for our clinical scholar faculty.

It is important to reiterate (as first noted in the literature overview for this chapter) that although the use of differentiated faculty appointment types is a growing trend, it has yet to be determined what effects this nationwide shift in hiring practices will have on a broad range of important higher education outcomes. Concerns in this area were expressed by Pharis (Art):

> In the last three years, we've been able to bring five new faculty into the department as nontenure-track faculty—these faculty are each appointed to a three-year term; they provide service, including committee work and advising, but their departmental responsibility to research is not as critical. These hires have improved the ratio between adjunct faculty, which was too high, and full-time tenure-track and

nontenure-track faculty. But I remain concerned that we still have too many adjunct faculty and not enough full-time faculty to contribute to the increasing service and to also fulfill the roles that only full-time faculty can provide.

Additional research is needed to shed light on whether the advantages offered by having a large proportion of alternative nontenure-track faculty appointments (the most immediate being financial flexibility) are balanced by the challenges they create. These challenges include, for instance, maintaining a shared academic culture that can effectively embrace different faculty appointment types, and fostering a high commitment to the institution among faculty who, by virtue of their alternative appointment type, are ineligible for the traditional academic rewards of promotion and tenure.

For more information on commonly used alternative faculty appointments, see Judith Gappa's (1996) report on the six common off-track models. Trower and her colleagues at the Harvard Graduate School of Education have also written a book about and have compiled a list in a CD-ROM of faculty appointment policies used in the universities across the country (Project on Faculty Appointments, 1999; Trower, 2000). In addition, several articles summarize appointment practices across universities and specifically in medical schools (Hearn & Anderson, 2001; Jones & Gold, 2001; National Center for Education Statistics, 2002).

How Are Faculty Members' Time Commitments Determined?

Many departments in our study apply a standard formula for how much time each faculty member is expected to spend on research, teaching, and service. (Faculty on the university's Duluth campus are unionized, and therefore have the most formal statements regarding time allocations.) Typically, there are upper limits on the number of teaching contact hours that can be assigned. In turn, this approach presumably puts a minimum on the percent of time that can be devoted to research and service. This illustrates a recurring theme from our interviews: In many departments, faculty research time is predicated on what is left over after time has been assigned to cover teaching.

Time allocation formulas serve as a starting point, but they are not immovable. For example, in Mechanical Engineering the guidelines for dividing a faculty member's time across the academic year are 50% research, 40% teaching, and 10% service, but these numbers do vary, with some individuals devoting 100% of their time to teaching activities. Most departments will allow faculty to adjust their time commitments when the circumstances demand it. Consider the following comments by Masten (Child Development):

> When I know that somebody needs time to write a big [grant] renewal, we try to shift things so that they have a little help with their teaching, or shift the load of teaching more into one semester. We try to stay flexible in order to provide the time and mental energy.... Keeping our teaching load reasonable is probably the single most important thing we do in this department, and we have had some advantages along the way because we were founded as a research institute. In our department we have all the teaching and outreach obligations that go along with a land grant institution, yet the research tradition is so strong that we've always organized our teaching is such a way that it doesn't burden any one individual, because that's counterproductive.

Staying flexible appears to be a common strategy—even a necessary one—for dealing with the ongoing tension between time spent on research and time spent on other faculty pursuits. Even in departments with differentiated faculty (e.g., tenure-track and clinical scholar track faculty), the proportion of time spent on research and teaching can be adjusted if, for example, a clinical scholar took on a major educational role or brought in a research grant.

How Do Faculty in These Departments Maximize Their Research Time?

"Maintaining the balance between teaching and research is one of the great challenges in a research university," noted Gladfelter (Chemistry). In our study, the most frequently cited strategies for optimizing the quantity and quality of faculty members' research time were as follows:

- Make the most of summers.
- Buy additional research time.
- Stack courses.
- Take advantage of protected time (new faculty).
- Take advantage of sabbaticals and semester leaves (midcareer and senior faculty).

Make the most of summers. In many of the departments in our study, faculty hold nine-month appointments. Consequently, their faculty tend to take advantage of the summer months to heavily engage themselves in research pursuits. "Faculty don't get paid in the summer, but I expect them to be doing research," said Bates (Chemical Engineering and Materials Science). "Some go away and continue to do their work elsewhere, but not too commonly. Most of us take summer salary out of our grants, so we're still paid. Not everyone can manage all of that, the whole summer, but certainly many do." In Cultural Studies and Comparative Literature, very few faculty members teach in the summer. "There's some financial sacrifice here," acknowledged Leppert, "but as soon as people get enough ahead, they use the summer to write." The Law School has a competitive grant program for faculty to help fund their summer research. These awards specifically cannot be used for course development and are preferentially awarded to projects that will ultimately result in publication.

Buy additional research time. Many (though not all) departments have formulas for determining how faculty who acquire external grants can buy out of teaching and/or service. For example in Psychology (Twin Cities campus), it takes 12.5% of a faculty member's nine-month salary to buy out of a typical course. In the biology department, they ask faculty to replace what it would cost to hire an instructor to teach their course, which usually turns out to be less than what a month's salary would be. Luepker (Epidemiology) reported that his department has "a very explicit system" for determining funding based on the time faculty devote to particular tasks:

> You get paid 7.5% for every credit you teach. . . . And I pay
> people 5% to be director of graduate studies, to be major
> chair, to run the seminars, things like that. That's how I
> divide up the state money and tuition. The rest has to come
> from research.

Stack courses. Collins (General College) used the term "stacking courses," whereby faculty can condense their teaching load in order to free up a future semester exclusively for research. Many faculty members go this route, teaching their eight courses over four semesters in blocks of three, two, three, and zero. Faculty in Cultural Studies and Comparative Literature often try to cluster their teaching into two days a week. Although this can make room scheduling a challenge, the Chair said his faculty find it well worth the effort to have uninterrupted time to focus on teaching and other days specifically allocated to research.

Take advantage of protected time (new faculty). Nearly all the departments in our study make special time arrangements to help new faculty successfully kick off their research programs. Here are some examples that emerged from our interviews:

- "In the first couple of years new [Psychology, Twin Cities] faculty are not given any committee assignments. Then it is modest up until they get tenure."

- "In General College, the tenure-track faculty have the equivalent of a year's release from teaching during the probation period. "

- "It's been a tradition in this department [Biology], especially with new assistant professors, that we give them a reduced teaching load in the first year they are here. We also reduce their service load. . . . We don't have them advise any undergraduate students during enrollment periods for their first year, and then we give them a reduced number of undergraduates to advise for the next two years."

The largest proportion of teaching release time is given to Nursing faculty in their first year. This is helpful, but "off-timed," according to Bearinger: "In the first year, you are so worried about walking into a class and embarrassing yourself if you are unprepared. You are working on getting together your syllabi, your lectures, and everything."

Take advantage of sabbaticals and leaves (midcareer and senior faculty). Among the most traditional strategies for facilitating the research productivity of midcareer and senior faculty are sabbaticals and leaves. Not surprisingly, faculty in these highly research-productive departments are often encouraged to take advantage of these opportunities for intense research activity. Leppert (Cultural Studies and Comparative Literature) said, "We spend a lot of time helping one another to develop research proposals. Consequently, we have a very high success rate on both the single-quarter leave and on the sabbatical supplement."

Gladfelter (Chemistry) said that he advocates as many people going on sabbatical and leaves as possible. "We can do that because there's a reasonable community of people around the Twin Cities who make their living by working at these temporary teaching positions in chemistry," he explained. Of course, not all disciplines have this luxury. The heads and chairs of particularly small departments noted that while sabbaticals and leaves can increase the research productivity and vitality of the faculty member taking the leave, the effects of such a leave can be hard on the faculty who remain. The inherent benefits and challenges regarding sabbaticals and other career development practices are described more fully in Chapter 12.

In Today's Academic Climate, Do Faculty
Have Enough Time for Their Scholarly Pursuits?

"There is *always* too little time," said Ben-Ner (Industrial Relations), echoing a common lament of the interviewed department heads. This lack of time applies to the full range of faculty roles, but particularly so for research-related activities. Consider the following representative comments from our interviews:

- "The one major barrier for most of us is time. The pressure of teaching and the pressure of committee work and administration is simply greater than it ought to be." (Psychology, Morris)

- "Most people's perception is they don't have any periods of uninterrupted time [to do research], much less significant amounts of time." (Ecology, Evolution, and Human Behavior)

- "I never have 40% of my time for research. Part of it is my fault, because I let teaching go overboard. Teaching is interesting and very dangerous in some ways, because it can be so rewarding that you end up spending most of your time doing that. . . . There is never a time I feel I am ready. Still, [sometimes] you need to say, 'okay, this is my research time.'" (Philosophy)

Sterner (Ecology, Evolution, and Human Behavior) shared his view of how the faculty time crunch affects not only the quantity of research that is conducted, but also the quality:

> I sense a slippage in the care that people are taking with their research under the pressure to keep publishing and getting grants and cranking out students. If I'm facing the decision to go back and do this experiment again because I have this little nagging doubt, but it's going to take three months, I better not do that. More and more, people are making the decision just to keep blasting ahead at full speed—for their own productivity and reputation . . . to get their next grant or another paper on the record, whatever. Just to crank out lots of stuff is pretty intense. The faculty aren't always able to devote the time needed to get the job done right. They're stretched to the limit.

In summary, it is essential that faculty have significant uninterrupted time to be highly research productive and, perhaps more important, to produce high-quality research. Getting this time is seen as increasingly difficult.

As a result, departments have become very creative in helping faculty optimally arrange their obligations and in differentiating faculty roles to allow faculty to focus on the job tasks at which they most excel and that they most enjoy. These strategies are helpful. But, as the roles of faculty become less similar and faculty have less in common due to their differentiated roles, leaders will need to increase their efforts to maintain a cohesive community, a research-conducive culture, and a positive climate.

Chapter 10 Review: Sufficient Time for Research

- A nearly even split between research time and teaching/service is common among faculty in these highly research-productive departments, but this does vary by discipline (mean = 45%, range = 10%–85% faculty research time, as estimated by the interviewed department heads).

- Some departments allow for a greater differentiation of roles, securing long-term contracts or instituting different promotion tracks for faculty with a greater interest in teaching than in research. However, when different appointment types and differentiated roles result in faculty no longer having common roles and responsibilities, increased leadership attention is required to ensure a cohesive community, a research-conducive environment, and a positive climate.

- Standard formulas for allocating time are used in some departments, but adjustments are common. Teaching is of considerable importance in these departments, and striking the right balance between research and teaching and service is a formidable challenge for their faculty.

- Faculty maximize their research time in a variety of ways. Those on nine-month appointments often spend their summers doing research. Some negotiate to buy out of teaching to provide more time for research. Most strive to arrange larger blocks of uninterrupted time for research. Departments build in flexibility so that faculty members can be given time to take advantage of unexpected research opportunities. It is common for departments to offer teaching release time and reduced committee appointments to their newer faculty, and many encourage their midcareer and senior faculty to take advantage of sabbaticals and leave.

- Despite these mechanisms, lack of sufficient work time for research remains a significant barrier in these departments.

11

Rewards

We try to celebrate the positive things as much as possible. We nominate faculty for awards and really do try to let them know they're appreciated. That's a morale booster. Faculty know that research is rewarded, that the rewards systems are there.

(Janice Hogan, Family Social Science)

LITERATURE SUMMARY
Research-productive departments distribute rewards equitably, in accordance with defined benchmarks of achievement. They promote the public recognition of their faculty and help stimulate the acquisition of intrinsic rewards such as conducting socially significant work, seeing one's work applied, and being part of a highly regarded institution. Other critical rewards for researchers include promotion and tenure, resources, recognition by supervisors or peers, and opportunities for responsibility and intellectual stimulation. Money can be a motivating factor or a disrupting factor; the latter occurs when faculty salaries are low compared to peers or when other inequities are perceived.

DEPARTMENT PRACTICES COVERED IN THIS CHAPTER
1) How do faculty rewards contribute to the research productivity of a department?
2) How are salary increases applied as a reward mechanism for faculty?
3) Besides salary increases, what other types of rewards are used in these highly research-productive departments?

What Does the Literature Say? _____

Bailey (1994) wrote,

> [It] is almost too good to be true: Researchers' commitment to research derives from intrinsic motivation (genuine interest in the task) rather than extrinsic motivation (tangible rewards). Personal challenge and stimulation derived from

> research may be what makes a productive and committed
> researcher.... (pp. 168–169)

This link between intrinsic rewards and high research productivity is found consistently throughout the literature. Researchers (and faculty as a whole) prosper when they feel like valued members of the organization, have opportunities to make meaningful contributions, are part of a culture that is a fit with their values, are part of an organization that contributes to society in ways they believe are important, are members of a highly regarded organization, and have autonomy in their jobs (Bland & Ruffin, 1992; Bowen & Schuster, 1986; Eckert & Stecklein, 1961; Green, Bellin, & Baskind, 2002; Gustad, 1960).

When researchers are asked to rate which rewards they value most, recognition and praise are the most highly rated (Hearn, 1999; Latham and Mitchell, 1976). This was confirmed in an experimental study reported by Latham and Wexley (1981), in which researchers were rewarded for productivity with managerial praise, public recognition, or money. Although all three rewards had a positive impact, money and praise had the greatest effect. Further, the authors noted, "the increase in performance due to the money over praise was so small as to be practically insignificant. Thus, from a cost/benefit viewpoint, it is most effective to give praise" (p. 190). Corcoran and Clark (1985), in their study of highly active faculty, found that recognition from colleagues and administrators emerged as one of four specific factors that supported faculty success. The other three were stimulating colleagues, a strong academically oriented administration, and adequate resources.

In more recent studies, recognition and money were found to be of equal importance to faculty. For example, The Institute for Research on Higher Education (2000) asked faculty what rewards and incentives they consider important; the top four responses were tenure, promotion, salary, and merit increases. In a survey study by Williams, Dunnington, and Folse (2003), money and recognition were deemed to be equally important features to faculty rewards systems. Money does seem to be a consistently important reward for a small subset of faculty. And it generally becomes more important when salaries are low in comparison to other comparable faculty or units (Blackburn & Pitney, 1988; Lewis & Becker, 1979). For example, Pfeffer and Langton (1993) found that "the greater the degree of wage dispersion within academic departments, the lower is individual faculty members' satisfaction and research productivity and the less likely it is that faculty members will collaborate on research" (p. 382). Money also becomes an increasing source of dissatisfaction when no funds are available for travel, when copy machines don't work, when library holdings become limited and, in particular, when the lack of funding seems to indicate lack of community or governmental support for their institution or system (Bowen & Schuster, 1986).

The Institute for Research on Higher Education (2000) study is one of the few that specifically asked about the importance of tenure and promotion, which are perhaps the most concrete and enduring manifestations of colleague and public recognition. Based on their interviews of 378 faculty at eight research universities, three doctoral-granting universities, four comprehensive universities, and four liberal arts colleges, the authors concluded that "tenure and promotion continue to rank as the most commonly cited incentives for faculty, regardless of institutional type" (p. 54). Studies consistently find that faculty who achieve promotion and tenure are the most research productive— and continue to be productive over time. Bland, Center, Finstad, Risbey, and Staples (2004), in a study of full-time faculty at research and doctoral-granting institutions, compared the research productivity (e.g., article production) of new faculty hired on tenure track versus that of faculty hired on other types of tracks. Although both faculty groups reported spending similar amounts of time on research, those in tenure-track positions were significantly more research productive. This is likely a result of not only the incentive of promotion and tenure per se, but also the fact that many of the other research-facilitating features described in this book (e.g., mentoring, networking, and access to resources) are more likely to occur for tenure-track faculty. Still, the impact of a tenure system on research productivity should not be underestimated.

In sum, multiple types of rewards can work together to facilitate faculty research productivity. Although salary may come to mind first when thinking about rewards, it is, in the words of Hearn (1999),

> ... only one piece in a mosaic of elements comprising the environment for faculty productivity.... Alone, salaries are neither the most important motivators for faculty ... nor the most uplifting of topics.... A single-minded focus on reforming salary policy alone, without consideration of its place in larger institutional concerns, makes little sense. (p. 407)

Department Practices _____

"Ultimately, faculty do their best because they love to teach and do research. That's a reward in and of itself. I think many people feel that way." This quote from McMurry (Mechanical Engineering), one of our study participants, reflects the literature's finding that intrinsic rewards can act as powerful cata-lysts for faculty productivity. He was not alone among department leaders in expressing this idea. Ben-Ner (Industrial Relations) also noted that a key reward for faculty "is their satisfaction in getting the project/research done." Ek (Forest Resources) said that his faculty "take a lot of satisfaction from their own accomplishments in terms of playing a leadership role in society . . . pro-viding expertise and solutions, and making a difference."

Does this mean that these highly research-productive departments need not, and therefore do not, provide their faculty with extrinsic rewards for being productive in research? Quite the contrary. These departments provide many tangible rewards to their faculty. Typically, these rewards are fiscal (salary increases, research assistants, etc.); however, the value of praise and formal recognition was also frequently acknowledged—a particularly salient point, given the scarcity of resources that many departments have at their disposal. In this study, department heads/chairs not only described the types of rewards common to their environments, but also expressed a keen awareness of how such rewards can have a greater impact on their unit's overall productivity.

How Do Faculty Rewards Contribute to the Research Productivity of a Department?

Rewards, though granted to individual faculty, can positively affect entire departments. Departments may find, for example, that the frequent and fair distribution of rewards ultimately enhances their unit's reputation, contributes to a positive group climate, and reinforces a culture of high achievement.

Enhance reputation of the department. When the accomplishments of individual faculty members are recognized, particularly through high-impact publications, national leadership appointments, and prestigious fellowships, the department as a collective can reap benefits. Leppert (Cultural Studies and Comparative Literature) described this well, saying,

> What it really boils down to is trying to figure out as many ways as possible to plug your faculty into the concrete reward system of actual dollars, and also into fellowships and awards that will have national prominence in terms of their career paths. Because rightly or wrongly, as we all know, getting one helps you get a second one, and it also creates prestige for the department and the individual.

Masten (Child Development) noted that awards are "important to our own productivity, but also important to our reputation. This then feeds back into more opportunities." As one example, several department leaders reported greater ease in recruiting excellent faculty and graduate students by virtue of their department being highly ranked or their current faculty being well regarded on a national or international scale.

Contribute to a positive group climate. The importance of a positive and supportive sense of community to research productivity was described in Chapter 3. Climate can be directly affected by the presence or absence of rewards. Bernlohr (Biochemistry, Molecular Biology, and Biophysics) observed that nominating faculty for university-level awards not only helps to foster their careers, but also "makes people feel better about themselves and their workplace." Ames said his department (Clinical and Population Sciences) tries to "focus on the personal stuff" and not let any accomplishment go unrecognized—things such as a faculty member's graduate students getting their Ph.D.s, or someone being voted veterinarian of the year by the Wisconsin Veterinary Association. The effect of this kind of personal attention on climate is clearly noticeable. "The message that this sends out is we care about people, about their personal life, and that we're here to help them," said Ames.

Reinforce a culture of high achievement. Rewarding research productivity, whether through praise and recognition or monetary means, can also serve to reinforce a department's culture of research productivity. Celebrating productivity in research is "embedded in the day-to-day life" of the Institute of Child Development, where it is standard practice for the director to begin faculty/staff meetings by announcing any new achievements of their faculty, students, and staff. This act, Masten noted, positively feeds back into the institute's research culture.

Bates (Chemical Engineering and Materials Science) said his faculty know that their department's system for distributing salary rewards is competitive and based on a high standard of achievement:

> They are expected to be outstanding, to get into the National Academy, be the plenary speaker at every meeting they go to, bring in the big bucks, publish in the top journals, teach the great courses, get great student evaluations, and win teacher of the year.

Although no one faculty member achieves all of this, there are clear matrices for success that are understood to be part of their culture and the basis for their internal rewards.

One of the premier benchmarks of faculty achievement is promotion and tenure. Thus, departments use this mechanism to increase productivity in desired areas, for example, teaching, research, service. In Chapter 3, we described how in highly research-productive departments, a high level (quantity and quality) of scholarship in research is expected of faculty seeking to advance in the tenure track. These expectations are embedded in their culture and reflect the departments' overall research emphasis.

> Salary often is not the primary reward for research faculty. In the 1998 NSOPF, for faculty who listed research as their primary role, the number one reason that could entice them to leave their current institution was "Greater opportunities to do research" followed by "Good research facilities."

How Are Salary Increases Applied as a Reward Mechanism for Faculty?

As noted in the literature review for this chapter, salary is but one reward for faculty and clearly not the only source of faculty satisfaction. Indeed, when we asked the department heads/chairs in our study, "How do faculty salaries in your department compare to those in peer institutions," 50% (16 of 32 respondents) answered that they were "somewhat" or "significantly" lower. This suggests that other types of rewards help to augment salaries as a source of faculty satisfaction and act as an incentive for ongoing productivity.

This is not to say that salaries are not important. In Chapter 2, for example, our study participants also noted the importance of providing desirable faculty recruits with a generous letter of offer. Prior studies highlight the importance of having equitable salaries for comparable faculty within a unit (Blackburn & Pitney, 1988; Lewis & Becker, 1979; Pfeffer & Langton, 1993).

In our qualitative work, we learned that when faculty productivity is monetarily rewarded in these highly research-productive departments, this typically occurs through salary increases based on merit. Increases are tied directly to a faculty member's documented productivity in designated areas, which include, at a minimum, research, teaching, and outreach/service. Typically, research is weighted heavily in the merit equation. This reflects the value that these departments place on research, as described by some participants in our study:

- "Research is a focal point for our evaluations at all levels. There aren't any faculty members in a position to ignore that. Our probationary faculty are intensely aware of the research expectation." (Psychology, Morris campus)

- "No matter how hard you try to say that teaching and clinical services are important, at the end of the day research is a pretty sure bet for the merit scores. This is a university emphasis. It just shakes out." (Clinical and Population Sciences)

- "We reward and recognize research by salary increases and [endowed] chairs, and everybody knows it. There are clear signals here what the value system is. If you have an extraordinary year or two or three combined with productivity and research, you will get a very large salary increase. If you have some dry years it will be reflected." (Law)

Within the general rubric of research productivity, a variety of scholarly activities can be factored into faculty merit rankings. "We have a long list of contributions that you can make in research," explained Hicks (Biology), "all the way from earning national awards and writing books, to serving on different research committees or reviewing manuscripts. Certainly getting your own grants and publishing papers are very high, and people get the most recognition for that." The Pharmacology faculty have developed a very detailed set of merit criteria which reward faculty for having given seminars, served on an NIH study section, and published papers with a high impact factor. Across departments, the number of published journal articles has traditionally been an important benchmark.

Despite sharing an overall view that fiscally rewarding research is important, each department reported having unique criteria that govern the distribution of salary increases. Whereas the scholarship committee in Pharmacology deliberately weighs research most heavily (65% of the merit score, 25% for teaching and 10% for service/outreach), other departments have developed criteria that formally equalize the value of research and teaching. General College uses a 20-point system for their annual merit scores: eight points for research, eight points for teaching, and four points for professional and university service.

Some departments' leaders described the struggle they face trying to quantify faculty achievements in nonresearch areas. As McMurry (Mechanical Engineering) explained,

> When I evaluate merit raises, I look at productivity in research, teaching, and service. I try to rank them appropriately, but it turns out that research ends up playing a very important role, because it's not so difficult to find that someone is much more research productive than someone else. It's much more difficult to show that someone is a

much better teacher than someone else. Actually, it's an interesting challenge to me as a department head. I would say as a result, research ends up playing a very important role in terms of one's annual assessment.

No merit system can overcome all difficulties—the primary one being the lack of any funds to distribute. Nonetheless, numerous department heads/chairs emphasized the importance of instituting a rewards distribution process that is developed by faculty and consistently applied by the current leadership. Often, heads/chairs or deans make the final decisions regarding salary increases. It is common for these leaders to rely heavily on recommendations produced by an executive review committee whose members are elected by the faculty and/or appointed by the head. A few department leaders reported using a more informal review system where the head asks faculty for an updated curriculum vita and a brief summary of what they have accomplished during the year, along with a list of their publications and other supporting materials. The head then meets with each faculty member individually to discuss the amount of salary increase warranted based on the faculty member's contributions to research, teaching, and service.

Although structure is important, merit systems are not necessarily static. Rewards criteria and processes can change in response to factors such as the current fiscal environment or a perceived need to very visibly reward faculty. In General College, during years when no money is available for raises, faculty efforts are counted toward the next year. Some departments try to account for achievements over multiple years, despite the necessity of conducting reviews on an annual basis. "If somebody has no publications in a given year, but it's just a low point, I'm not going to recommend a zero or one-percent salary increase, especially if their contributions have been significant in other places in the department," explained Gladfelter (Chemistry). Some colleges and departments have successfully experimented with one-time salary bonuses as a type of carrot to motivate productivity, whereas others have deliberately steered away from them, preferring instead to use base salary increases as a sign of the department's long-term investment in their faculty.

Besides Salary Increases, What Other Types of Rewards Are Used in These Highly Research-Productive Departments?

Indirect cost return. Another financial reward used in some departments is the return of indirect grant dollars (i.e., grant dollars awarded to cover an institution's facilities and administrative costs) to faculty who are successful in acquiring external funding. For the departments in our study, the university takes a portion of the indirects for services it provides to researchers. Each of the colleges and departments then decides how to distribute their portion. "My view is to reward the person financially, personally, with augmentation, and also to reward the program by providing financial resources for that person's program," said Simone (Oral Sciences). "When people receive grants and there are IDCs [indirect costs] from those grants, parts of those IDCs and salary recovery should go back to the investigator." Other department heads/chairs provided some specific examples of this practice in action:

- In Applied Economics, half of the faculty salary savings generated by grants is returned to the principal investigator for use in his or her research program. "That gives them some extra money to work with," said Eidman. "They can use it for trips, or computer equipment, hiring research assistants, whatever."

- The Department of Medicine uses some of their indirect cost returns and central dollars together to fund a "research incentive plan." In this plan, faculty are provided with a certain percentage of their indirect costs to use as flexible spending dollars for their research programs or as salary compensation. According to the department chair, this reward is a particularly strong incentive for junior and midlevel faculty. The system is designed to make it harder for more senior faculty (those with higher salaries) to qualify.

- In the biology department, one third of indirect monies is kept by the college, one third is given to the department head for use at his/her discretion, and the remaining third is returned to the principal investigator on the grant.

Public recognition of research achievements. Money isn't everything, so the saying goes. And so it is with faculty rewards. As noted earlier, praise and recognition are also highly effective means of increasing faculty productivity—potentially even more effective than monetary rewards. Consider these comments from Masten (Child Development):

> We are interested in each other's work. There's a tradition of being interested, so when people are fond of a paper they have written, they distribute it to their department colleagues. When one of us gives a major address or receives a prestigious award, we attend if we can. That way, people are recognized, they are encouraged to do research by the

atmosphere and by the reward system in the university and department.

This idea was clearly echoed by other department leaders in our study, who described the many strategies they use to visibly acknowledge their faculty's achievements.

The School of Nursing puts up a bulletin board in their building to illustrate the research achievements of their faculty, while the family social science department distributes an electronic newsletter for graduate students and faculty to acknowledge published articles and acquired grants. Several heads/chairs reported regularly emailing faculty so as to visibly congratulate them on their achievements. Others rely on their web pages, where their faculty's curriculum vitae are placed.

The Department of Oral Sciences uses the public relations office in their college to get information on outstanding faculty accomplishments (e.g., a high profile paper) to the appropriate networks. This practice encourages young faculty to learn how to promote themselves and make themselves more visible.

The Department of Cultural Studies and Comparative Literature publishes a yearly "brag book" to showcase their faculty's research successes, along with the accomplishments of their students and staff. Leppert explained,

> I make sure that the right people see it. In part it is intended for internal consumption, but it's also intended for the dean and the provost and the president and the dean of the graduate school and so on.... I think it's really important for a chair to constantly be reminding his or her administration of the department's success.

The Law School has a similar practice. They annually publish a book describing their faculty's research activities. This is distributed to all faculty, but also disseminated externally, "for the rest of the world to see," said Sullivan. In addition, the spring issue of their alumni newsletter reports all the scholarship that was published in that academic year and identifies the faculty who currently hold their endowed chairs. "Again, it's another way of promoting, celebrating, and encouraging," said Sullivan.

Promotion and tenure. As noted in the literature review for this chapter, one of the most highly valued nonsalary rewards within academia is promotion and tenure. Certainly, there is money attached to being promoted and tenured and to the long-term commitment it provides. But, the power of promotion and tenure goes well beyond its financial value. The career-long public recognition value of having acquired promotion and tenure is a very powerful incentive, and when this is tied to research outcomes, as expected, it facilitates research. For example, when the organizational level goals for the School of Nursing and General College shifted to an increased emphasis on research, the level of research productivity needed to achieve promotion and tenure also increased. To help faculty successfully meet the requirements for promotion and tenure, departments devote a host of resources; these include, for example, generous start-up packages for new faculty (Chapter 2) and structured mentoring (Chapter 5).

Although promotion and tenure are powerful incentives, they have the shortcoming of being able to be used only once. Thus, the departments in our study skillfully use promotion and tenure, but also rely on other types of rewards mechanisms such as those detailed in this chapter.

Other "tangible" rewards. Finally, many departments, as they are able, reward their research-productive faculty through the selective allocation of resources such as graduate assistants, protected research time, or space. Some departments allow their researchers to occasionally buy out of a semester's teaching obligations. This provides them with more flexibility in their sched-ules and more time to spend on research. Several department heads/chairs also spoke of the value of nominating their faculty for internal and external awards, some of which carry great prestige and/or are tied to a substantial amount of research funding (e.g., university fellowships). Each of these types of rewards—resources, sufficient work time, brokered opportunities which include nominating faculty for awards—stand out in the literature as distinct environmental characteristics that facilitate research productivity. As such, they are discussed more fully in other chapters.

Chapter 11 Review:
Rewards _____

- Rewards granted to individual faculty members also benefit departments. Specifically, they enhance the department's reputation, contribute to a positive group climate, and reinforce an internal culture of high achieve-ment.

- Providing annual, merit-based increases to faculty salaries is the most prevalent reward mechanism in these highly research-productive depart-ments. Each department differs in its approach to evaluating and ranking faculty, but all place a heavy emphasis on research in their merit schemes.

Finding better ways to appropriately document and reward effective teaching is often a challenge for these departments.

- Rewards can take many forms: the return of indirect grant dollars to the faculty member, the granting of protected research time, the provision of increased and/or improved space, or the allocation of research assistants. One particularly effective reward involves publicly recognizing the research achievements of faculty via alumni newsletters, centrally located bulletin boards, announcements at faculty meetings, and so on.

12

Brokered Opportunity Structure

The university has lots of honors and other mechanisms for making people feel better about themselves and the workplace. Sometimes we just need to take advantage of those existing opportunities, whether for teaching, research, or service.

(David Bernlohr, Biochemistry,
Molecular Biology, and Biophysics)

LITERATURE SUMMARY

A sense of being stuck in one's career results in low productivity, disillusionment, and disengagement. To avoid this, research-productive departments proactively create and broker opportunities for their faculty's ongoing professional development (e.g., awards, fellowships, team teaching, opportunities for specific training). The result is that faculty of all ages and career stages remain active, energized, and ultimately, productive.

DEPARTMENT PRACTICES COVERED IN THIS CHAPTER
1) Why do all faculty need brokered opportunities?
2) What types of opportunities do these departments apply to prevent or overcome obstacles to faculty growth?
3) Who in the department is responsible for brokering growth opportunities?

What Does the Literature Say?

A lack of organizational opportunities or a feeling of getting stuck in one's professional development can result in faculty disillusionment and declines in their productivity (Bland & Bergquist, 1997; Boice, 1986, 1993; Corcoran & Clark, 1985). Stuckness has a particularly negative impact if it happens early in a career, and if the faculty member sees his or her colleagues continuing on an upward track. Midcareer faculty can also experience an unwelcome plateau in their work life if, for example, they do not keep up with the continual knowledge and technology explosion, or if they experience a sense of declining options for scholarly contribution as they proceed through life stages (American Association for Higher Education Task Force, 1984; Finkelstein, 1996).

The good news is that faculty can emerge from (or even completely bypass) stuckness, with no dramatic declines in their productivity. They do so by continually creating new professional opportunities for themselves. Importantly, facilitating the ongoing growth of faculty is not an individual effort. Vital faculty are, in most cases, fortunate enough to have colleagues or department heads who alert and encourage them to find ways to overcome barriers and continue to be productive, such as applying for a fellowship or sabbatical, trying on a different role, or team teaching a related course.

To prevent and overcome stuckness for faculty at all levels, institutions must be proactive in brokering professional development opportunities for their faculty (for example, by providing multiple ways for faculty to be continually updated in both their content area and relevant technology). Katerndahl (2000) found a significant increase in research productivity among faculty who attended methods conferences on research compared to matched controls who did not. The institution's essential role in the preventing or overcoming of stuckness is underscored by Rice and Finkelstein (1993):

> . . . vitality seems to be associated with the availability of opportunities subject not only to individual motivation but very much to organizational brokering and entrepreneurship . . . (p. 14). The challenge here is one of organizational development. Senior faculty, especially, need multifaceted organizational structures that will encourage them to broaden their horizons, approach their work in different and imaginative ways, and find new opportunities to grow and change. (p. 17)

Department Practices

One way in which the departments in our study attempt to limit faculty stuckness is by first hiring the most driven faculty they can find, particularly candidates who possess a strong motivation to conduct research (see Chapter 2). This recruitment practice can be viewed as a preemptive strike to preventing career stuckness down the line. The success of this approach was noted by several leaders in a variety of disciplines:

- "We don't have to encourage faculty. We actually have the opposite problem, since they are an entrepreneurial bunch of people to start with.

Sometimes it's like we're holding them back, saying, 'This is the rule: you can't do everything you want to do.'" (Public Affairs)

- "A large number of my faculty are aggressive, enterprising, and ambitious. They want to succeed, and strive to get a big name in the world of research. They have excellent research ideas and are always on the lookout to write extramural research grants." (Veterinary Pathobiology)

- "Most of our faculty are pretty motivated themselves. They want to and try to get into the National Academy of Sciences or be invited around the world to talk." (Pediatrics)

- "Because we have a research-oriented faculty, I have no trouble encouraging senior faculty to apply for awards. In fact, they are always applying for them. . . . There's nobody on the faculty who doesn't publish virtually every year." (Cultural Studies and Comparative Literature)

This is not to say that faculty in highly research-productive departments have no need for brokered opportunities. Rather, a major reason that these faculty do not get stuck is precisely because their home departments first understand the natural growing pains that faculty can encounter over the course of an academic career and then help their faculty to respond to emerging career obstacles in productive ways.

In short, all faculty need brokered opportunities to minimally overcome and optimally prevent obstacles to their continued growth and vitality. This chapter outlines some of the most frequently encountered sources of faculty stuckness (e.g., lack of financial resources, academic burnout), followed by examples of the many successful methods these department use to redirect and rejuvenate their faculty. Typically, these opportunities are brokered through the active involvement of department leaders and other productive senior colleagues.

Why Do All Faculty Need Brokered Opportunities?

For most faculty, an academic career is a lifelong career. Even the most successful faculty member can run into obstacles over the course of 40 to 50 years of academic work. These obstacles vary widely, from personal circumstances that distract a researcher's attention to the trauma of institutional restructuring. There are, however, some common obstacles that the department heads/chairs in our study identified and, accordingly, seek to prevent or overcome through brokered opportunities. These obstacles include:

- Lost spark.
- Lack of time.
- Change in work environment.
- Lack of financial resources.

Lost spark. Occasionally faculty members become stalled in their work or lose the passion they previously had for their topic. "People become worn out, burnt out, or disillusioned," acknowledged Eidman (Applied Economics). To combat this, he tries to anticipate when faculty are in danger of getting into this position and takes preventive action, such as alerting them to new professional opportunities in a different, but related topic area. Pharis (Art) also voiced a need to provide some type of mentoring to "faculty who maybe have been stuck in the ranks forever and can't quite get themselves unstuck, even though they're plenty bright and have talents."

Lack of time. A frequent obstacle for faculty is a lack of sufficient time to devote to research. Departments have a limited number of faculty to perform the necessary responsibilities in teaching, advising, research, service, outreach, administration, and, for clinical departments, patient care. This time crunch can fiercely take hold when faculty attain the status of associate professor, as one of our interviewees, Garavaso (Philosophy), vividly recalled:

> It was horrible when I became associate professor. For three or four years I didn't publish anything; I was too busy. You hear about too many responsibilities for people as soon as they get to be an associate. That was the worst time in my life.

Klinger (Psychology, Morris) similarly observed, "Midcareer faculty are the people that are most tapped for committee assignments, administrative assignments, and numerous other things. They get involved in many ways, and the time squeeze on them is terrible."

Change in work environment. Today's academic institutions are in continual flux, and faculty stuckness can be an undesirable side effect of environmental changes (e.g., merger with another unit, redefinition of mission and goals). Highly productive research faculty might find themselves expected to perform under an entirely new set of rules less conducive to research. One example is when medical school departments ask their physician investigators to increase their provision of patient care. Of course, organizational change can actually be invigorating if research-productive faculty members now find themselves in an environment that is even more supportive of research than was their previous setting. For less research-productive faculty, however, being forced into an environment with an intense research emphasis can present its own challenges. At the time of our study, the Department of Epidemiology had recently merged with the program in maternal and child health. As a result, tenured faculty from the latter program were experiencing a form of culture shock, and the department as a whole was struggling with how to best support them.

Lack of financial resources. Research funding is almost always difficult to attain, even for faculty members engaged in hot topic areas. Facing the most difficulty are those who find that their particular research area is no longer well supported by funding agencies. "There are fads to funding just like there are fads to clothing," said McMurry (Mechanical Engineering). "People may be working in an area deemed to be really important when they first got their Ph.D., but which 20 years later is less popular, even though it might still be important." In the Department of Family Social Science, Hogan encourages faculty members who are nontenured and have yet to acquire major external funding to read requests for proposals put out by funding agencies, "to see if their interests don't need a shift. Faculty really are trained into a niche, but if that niche isn't fundable, how far can you really go in creating new knowledge?"

What Types of Opportunities Do These Departments Apply to Prevent or Overcome Obstacles to Faculty Growth?

Within a department, faculty can be at different levels of productivity and experience different obstacles to growth. Each level and/or obstacle might require a different type of brokered opportunity to keep the faculty member moving forward in research. The department leaders we interviewed described their strategies for retaining, refocusing, and rejuvenating each of their faculty, in accordance with where the faculty member falls on a research continuum:

- For top researchers, they proactively offer incentives (e.g., endowed chairs, high-profile awards) for them to remain at the university as high achievers.

- For excellent researchers stretched thin by other responsibilities, they encourage focused research time through sabbaticals and semester leaves.

- For lost researchers—those stuck, disillusioned, or displaced in the university system—they provide mentoring, resources (e.g., travel or professional development funds), and other inspiration to help relight the research flame.

Brokering opportunities for top researchers. Every highly research-productive department has some research stars—faculty members who spend the majority of their time on research and are currently well funded and productive. For this subset of faculty, the department's goal is to keep them well funded and productive. A related goal is to simply keep these prominent researchers at the university, despite attractive recruitment offers from other institutions. Gladfelter (Chemistry) acknowledged this pressing need to retain their most high-achieving faculty:

> We went through a big hump of retirements and new hires in the 1980s and 1990s. Now, the careers of these new hires are on a great upward slope. Eventually we hope to reward excellent performance with endowed chairs. Our challenge for the immediate future is to retain this group of outstanding faculty until we raise the funding to support such awards.

In our study, the most frequently cited brokered opportunity for top researchers was to nominate them for endowed chairs or professorships. These include the university's prestigious and resource-rich McKnight awards (distinguished professorships for midcareer faculty, land-grant professorships for junior faculty). These awards serve to honor and financially reward some of the highest achieving faculty across the institution. And they have the added benefits of attracting the brightest scholars to the university and providing administrators with the leverage to act quickly when there is a need to retain a faculty member.

The purpose of any endowed chair is to provide the chair holder with the resources needed to continue his or her substantial contribution to teaching, research, and public service. The Law School uses its approximately 30 endowed chairs to reward its top scholars. The chair term is limited to seven years, which acts as a built-in incentive for these faculty members to continue to produce at a very significant level. Within the Institute of Public Affairs, the five endowed chairs carry a substantial annual income ($200,000 to $500,000) "which gives these faculty members all the resources they need to be productive," said Archibald. One such resource is time. At the Institute of Child Development, for example, the only faculty members allowed to buy out of their teaching responsibilities (to create more time for research activities) are chair holders and faculty with career development awards.

Departments also broker opportunities for their exceptional researchers by nominating them for high-profile awards in their discipline. "Awards are one very important way that a chair and other senior people in the department can reward and encourage productivity among people at all levels," observed Masten (Child Development). During our interview with Bates (Chemical Engineering and Materials Science), he outlined some of the recent awards his top researchers have received, but also stressed that his department and the university could do much more in the way of nominating their faculty:

> We don't pay attention to this the way some of the private schools do. . . . The people are here, no question about it. For some, it's just a question of actually sending in the nomination. We could put two or three more people in this department into the National Academy of Sciences. We just have to pay attention to it.

Brokering opportunities for excellent researchers stretched thin by other responsibilities. In addition to their star researchers, these departments are sustained by a core of productive faculty members who, though also excellent and high achieving in research, choose to spread their time more evenly across the academic tasks of research, teaching, advising, service, and administration. These responsibilities, while important to the overall vitality of the individual, the department, and the larger university, put these faculty members at risk of losing their edge in research. Notably, it is the nonresearch activities (office hours, committee meetings) that typically occur on a strict schedule, leaving research as the only task flexible enough to be put off to another time. This trend can, over time, have negative consequences on a faculty member's research program. If these faculty are to stay on track and maintain their excellence in research, it is essential that they have protected time to focus solely on the research enterprise.

For faculty who are heavily task-diversified, sabbaticals and semester-long leaves are particularly appropriate brokered opportunities. By participating in them, faculty members can steer their research in a new, promising direction, or otherwise stimulate their future productivity. Consider these recent success stories shared by the department heads/chairs in our study:

- A staff member in Chemistry took a six-week leave to develop instrumentation at Argonne National Labs that could be used for his projects and, potentially, those of other researchers at the university.

- In Chemical Engineering and Materials Science, a tenure-track faculty member took advantage of a prestigious opportunity to run a seminar at the Theoretical Institute of the University of California–Santa Barbara.

Leppert (Cultural Studies and Comparative Literature) spoke fondly of the first sabbatical he ever took. "It was so wonderful that I promised myself I would take one whenever I was eligible." Several other department heads/chairs spoke avidly in support of sabbaticals and leaves. "We do a lot to encourage them and usually have about two or three faculty participating in them per year. It's part of our culture that you have to go out and rebuild your capital," said Eidman (Applied Economics). McMurry (Mechanical Engineering) said he "takes a very strong stand" in promoting semester leaves and sabbaticals. "I feel that faculty really need that time off, so I do whatever I can to make it possible. . . . The rest of us have to pick up the slack in teaching, but I think we are doing well."

> **Nationally, How Many Research Faculty Are on Sabbatical at Any Given Time?**
>
> During the fall of 1998 only 2.5% of the research institution faculty responding to the 1998 NSOPF indicated that they were on sabbatical.

The prior comment by McMurry touches on the reality that these departments do face difficulties in facilitating sabbaticals and leaves, as do the faculty seeking to take advantage of them. Departments have the challenge of spreading teaching, student advising, and committee work over a thinned-out faculty and in many cases covering the costs of hiring replacement instructors to meet their curricular demands. As Klinger (Psychology, Morris) said, "When you're as small as we are, when one person goes on leave, the whole area of the discipline goes on leave." Other department leaders described having to overcome faculty members' fears that their absence will hurt the department. As Campbell (Psychology) put it, "Everybody says, 'If I'm away from the place for a year, what will happen to this operation?' As a result, far fewer are taking advantage of sabbatical opportunities than should be." Some faculty also shy away from sabbaticals given the financial deterrent of having to give up half their salary or otherwise find external funding to supplement their income.

These challenges, though daunting, do not undermine the importance of brokering research-release time for faculty. On the contrary, they underscore the vital role that departments play in not only encouraging these options, but also helping their faculty overcome barriers to securing them. The end return on these investments is nearly always a more rejuvenated, more productive faculty member.

In some circumstances, simply bringing up the topic is enough incentive. Bernlohr (Biochemistry, Molecular Biology, and Biophysics) explained, "I probably haven't been very proactive at encouraging sabbaticals—it's not intentional. I asked this year if anyone was interested in sabbaticals, and we do have one individual who is on a single-semester leave because of that."

Many department heads agreed that the university's semester-leave policy, which guarantees faculty their entire salary during the leave, provides a fiscally attractive option for many faculty. "I think the single-semester leave program is of inestimable importance. It's not typical in universities to have a single-semester leave at full pay," said Leppert (Cultural Studies and Comparative Literature). Departments must still deal with the void created by the faculty member's short-term absence, but many find creative ways of filling it. Here are some examples:

- The Institute of Public Affairs uses endowed funds to help hire replacement instructors.

- Ascerno (Entomology) has an expectation that faculty will "make arrangements to cover the important parts of their position, for example, the teaching," so that the department can secure protected research time "without going through a lot of red tape."

- In many departments, faculty willingly do whatever they can to cover the responsibilities of faculty on leave, knowing that their turn is coming up and that they will want the same coverage.

- The Department of Medicine earmarks some funds in its budget specifically for faculty leaves and sabbaticals. It also has a policy of using the National Institutes of Health salary caps in determining leave and sabbatical salaries, which makes it more feasible for the department to cover a physician's salary.

- The university also awards sabbatical supplements of up to an additional $30,000 or 30% of a faculty member's salary.

Brokering opportunities for lost faculty—those stuck, disillusioned, or displaced in the university system. Finally, there is a small group of faculty with the potential to be good researchers who have perhaps lost focus, are facing a need to shift to a new research area, or, due to a merger or change in their department's goals, are suddenly expected to be more highly research productive at midcareer.

Fortunately, for every potential obstacle, there is typically one or more ways of overcoming it. Many departments in our study encourage their faculty to take sabbaticals; some provide professional development funds for faculty to receive advanced training in research; others facilitate networking with prominent researchers by providing travel support or by inviting outside speakers to the department. Here are some additional examples from our qualitative data set:

- *Departments can successfully broker connections, for example, by pairing stuck faculty with other active investigators.* Luepker (Epidemiology) shared a story about a faculty member in nutrition who for 14 years taught class after class, but since connecting with other research-productive faculty has turned into an "outstanding" externally funded researcher, publishing numerous peer-reviewed articles each year.

- *By focusing attention and resources on promising researchers, departments can find diamonds in the rough.* Pharis (Art) recalled suggesting to a faculty member that he cut back on his teaching and increase his grant writing and studio work. "He wasn't familiar with the [grants] system. We were able to help him with the writing of some of these grants and let him know when some things came up that seemed appropriate for him. ... Within the last two years, he's gotten three or four grants, and his work is really going well."

- *Some faculty benefit from a formal change in their appointments.* The head of Applied Economics described how one of his faculty with an extension appointment dramatically improved his overall productivity—including his research contributions—since engaging himself part-time in undergraduate teaching.

- *Travel for the purpose of professional networking can reinvigorate stuck faculty.* As Gengenbach (Agronomy and Plant Genetics) said, "Even going to a two- or three-day meeting or workshop always gets me revved up to come back and try new ideas and ways of doing things. Not that I always do it, but at least it gets the juices flowing again."

- *Departments can offer workshops to update and/or supplement their faculty's skill sets.* Bearinger described how in the School of Nursing "we've taught people about NIH, about specific types of grants, how to do posters, how to be your own writing consultant, how to submit grants using EGMS [Electronic Grants Management System]. I've taught how to present your research from the platform, doing a ten-minute presentation. ... I think those research seminars were a huge shift in skill building."

To supplement these examples, we encourage readers to explore the many other chapters in this book that touch on the theme of encouraging faculty growth at all career stages. These strategies include facilitating informal or formal mentoring (Chapter 5), arranging for limited-time reductions in faculty teaching and service commitments (Chapter 8), routinely applying reward systems to motivate faculty work (Chapter 11), and providing regular opportunities for faculty involvement in governance (Chapter 14).

Who in the Department Is Responsible for Brokering Growth Opportunities?

Opportunities for faculty growth and recognition may be abundant but are unlikely to produce fruit without active brokering by other members of the organization. Indeed, many stuck faculty have tremendous difficulty becoming unstuck without a nudge from others—the department chair, other productive local peers, or members of their professional network.

This is no secret to the department heads/chairs in our study. As Bernlohr (Biochemistry, Molecular Biology, and Biophysics) observed,

> Our department has more McKnight professors than many departments do, yet we all have equal opportunity to apply, put the dossier together, write nomination letters. . . . I'm not convinced, quite frankly, that we have truly better faculty than everyone else does. We may simply be more avid in putting those things together.

Heads/chairs play a particularly important role in developing and maintaining a brokered opportunity structure in their departments. They might perform specific tasks, such as creating an award nominations packet, juggling faculty assignments to cover faculty duties during leaves and sabbaticals, or lining up money to support faculty travel or training.

In Pediatrics, Moller will forward award notices to the department's awards committee and encourage division heads to nominate a faculty member identified as a good fit for a particular award. "Other times I'll send out something broadly to the faculty, saying nominations are open and we're willing to accept individuals. Usually a division head puts together the packet for the awards," he said. Bates (Chemical Engineering and Materials Science) also enlists the assistance of his most experienced and renowned faculty:

> Gus Aris has been very helpful with some of these nominations—he's made academy nominations and award nominations, because he's emeritus. I actually have him right in the main office so that he's close to people who can help him. He's a remarkable guy. He's been extremely generous with his influence and his time.

These tasks require a fair amount of effort, but the department leaders we interviewed were more than willing to perform them, given the desirable end product—a well-funded, highly recognized, more productive faculty member. Their belief in the value of brokered opportunities is reflected in comments such as the following:

- "The things we do, such as the McKnight program, are laudable. It's a remarkably competitive environment for grant dollars and students. Any activities that we can initiate to help our faculty succeed are good." (Chemistry)

- "Since the university implemented the McKnight awards, all five of our qualified junior faculty have received it. . . . The availability of these awards and our success at receiving them has played a major role in fostering the career development of our junior faculty and, concomitantly, the reputation of our department." (Child Development)

In conclusion, brokered opportunities, particularly those offered to the highest achieving faculty, benefit more than the individual. Many of the interviewed department heads/chairs spoke with pride about the type and number of awards their faculty have received and how this has reflected well upon their department as a whole. As Pharis (Art) summarized, "It brings an attention to this department which I think it hasn't had, and which it deserves and needs. . . . It elevates the whole range of activities that we do here and sheds some light on us in a different way."

Chapter 12 Review: Brokered Opportunity Structure _____

- All faculty, no matter how vital and productive, need continual opportunities to develop and grow in their profession. Without their institution's active engagement in brokering such opportunities, faculty can fall victim to common obstacles to productivity (e.g., lack of sufficient time, inadequate resources, outdated skill sets, a sense of disillusionment with the research enterprise).

- Highly research-productive departments tailor their use of brokered opportunities to coincide with their faculty members' unique productivity levels and/or career stages. Whereas their research stars might benefit most from endowed chairs and high profile awards, other researchers might have a more pressing need for things such as focused research time (sabbaticals, semester leaves), stronger working relationships with other successful colleagues, or a change in appointment type.

- Ensuring the presence of opportunities for faculty growth and development is only the first step. Department heads/chairs (and oftentimes other senior faculty) must also encourage their colleagues to seize existing opportunities, help clear a path for them to do so, and suggest/create new opportunities as needed to keep a faculty member thriving.

13

Faculty Size and Diversity: The Right Mix of Expertise and Experience

I firmly believe that we need to be larger to stay competitive because there are good national data that research is concentrating in more research-intensive schools. The question is, are we going to be one or not? The only way to do that is to grow.

(*Jonathan Ravdin, Medicine*)

LITERATURE SUMMARY
Research groups tend to be more productive when they are larger, when they have some continuity in their membership, and when their membership is diverse. Here, diversity is defined as faculty members having different technical backgrounds, coming from related yet varied disciplines, offering different approaches to problem solving, and being at different stages in their careers.

DEPARTMENT PRACTICES COVERED IN THIS CHAPTER
1) How does faculty size impact the research productivity of a department?
2) How does faculty diversity (in expertise and experience) influence research productivity? How close do these departments come to having their desired faculty mix?
3) What strategies can be used to attend to faculty size and diversity? What challenges do departments face in trying to do this?

What Does the Literature Say? _____

Several studies of research productivity (in groups, departments, and institutions) have found that performance increases as the group size increases (Blackburn, Behymer, & Hall, 1978; Bland & Ruffin, 1992; Johnston, 1994; Jordan, Meador, & Walters, 1988; Manis, 1951; Pineau & Levy-Leboyer,

1983; Smith, Baker, Campbell, & Cunningham, 1985; Wispe, 1969). In general, there is little research productivity in groups of less than three to five members. Thereafter, a linear relationship emerges between the size of a group and its outcomes, such as resources accumulated, products produced, and recognition received.

Dundar and Lewis (1998), in their analysis of National Research Council data on research universities, found that ". . . program and departmental size in numbers of faculty is, indeed, a strong predictor of average publication" (p. 622). They further found that having a large percentage of the faculty publishing, rather than having just a few prolific members, significantly increased a department's research productivity.

The finding that size is a virtue where research productivity is concerned is congruent with what we know about other research-facilitating features of the workplace. For example, larger groups might be expected to have greater resources. Also, members might have more opportunities to engage in lively debate with colleagues who think differently from themselves. According to Pelz and Andrews (1966), such "intellectual jostling" can be beneficial. When they looked at the impact of research group members having diversity in training, technical backgrounds, and ways of thinking, they found that greater diversity is positively associated with research productivity. The caveat to this is that diversity must be balanced by common group goals and values. Other researchers similarly found that increased diversity increases group productivity (Blau, 1976; Pelz, 1967; Smith, 1971; Steiner, 1965).

Continuity within a group can also positively impact its productivity. Pelz and Andrews (1966) found a positive correlation between the length of time a research group stayed together and its members' productivity. They did note, however, that when colleagues have worked together for over seven years, it is especially important to work at maintaining a climate of "creative, supportive tension." In the absence of such efforts, older groups can begin to lose their atmosphere of intellectual competition, group cohesion, and enthusiasm.

Department Practices

Throughout this book, we have been addressing, albeit subtly at times, the importance of a department's faculty structure (size, diversity) on its productivity. Recall that in Chapter 2 we learned that research productivity hinges on having the right people—people with a drive to conduct research, who adhere to the highest standards of excellence, and who work competitively, yet cooperatively with their local colleagues in an intellectually stimulating way. From recruitment to retirement, it is the faculty who make the research happen.

According to the literature, of particular importance to research productivity is having a faculty of adequate size, continuity, and diversity with respect to members' disciplinary backgrounds and approaches to problem solving. Below, we describe commonalities and differences in how the interviewed department heads/chairs view faculty size and diversity and how they struggle to ensure the right mix of faculty.

How Does Faculty Size Impact the Research Productivity of a Department?

The highly research-productive departments in our study have a fairly large complement of full-time faculty (mean = 28 faculty, mode = 18, median = 22, range = 11 to 101; see Appendix E). What these numbers do not tell us is how much emphasis the leaders of research-productive departments truly place on faculty size. Is size as important to the research productivity of these departments as the prior literature would indicate? Why or why or not?

Some insight can be gained by reflecting on the content of previous chapters. First, recall from Chapter 12 that faculty in smaller departments sometimes find it difficult to take sabbaticals because their absence would leave large, difficult-to-fill holes in the curriculum. Second, a larger faculty, particularly one with an involved core of midlevel and senior members, offers a stronger mentoring capacity for assisting more junior members (Chapter 5). Third, being surrounded by a greater number of research-productive colleagues can provide faculty with more opportunities for communication with peers (Chapter 7), and possibly in-house collaborations (Chapter 6). In these ways, faculty size appears to play a mediating role in a department's overall productivity; it gives some of the other research-facilitating characteristics a greater chance of succeeding.

Feldman (Health Services Research and Policy) identified another advantage to departments' having a critical mass of faculty researchers: With more faculty involved in more areas of research, his department as a whole can hold a diverse portfolio of research projects. This strategy has helped shield them from severe funding shortfalls. The department continues to thrive, even when a research area loses popularity with funding agencies or otherwise hits a dead end. "You can't do what we're doing with five people," Feldman said. "We've been fortunate since the division's beginning over 20 years ago to have the necessary critical mass. I was here just after it got created in 1978, and even then we started off with about a half-dozen faculty members."

In a good-sized department, "you can have more expertise and have people involved in narrower areas of research," said Moller (Pediatrics). In contrast, smaller departments may find themselves better served by hiring specialized generalists—people with expertise in a specific knowledge area, but who
can also move easily between areas so as to meet the department's overall
needs. Ben-Ner (Industrial Relations) offered up this illustrative example:
"Unlike other departments, in ours, the interdisciplinary approach has to
reside in every person. Every person has to be a Jack-of-all-trades and, by
necessity, kind of do everything very well."

"Size matters, pure and simple," according to Ravdin (Medicine). Given
this conviction, he has pursued a strategy of aggressive growth during his leadership. One of his aims is to boost the department's overall ranking in NIH
grant dollars awarded: "We've got great quality, and the reason we're not in
the top 20 is capacity. We've got to come to grips with the fact that to remain
in a competitive environment, we're going to have to be larger."

Ravdin did acknowledge (as did other department heads/chairs in our
study) that larger faculty groups need careful leadership if they are to succeed.
Leaders keep the department's overall vision in front of the faculty and help to
ensure that all parts are supporting the whole (see Chapter 14). Indeed, recall
from Chapter 3 that having a shared set of goals that coordinate faculty work
is another important characteristic of the research-productive organization.

Ascerno (Entomology) voiced an additional caution that using faculty
growth as a criterion of success should not override the need to provide current faculty with the resources they need to succeed:

> I think that, at some point, we should set sort of an ideal
> size [for departments]. . . . Then, instead of converting every
> open [new or retired] position to a new position, we take
> that money and run that back to support the faculty. To me,
> that makes a lot of sense, and then empowers the faculty.
> They see that they are important as individuals, that they're
> getting the support they need, and I think it helps to up
> their productivity.

This theme of providing faculty with the resources they need for research
productivity is addressed more fully in Chapter 8.

Finally, although the emphasis of this project was on defining strategies
for facilitating research, a few department leaders also commented on how
faculty size affects other areas of faculty work. For example, Archibald (Public
Affairs) made mention of their small student-to-faculty ratio: "This makes

the students happier, because they have more contact with faculty, which then makes our faculty more productive." Similarly, Moller (Pediatrics) remarked that having a large faculty base is an advantage, because "you can spread responsibilities around more, and it's better for education."

How Does Faculty Diversity (in Expertise and Experience) Influence Research Productivity? How Close Do These Departments Come to Having Their Desired Faculty Mix?

Intimately tied to group size is group composition. According to the literature, the most productive research groups are diverse with respect to their members' areas of expertise, technical backgrounds, research approaches, and experience. By drawing on their members' breadth of experience and diverse ways of thinking, these groups can work synergistically to achieve their shared research goals.

Do the academic leaders in our study agree with this? In what ways is faculty diversity of this type a driving force behind their research productivity? In this section, we present our study's qualitative findings on two related areas of diversity—faculty expertise and experience.

Diversity in expertise: Mix of skills, approaches, and training. Sterner (Ecology, Evolution, and Behavior) got right to the heart of the matter when he said, "Frankly I don't want another faculty member in the department who does what I do. It doesn't do you any good. I want people who are different."

Another indication that these highly research-productive departments value diversity is the emphasis they place on interdisciplinary research. (This topic is discussed in depth in Chapter 6.) Their faculty recognize the potential for generating new knowledge when the research approaches of different disciplines are merged. Accordingly, many of their faculty members actively forge collaborations with colleagues, be they in other departments, in other universities, or in industry. Collaborations within a single department are also possible, provided the right mix of faculty is present.

Some of the most outspoken proponents of a diverse faculty base were the department heads/chairs in clinical and professional schools. Consider these reflections of Simone (Oral Science) in the School of Dentistry:

> At one time I thought that clinical departments should do clinical work and basic science departments should do research. But after thinking about it more and more, I think there's probably more importance to having a good mix in each department, because the ultimate goal is to have the basic sciences taken to the clinic. In medicine, we hope to

bring new discoveries and approaches from basic research to the bedside, and if the two remain separate for too long, this just doesn't get facilitated.

Others shared a similar view. Vayda (Diagnostic/Surgical Science) noted that their more clinically oriented dental faculty have successfully participated in research by virtue of collaborating with their tenure-track colleagues. Similar advantages are realized in Veterinary Medicine, explained Ames (Clinical and Population Sciences):

> A lot of times, the clinician is the one who is thinking through the logistics of the animal side of the experiment, and the basic scientist is thinking through the "what's the best methodology to test this hypothesis" sort of thing. . . . These kinds of relationships are the key for people with heavy clinical commitments to getting research done.

Diversity in experience: Mix of junior, midlevel, and senior faculty. From our interviews we discovered that these highly research-productive departments are concerned about another area of faculty diversity: having the right balance of senior, midlevel, and junior faculty members. Each has a unique and important contribution to make within the department. For example, Warthesen (Food Science and Nutrition) commented that the junior faculty bring in new ideas and write the most grants and peer-reviewed articles, "maybe out of fear of not attaining tenure," he acknowledged, "but that's okay. It makes the department productive." In turn, the senior faculty know the ropes, which is also critical. They bring in the big grants, cover faculty during leaves, and generally keep the department running smoothly.

> "Research on the power of the (numerical) minority in groups has also uncovered some intriguing findings regarding the positive effects a newcomer can have on a group. For groups seeking to be more innovative and effective, newcomers may be an overlooked source of innovation." (Cini, 2001)

The importance of senior faculty is also reflected in the literature, which finds that continuity in group membership, institutional memory, and a strong mentoring capacity are all characteristics of research-productive groups. Still, it would be unwise for a department to fall short in continually bringing in junior faculty or new, but seasoned faculty. New members introduce different perspectives to the faculty mix and, in doing so, help foster an environment of positive intellectual competition—which, according to prior studies, is another hallmark of research-productive groups.

Despite the obvious advantages to having an experience-diversified faculty, very few of the departments in our study actually had what their leaders would consider an optimal mix of assistant, associate, and full professors. Events frequently interfere with the realization of this goal. A few such circumstances voiced by our study participants are the availability of funding for new faculty lines, the extent of faculty turnover due to moves or retirements, or a department's track record in successfully closing the deal during periods of faculty recruitment.

Most commonly, the departments in our study were top heavy, with a large cadre of full professors but very few junior faculty. Because of the major growth in higher education in the 1970s, there are many departments where a large proportion of the faculty members are full professors and in their 50s or 60s. A few departments in our cohort were skewed in the opposite direction, with a heavier concentration of junior, nontenured faculty. Sometimes, the vagaries of funding resulted in unusual mixes, such as in Biochemistry, Molecular Biology, and Biophysics, which has a bimodal mix of faculty. Bernlohr explained:

> Currently we have a cadre of seven assistant professors, we only have a few associate professors, and everyone else is a full professor. That somewhat mirrors the university's hiring program, where we went through a lull and now, because of the molecular biology initiative, we are back hiring again.

What Strategies Can Be Used to Attend to Faculty Size and Diversity?

Once again, faculty recruitment and selection comes to the forefront. Currently, the primary concern of many departments is the large proportion of faculty who are likely to retire in the next 10 years. When will they retire? How will multiple retirements be handled smoothly? The need for combined retirement and recruitment planning was voiced again and again by interviewees:

- "With the exception of two people, we are 100% tenured. That means a different kind of management. I call them, 'mature assets.'. . . So, we need to look down the road at age planning." (Public Affairs)

- "When recruiting, we need to look at age. Otherwise we will end up in the same situation that we are in now, where we have 80% of the faculty retiring at the same time. We need to balance age by hiring some senior-level faculty and some junior faculty. Without careful management, it's going to be chaos if we don't have the faculty to provide the support, mentoring structure, ability to do service, and so on." (Art)

- "We had a review, an external review, about maybe six years ago. And they said, we have talked to this faculty, and there are a bunch of you that are retiring. You have got to think about this. As a top-heavy department you will be out of business very shortly without thinking this one through." (Family Social Science)

Among our study participants, it was less common for departments to have a majority of junior faculty. Those that did, however, also adopted strategies during their recruitment phase so as to maintain the department's culture and climate. Leppert (Cultural Studies and Comparative Literature) shared this scenario:

> We are a faculty of 14 with a lot of new hires, because six years ago we were a faculty of five. Some of the people we have brought in have been senior or early/midcareer, so they are not brand-new Ph.D.s. But we have hired about three new Ph.D.s among them. This has presented a real challenge in terms of acculturating, but we have been very careful in choosing people who we think will be a good fit.

Paying careful attention to hiring and retention is the primary means by which departments can build the right size and mix of faculty. As a concept, this sounds simple. In practice, this is no easy task. Recall from Chapter 2 on recruitment that these departments, while seeking diversity in experience and background in new faculty hires, also try to attract faculty who have a passion for research, who demonstrate a high degree of collegiality, who match the department's goals and culture, who can meet their curricular needs, and so on. Balancing all these considerations is a challenge, even without the added complexities of institutional and national funding trends and the inordinately large number of anticipated faculty retirements over the next ten years. Effective leadership and governance will be needed to navigate these waters. The importance of these two critical components of the research-productive environment is the topic of our next chapter.

Chapter 13 Review:
Faculty Size and Diversity _____

- Having a large, stable complement of faculty is associated with high research productivity. Greater size increases the likelihood that many of the other characteristics associated with research productivity are present, such as colleagues with whom to collaborate, resources, mentoring, networks, and so on.

- Diversity among faculty with regard to career stage, related disciplines, and research methods positively influences research productivity. A good balance between senior and junior faculty gives considerable vitality to a department.

- Maintaining the right mix of faculty can be difficult, given the vagaries of higher education funding. Careful recruitment planning in terms of future research foci and faculty career stages is needed to help achieve the right mix.

- As departments achieve greater size and diversity, the importance of effective leadership and governance also increases. The challenge leaders face is uniting a diverse faculty around common goals, a shared culture, and a fair rewards system aligned with these shared goals.

14

Leadership and Governance

We are all equals on the faculty. As department head, I may
have the power to make some decisions, but if I make the
wrong decision frequently enough, I won't be in this job.

(Russell Luepker, Epidemiology)

LITERATURE SUMMARY
The leaders of research-productive groups are consistently seen as
excellent, productive scientists. They internalize the group's mission
and keep the research emphasis clear to the group. They also use a participative governance style, with formal mechanisms and expectations
for all members to contribute to decision-making. High-quality information is readily available. Members have a sense of ownership in the
organization. They believe that their ideas are valued and that they
have an important role to play in the future of the organization.

DEPARTMENT PRACTICES COVERED IN THIS CHAPTER
1) What key roles do department leaders play in creating an environment conducive to research productivity?
2) How is participative decision-making facilitated in these highly
   research-productive departments?
3) How do department leaders balance a need to involve faculty in
   governance with using faculty time wisely?
4) Does continuity in leadership matter?

What Does the Literature Say? _____

Leadership is perhaps the most influential environmental variable affecting
research productivity. To quote Blackburn (1979), ". . . nearly every positively
correlated [with research productivity] factor resides in administrative hands"
(p. 26). It is the leader who heavily influences the presence or absence of all
other institutional characteristics—from setting clear goals and maintaining a
research emphasis within the group, to developing fair, effective reward systems and allocating funds for needed technical resources.

In a study by Dill (1985, 1986b) of research groups in Europe, the leader was found to account for much of the variance among groups' productivity. Dill (1985) suggests that it is the leader's prior research experience—an understanding of the culture, necessary skills, national network, and so on—that allows him or her to best facilitate research productivity. Other studies of productive units similarly concluded that the leader must be perceived as a highly skilled scientist (Andrews, 1979; Dill, 1982; Drew, 1985; Sindermann, 1985). For example, Andrews (1979) found that group climate (a correlate of research productivity) was most positive when the leader was perceived as highly knowledgeable in the field, well-qualified technically, hard-working, and supportive of others' work.

Another predominant finding from the literature is a high, positive correlation between research productivity and a specific style of leadership, namely, assertive participative governance. In their synthesis of studies of successful research groups, Bland and Ruffin (1992) report that leaders who use a participative approach to decision-making exhibit a distinct set of characteristics: 1) They hold frequent meetings with clear objectives; 2) they facilitate good leader-member relationships by way of open communication; 3) they allow the expression of all points of view; 4) they share information openly and completely; and 5) they vest ownership of projects with all group members (Birnbaum, 1983; Dill, 1986a; Epton, Payne, & Pearson, 1983; Hoyt & Spangler, 1978; Locke, Fitzpatrick, & White, 1983; Pelz & Andrews, 1966; Pineau & Levy-Leboyer, 1983).

Further evidence of the positive impact of participative leadership is the finding that highly productive units tend to have flat and decentralized organizational structures, in which individual members can act with high levels of autonomy (Bean, 1982; Birnbaum, 1983; Epton, Payne, & Pearson, 1983; Okrasa, 1987; Rice & Austin, 1988). Okrasa (1987), for example, found that research units with a decentralized structure had both greater overall research productivity and more consistent research productivity across members. Decentralization does not mean anarchy, however; recall that research-productive groups also have a shared culture and clear, commonly understood goals that coordinate members' work.

This overarching profile of the effective research leader—one who facilitates group productivity through the pairing of some structure with highly participative governance—is echoed in the literature on effective department heads and higher education leaders (Bensimon, Neumann, & Birnbaum, 1989; Bland, Starnaman, et al., 1999; Lawrence & Blackburn, 1985; Rice & Austin, 1988). Notably, Rice and Austin (1988), in their study of more than

100 high-morale colleges (identified via a faculty survey and site visits) found that "*every* one of the top-ten colleges with high morale and satisfaction had leadership that was aggressively participatory in both individual style and organizational structure" (p. 54). Bensimon et al. (1989), in their review of educational leadership, found leader effectiveness to be related to two overriding concepts: initiating structures—which includes establishing clear coordinating goals, emphasizing the priority goals, and aligning rewards with goals—and using considerate behaviors, defined in most studies as including the same behaviors characteristic of an assertive participative style of governance (Hemphill, 1955; Hoyt & Spangler, 1978; Knight & Holen, 1985; McCarthy, 1972; Skipper, 1976).

Department Practices

In our study, the leaders of highly research-productive departments were asked, "What do you think are the most important things you do as a leader of this department, and what other department leaders do, to support the research productivity of the faculty?" A related set of questions queried them about their department's structure of governance, methods of decision-making, and the degree to which faculty have a voice in important decisions. Their responses, summarized below, were strikingly congruent with findings from the literature: that is, highly research-productive departments have leaders who proactively facilitate research through 1) a comprehensive set of leadership roles and responsibilities, and 2) a flat or decentralized organizational structure supported by shared goals and assertive participative governance behaviors.

What Key Roles Do Department Leaders Play in Creating an Environment Conducive to Research Productivity?

Although the interviewed heads/chairs spoke humbly about their roles, it is clear that their leadership is pivotal to the research excellence of their departments. They described, for instance, their practices of helping faculty maintain their professional networks by financially supporting travel, of nominating faculty for research honors and awards, of arranging faculty office/laboratory space so as to facilitate local collaborations, and of recruiting and hiring new faculty who are driven to conduct research and who bring a desirable depth and breadth of research expertise to the department.

These examples illustrate a dominant theme that emerged from our qualitative study and which is echoed in the prior literature: The leader of a research unit has a tremendous capacity to influence the presence—and preservation—of all the other environmental characteristics that facilitate its members' productivity.

In this chapter, we begin by highlighting for readers four of the more overarching leadership roles that, according to our study's participants, are pivotal ways in which they support their faculty's research endeavors:

- Keeper of the vision

- Manager (of money, space, people)

- Department advocate

- Peer model (of researcher, teacher)

Keeper of the vision. We noted in Chapter 3 that highly research-productive departments have well-defined, shared goals focused on research. Consistent reinforcement of those goals is thus one key role—perhaps *the* key role—that department leaders are called on to play. "The department head is the keeper of vision," said Ek (Forest Resources) "I think the department head's role with respect to vision is to remind folks why we are into something, to create a place where they can come to understand some of the context of their work."

The importance of this role cannot be overstated, and, given its importance, the task of keeping a research-centered vision alive requires a significant commitment. Consider these comments from Ravdin (Medicine):

> I think the critical thing is that you set an aspiration, a goal. You articulate those goals and that vision to the faculty. You find resources to allow people to succeed, you sustain the passion, the vision, and the involvement over a long period of time.... I still am amazed at how much vision you have to provide as the chair. It just doesn't happen another way. You need to express it, and you need to be personally involved.

Manager (of money, space, people). In addition to the role of visionary, department heads/chairs must act in the very pragmatic role of manager. Budget, salary, space, and personnel are just a few of the many areas that demand a manager's day-to-day attention. Much has been written about strategies for attending to the diverse management responsibilities of a department chair (Creswell, Wheeler, Seagren, Egly, & Beyer, 1990; Gmelch & Miskin, 1993; Hecht, Higgerson, Gmelch, & Tucker, 1999; Knight &

Trowler, 2001; Leaming, 1998; Lucas, 1989; Lucas & Associates, 2000; Seagren, Creswell, & Wheeler, 2000; Tucker, 1984; Walvoord et al., 2000). In our study, Bates (Chemical Engineering and Materials Science) summarized well the significance of the managerial tasks that he takes on:

> I see myself as paying attention to a lot of details, none of which individually is so important that it would hurt the department if something didn't get done, but which collectively can lead to an erosion in how the department functions. . . . I spend a lot of attention on space and on budget. The way IT [the Institute of Technology] works, we have the whole budget in the department, and it's very easy for the department to go belly-up. That has to be paid attention to. . . . All of these details are clearly as important as the visionary details which everyone would normally think of a leader talking about. . . . It takes time to correct space inequities, budget details, so that's where a lot of my time goes, worrying about those details. . . . I hope most of the faculty don't even know this. It's not something that they should have to worry about.

Increasingly, many academic leaders are being called upon to not only manage their existing resources, but also to help secure new funding streams. The head of Pediatrics was just returning from a fundraising event when we interviewed him. The Department of Chemical Engineering took the step of hiring a professional development officer. This position, split with the Institute of Technology, was created to help Bates and other department heads in the Institute raise money for endowments, chairs, professorships, and fellowships for graduate students.

Of course, in addition to managing finances and other resources, a department chair also "needs to be able to manage people—their egos, and the incredible bickering that can go on, " said Garavaso (Philosophy). As Pharis (Art) aptly stated, "This job is not necessarily about resources, it's about relationships." Leaders who successfully tend to their faculty and staff's interpersonal issues can reduce conflict and, in turn, have a positive influence on many other research-facilitating features of their environment (e.g., group culture and climate, communication, collaboration).

Department advocate. The influence of department leaders extends beyond their immediate home turf. Another responsibility of effective heads/chairs is to champion their department's successes at the level of the larger institution (college, university), and in turn to lobby for resources that will keep their departments thriving. Leppert (Cultural Studies and Comparative Literature) explained the importance of making sure that his department is widely known by upper-level university administrators as a highly research-productive unit:

> If you just think of CLA [the College of Liberal Arts] with 30 departments and something like 15 research centers, I think it's really important for a chair constantly to be reminding his or her administration of the department's success. I have found that maintaining contact with my superiors all the way up to the president is one of the ways to build a department. . . . To put it differently, if you are very successful, but the only people who know it are on the outside, the people in your discipline, you are really short-changing yourself in terms of how universities function. You have got to function with resources, and if you are not telling the people who have resources that you are worth it, you are not doing your job.

Peer model (of researcher, teacher). Finally, in any discussion of leadership roles, it is vital to remember that department heads/chairs are faculty members, too, with the same or similar expectations for productivity in research, teaching, and so on, as their faculty colleagues. The importance of leaders being able to model productive scholarly behaviors was expressed by numerous participants in our study:

- "I teach half time and I keep a research load. . . . I just don't think administrators at any level can exempt themselves from the work of the faculty." (General College)

- "The department head needs to be a very good scholar and a very good teacher. Faculty can't respect an administrator who doesn't do these jobs as well as they do, or better." (Philosophy)

- "Although I spend a lot of time administrating, I am another faculty member

The 1998 NSOPF looked at research productivity for the 242 respondents who identified themselves as a department chair or head. Of these, 221 participated in research activities. On average:

- they spent 12.5% of their 58-hour week on research activities

In a two-year period they averaged:

- 3.7 solo creative works or juried media
- 4.5 joint creative works or juried media

and try to set an example. Actually, I'm 80% NIH funded, so I carry my research weight like anyone else around here." (Epidemiology)

- "I teach a course a semester, and I normally have 90 to 100 students in that class, which is a big load. As the provost said to me recently, you teach nearly as much as your full-time faculty teaches. First, I love to teach. Second, it sends a signal that I am doing the same kinds of things they are doing." (Law)

Prior studies have found that the leaders of highly research-productive groups are themselves productive researchers. Accordingly, in the brief written survey included in our study we asked these faculty leaders, "In your discipline, how highly regarded are you for your research?" On a five-point scale, nearly all respondents rated themselves as "extremely highly" (scale score = 5) or "highly" regarded (scale score = 4) in their discipline for their research. In their qualitative responses as well, study participants expressed a belief that academic leaders need to be good scholars—to have experience in conducting research, to be successful in grant writing and publication, and to have strong links to the major people, funding agencies, and industries in their discipline.

Being (or having been) actively engaged in research, these department leaders can identify with the struggles faculty members face in building and sustaining a strong research program. They approach their work with the ethic and socialization of a researcher. And they understand the obstacles that researchers can encounter. As Sullivan (Law) observed,

> I sometimes struggle in the loneliness of research and writing and editing. I understand when somebody is having some difficulties. I am empathetic in that regard. Because I am close to it, I can help them through it, whatever hurdle they are facing.

Specific examples of such hands-on support are provided in other chapters, for example, Chapters 5, 6, and 12.

How Is Participative Decision-Making Facilitated in These Highly Research-Productive Departments?

Thus far, we have focused our discussion on the many diverse roles that department heads/chairs are asked to perform. But departmental governance is by no means a one-person undertaking. As noted in the introduction to this chapter, a key feature of effective leadership in research-productive organizations is the use of an assertive participative approach, whereby leaders allow the expression of all points of view and vest ownership of projects with all group members.

Congruent with this finding, the department leaders in our study spoke eloquently of the importance of securing their faculty's input and involvement in decisions. They also described their practice of regularly soliciting and applying such input. Consider these representative examples from our qualitative data set:

- "I have tried to get rid of as much unilateral department chair decision-making as possible. . . . I think this is important, because it gets people involved, it makes people feel empowered, and it makes them feel like they're a part of a team." (Finance)

- "Ours is sort of a Quaker-like group. We all want to be there for everything. There is a history of faculty being very involved in all kinds of decisions." (Family Social Science)

- "I think we are democratic to death. We discuss everything." (Philosophy)

In our study, we did not collect observational data on our study participants' actual behaviors, nor did we interview faculty members to get their perspective on their department's leadership and governance practices (which might have differed from those expressed by the interviewed heads/chairs). However, at least in the abstract, those interviewed did endorse the participative governance approach which prior studies have found to be widely used in research-productive organizations. They expressed a commitment to transparency and fairness in their information sharing and decision-making. And they reported having a variety of formal structures in their departments that encourage shared governance. Commonly used structures and strategies for facilitating shared governance included the following:

- Decentralized organization (associate and vice chairs, division directors)

- Committees (consultative, standing, ad hoc)

- Faculty meetings

- Faculty retreats

- Frequent, substantive, open communication with faculty

Within these structures and strategies, there was great variance from department to department in how they were applied. In large part, how many structures and to what degree these structures were necessary appeared to depend on the department's size.

Decentralized organization. Most of the larger departments in our study rely on additional levels of leadership to help with day-to-day management.

Common examples are vice chairs for education or research, and directors of graduate or undergraduate education. In some departments, faculty members will direct divisions that represent the major research, training, or clinical areas of the department. These governance structures might change over time, for example, when new research areas became prominent or when innovations such as technology require division status.

The ongoing roles of these additional leaders are to manage their section, to gather input from and represent the faculty, and to provide advice to the overall department head/chair. Ravdin explained how this type of governance works in the Department of Medicine:

> In large units like this you have to have distributed leadership. The democratic activities need to be more at a division rather than at a department level. . . . They [divisions] are small enough units that the faculty and the divisional director can meet on a regular basis, make consensual decisions, and decide on an agenda. Then, on a department-wide basis, I meet three times a month with the division heads and vice chairs. I won't do anything without discussing it with them. Our department faculty meeting that we have once a month ends up being more informational, because it's too large a group.

Division leaders and associate or vice chairs typically play more than an advisory role; it is common for division leaders to have significant decision-making authority. For example, area directors in the Twin Cities campus psychology department "have virtually total authority over the selection of graduate students, graduate student evaluation and progress, courses, and curriculum," said Campbell. Faculty serving in such roles learn firsthand about the nuances of academic leadership. In this way, decentralized organizations can groom future department heads/chairs. Again, Campbell:

> [Leadership succession] is a huge problem that we must constantly grapple with. . . . The associate chair rotation will be valuable. We also have some people who are younger who are getting experience in various parts of the college management [such as] being on the executive committee in the college. What we must start doing is more rotating of people through key jobs and getting more people familiar with how the department and college operate.

A decentralized structure is a distinctive feature of not only individual departments, but also the University of Minnesota as a whole. This was noted by several study participants who reported playing an active role in helping their respective colleges and the larger university succeed. Just as they value their own consultative committee to help them govern the department, they view themselves as part of a larger consultative team that helps their college succeed. Ravdin said,

> I spend half my time, maybe a little less, on leadership activities external to being head of Medicine because I feel that is the only way to succeed internally with our mission. . . . That's not helping me directly with managing the department, but it is a way for me to contribute to the overall environment.

The heads/chairs of Art and Entomology also commented on the need for departments to act as part of the larger college and university's team. They actively promote this by encouraging their faculty to participate in college and university-level governance. This helps their faculty become involved and visible at all levels of decision-making across the institution.

Committees (consultative, standing, ad hoc). Committee work is a part of faculty life. But it is also one of the primary means by which academic departments encourage shared governance.

Most of the departments in our study have a consultative committee that meets frequently with the department head/chair, typically once a week or every other week between the full faculty meetings. Consultative committees are charged with gathering input from the larger faculty group and then bringing that input to the decision-making table. The members of consultative committees might include the department's vice or associate chairs, division directors, chairs of key faculty committees, and additional representatives elected from the faculty. Some committees include elected representatives from other employee groups such as staff or graduate students. This inclusionary practice gives department leaders the benefit of full community voice.

In addition to consultative committees, most research-productive departments have a strong standing committee structure organized around specific topic areas. Members are selected by faculty vote or appointed by the chair. Having committees perform ground-level tasks in specific areas and then report back to the larger faculty body with recommendations can ensure a participative approach to governance, while saving time for the faculty as a whole.

The Department of Pediatrics recently created a research council, "which is maybe six people, all with NIH grant support" said Moller. "They helped develop the response to one of those research priorities in the Medical School, and they're looking at what type of infrastructure we need for helping support research." They also have a board to run their clinical activities and have formed a pediatric educational council that is responsible for implementing the education program.

Although the number of standing committees varied by department, our interviews confirmed that highly research-productive departments significantly use committee structures as a way to ensure faculty input into decisions. The Law School is one example. Sullivan explained,

> All policy decisions go through a committee structure first. . . . I haven't counted them, but I would guess we have maybe 20 different committees: admissions, appointments, awards, career services, clerkships, consultative committee to the dean, educational policy, graduate and international programs, grievances, honor code, interdisciplinary appointments in joint degrees, academic journals, post-tenure review, etc.

For such extensive committee structures to run smoothly without a breakdown in communication, it can be helpful to have an administrative staff structure that mirrors the committee structure. In Child Development, for example, a staff member helps to track all committee activities. "She makes sure all these committees know what the others are doing," said Masten. "That's why we have ex officio communication here, so that there is an intertwined, interconnected structure in the department."

Among the departments in our study, there were a few exceptions to the significant use of standing committees. Bates (Chemical Engineering and Materials Science) said he tries to ask faculty to spend very little time on committees and in faculty meetings. Instead, he uses a team of the four directors and the executive officer as an advisory group. This is a relatively small department, however (about 30 faculty), and faculty do all meet every Friday for lunch, which provides a time to informally discuss department business when necessary.

A few departments prefer ad hoc committees in lieu of numerous standing committees. These ad hoc groups address specific issues as they arise before bringing them to the faculty as a whole. Hicks (Biology) described his department's selective and varied use of committees in this way:

If we have a short-term problem that's very focused, we'll form a work group. Three or four colleagues develop a solution. Then we bring that solution to the department meeting, explain it, vote on it, and move on, rather than have 20 people try to develop a solution. We have ad hoc committees, which are for longer term [issues]—a year-long problem or even a couple of years, but not something that's continuing. Then we have standing committees that everybody knows about that are always doing something, like a curriculum committee. So, we have tried to resolve things or provide a solution before we walk into a department meeting. We can then discuss that solution rather than discussing a problem and bemoaning it.

Faculty meetings. The faculty meeting is one of the most traditional forums for faculty governance. It is there that faculty are drawn out of their specific divisions and reminded of the collective short- and long-term goals of the entire department, as well as those of the larger institution (e.g., school, college, university).

Departments typically hold regular faculty meetings, occurring monthly or quarterly. These meetings are used for votes on major decisions and for sharing information about activities across divisions. Hicks has found it useful to limit their meeting agendas to issues that require the discussion of all Biology faculty members. Setting timelines for each agenda item and sticking to those as best as possible has also helped increase his faculty's participation.

All but the smallest departments try to discuss topics within committees before bringing issues to the whole faculty. This is particularly essential when dealing with conflicts and more sensitive department-wide issues:

- "I would never go into a graduate faculty meeting knowing there is a contentious issue without doing a lot of background work. From previous directors I learned it was important to be prepared, and that is part of the way consensus building occurs. We have some strong-willed faculty with very different points of view, and the reality is there are going to be people who will have some clashes. We try to handle them in smaller groups and meetings so we can build a consensus before we get into a room as a large group." (Child Development)

- "If there's an issue to be discussed that will affect an individual, group, or area, I will meet with those involved to get their input. That takes a reasonable amount of time, but it's better than trying to resolve a difficult or complex problem in a faculty meeting without adequate preparation. Laying the groundwork will help faculty converge on a decision." (Chemistry)

Faculty retreats. In addition to faculty meetings, many research-productive departments hold off-site faculty retreats to allow for decision-making in neutral territory. "We discuss issues that are important to us, all the way from problems with operations, curriculum development, and research strategies, to what kind of a position we want to make a bid for this next year," explained Hicks (Biology) "It's been a good team-building tool, and we have always done it away from the university, where it's not the same conference room where we have faculty meetings and debates. What that's done is get us ahead of the game."

According to Gladfelter (Chemistry), retreats are valuable in allowing faculty to escape the routine, the immediacy of daily issues, and instead look creatively at the department's future.

> It's very difficult in the academic year to sit down at a faculty meeting for this type of general discussion. We have faculty meetings once a month, and I try to keep those to an hour if I can. Often there are pressing issues such as hiring and resource allocation that have to be addressed at these meetings. By minimizing discussions of such issues at the retreat, we could focus on longer-term issues. We generated a lot of neat ideas, many of which have been implemented.

Frequent, substantive, open communication. All of the interviewed department leaders spoke of the importance of proactively and frequently communicating with their faculty as a means of facilitating shared governance. These departments use multiple forms of communication, besides the aforementioned committees, faculty meetings, and retreats. All of the department heads spoke of making extensive use of emails—both messages relevant to the full faculty and individual messages of import to specific members. Some departments also continue to use traditional print media (newsletters and the like), one example being the *News On Wednesday* publication put out by the Department of Educational Psychology.

Many heads/chairs regularly walk around their department to informally interact with faculty on a daily or weekly basis. Collins credits past deans for facilitating good communication within General College: "Jean Lupton was a very gregarious person. She sort of insisted on a social environment that valued people talking with each other. David Taylor [the current dean] is the same way." Collins added that serendipity has played a part, in that they are a smaller college whose faculty have been successful in maintaining good working relationships with one another: "We don't have people here who are not talking to each other."

Yearly faculty reviews (meetings and/or written reports) are another common mechanism of communication. Ek (Forest Resources) holds hour-long annual review meetings with each faculty member to provide them with feedback on their performance and also to solicit their opinions on how to develop the department as a whole.

> We talk about what they plan to do in the future, what are their strengths and limitations in trying to get those things done, etc. Then I ask about their level of interest in what they are doing and seek their suggestions on where they and the department need to go. I ask not only about direction for the coming year, but over the next several years. Suggestions from this part [of the review meeting] can be very helpful.

Again and again, the participants in our study talked about the need to keep the lines of communication open and to make complete information, particularly budget information, readily and routinely available to faculty:

- "Overall the most important role [of the department head] is to communicate, and to make sure that we don't have a breakdown either between me and the rest of the faculty, or among the faculty themselves." (Agronomy and Plant Genetics)

- "We are an open book with all of our financial information." (Medicine)

- "To be a chair, at least of this unit, and perhaps any good unit . . . you have to be incredibly fair and transparent in the things you do. I'm perfectly willing to say, 'Come and look how we got there.' I present the budget every year to the faculty. I say, this is how I spent the money we had. And we can argue about it. If good arguments are made, we'll have a different budget. I think being transparent and open is important." (Epidemiology)

How Do Department Leaders Balance a Need to Involve Faculty in Governance With Using Faculty Time Wisely?

It is indeed a balancing act to meaningfully involve faculty in department governance while respecting their other work commitments. All faculty members want to be appropriately involved in decisions, but just what is appropriate varies from one department to another. Each department seems to have come to the right balance carefully and over time, using faculty input, the leader's best judgment, and trial and error:

- "There is an interesting combination here. There is an understanding that we give the chair a lot of authority to make decisions, but we expect the chair to know when others should be consulted. It has taken me a couple of years to get the nuances of this type of leadership. . . . Of course I make mistakes along the way. Sometimes, if I'm not sure, I'll ask some of my wise mentors." (Child Development)

- "We have faculty meetings, and I try to keep everyone informed as well as I can. I definitely try to work through committees to get policy issues discussed, alternatives debated, a proposal put forward. I'm officially a head, and I do have more powers than a lot of chairs, if you read our documents. However, there is no doubt in my mind—or I think anybody else's—that if I were to overstep my bounds I would know about it very soon." (Applied Economics)

- "They [faculty] don't need more stuff crossing their desks—more microdecisions or whatever. I just try to do everything I possibly can, and then when I need input I try to restrict it to a committee or several select people. I go to the whole faculty for deep issues like hiring." (Ecology, Evolution, and Behavior)

- "On the one hand, as faculty we all say, 'We want to be consulted.' On the other hand, we all say, 'Leave us alone. Let us do what we want, and take care of the stuff for us.' It's always this balance; it's a very difficult balance. They want leaders to lead, but not too much. So, we have a governance mechanism that tries to balance this. There will be faculty who will say we're very consultative, we're totally open. And there will be faculty who say that I make all the decisions, and they don't get any input into it. You just keep working on it." (Medicine)

Does Continuity in Leadership Matter?

This need for department heads/chairs to "just keeping working on it" suggests that continuity in academic leadership can be advantageous. Indeed, several of the departments in our study were characterized by an extraordinarily low turnover in their leadership. Child Development, for example, has had only seven directors over 75 years, and McMurry is just the sixth head in Mechanical Engineering's 100-year history.

Despite problems that could arise with longer leadership terms, most of those interviewed shared the view that leadership stability is a strength.

According to Warthesen (Food Science and Nutrition), "The advantage to continuity is that year to year you are giving consistent notes to faculty about values, about their performances, about their improvement, about what they need to work on." He went on to explain that sometimes, with the chair system (chairs are elected typically for a one- to three-year term), a faculty member who isn't getting good signals from the leadership can ignore these, and instead wait for or initiate a change in leadership.

In conclusion, the department leader is a key person, perhaps the key person, in determining if a department is highly research productive. These leaders do so by embodying the values and culture of academe (e.g., preeminence in research, excellence in teaching) and by rigorously attending to the many environmental features that facilitate productivity in research.

This is no small task, and new leaders might find themselves thrust into this role feeling unprepared. Precisely with this in mind, we created this book to provide department chairs and deans—or others charged with facilitating research in their institution—with two sets of preparatory information: 1) a sampling of specific research-facilitating strategies that others have used successfully, and 2) a summative body of literature to undergird these practical approaches. We encourage readers to spend time reflecting on this rich body of information; the value is truly in the details.

Chapter 14 Review:
Leadership and Governance _____

- The leaders of highly research-productive departments are charged with keeping the research mission in front of the faculty. They spend a great deal of time attending to the management details of running a department and serve as successful peer models for other faculty. In addition, they are conscious of advocating their department to higher administrative levels and of being responsible for the success of their larger host institutions.

- In these departments, heads/chairs appear to have adopted a participative approach to governance. They purposefully establish structures that facilitate this approach (e.g., a decentralized or more horizontal management structure, frequent communication with faculty through different media) and actively use these structures to ensure shared governance. The size of a department is particularly influential in determining the number and type of governance structures put into place.

- Over time, these departments have adopted their own unique ways of balancing two desirable governance features: strong faculty participation in governance and the time-saving benefit of leaving certain decisions in the leaders' hands, without extensive faculty consultation.

- Longevity of leadership is a defining characteristic of many departments in this study. One cited advantage to leadership continuity is greater efficiency in the role (once the learning-curve period has passed). Another is greater progress toward faculty members' individual goals and the department's collective goals.

15

Final Take-Home Lessons

The highly research-productive department is a carefully constructed mosaic of individual, environmental, and leadership features. When this mosaic is developed and continually nurtured, the result is synergistic—it creates a research-conducive organization that is more than the sum of its parts, and it yields researchers who are better (i.e., more productive) than they would be elsewhere.

In the preceding chapters, we described the many strategies used by departments to help faculty achieve the highest levels of research productivity. At this point, we suspect that you, the reader, have taken mental stock of your own institution's environment for research and, having done so, are experiencing a reaction that falls somewhere on the following spectrum:

- You are excited that your department or larger institution already has all (or nearly all) of the essential features described in this book. As such, you are confident that your faculty will stay the course of being highly research productive.

- You are encouraged that your department or institution has some of the essential features described in this book, even though other features are missing or weak. This being the case, you are wondering, how can you build on what you already have? Is what you have good enough?

- You are concerned that your department or institution lacks most of the essential features described in this book. Given this, you are wondering where to start. Is there a subset of features that are more critical than others? What first steps might you take toward laying the foundation for sustained vitality in research?

Regardless of where you fall on this continuum, five overarching take-home lessons from our qualitative study are worth considering:

1) The complete mosaic of research-facilitating features, working together, will yield the most research-conducive department.

2) Although having all the features is ideal, there is a subset of seven features that, in our assessment, are most essential. Of these seven, "Clear Goals" and "Leadership" stand out as the most important.

3) Constant vigilance is required to maintain an enduring research-conducive environment.

4) By formally assessing the presence and strength of the research-facilitating features, departments can identify areas needing special attention.

5) Implementation of all the features can occur by any number of specific strategies, fine-tuned to best fit the local environment.

The Complete Mosaic of Research-Facilitating Features, Working Together, Will Yield the Most Research-Conducive Department

In the process of analyzing our qualitative data, we were struck by an inescapable lesson: When it comes to research-productivity features, more is definitely better. In the most successful departments, nearly all of the research-facilitating features are present. Moreover, these features constructively reinforce and play off one another. This means that implementing a feature, or removing one, can create a ripple effect with wide-reaching consequences.

This point is critical. Thus, we tried to emphasize it in several ways throughout this book, beginning with the introductory chapter that unites the features into a single "model of the research-productive organization." In subsequent chapters, even though we discuss the features individually, we routinely refer to other chapters to emphasize the push-pull effect that the features have on one another. Throughout the text, we use words and phrases such as "intertwined," "interdependent," "interplay," and "mutually reinforcing." And here, in the concluding chapter, we punctuate this lesson one last time. Consider the following examples gleaned from previous chapters:

- Rewarding faculty for research achievements through recognition and awards (Chapter 11) positively feeds back into a department's reputation. This in turn can make it easier to build up other features such as recruiting exceptional faculty researchers (Chapter 2) and emphasizing research as a priority goal of the organization (Chapter 3).

- Encouraging frequent and substantive communication among faculty (Chapter 7) can help promote a culture of collaboration (Chapter 6), stimulate informal mentoring (Chapter 5), and encourage participative governance (Chapter 14).

In general, adding features can be expected to have a positive, additive effect on research productivity. But, precisely because these features are so intertwined, attending to some while neglecting others can actually have a detrimental effect on an organization. A study by Denton and Hunter (1997) vividly illustrates both of these points. They report the impact of implementing seven mechanisms to increase the amount of external funding acquired by faculty in a college of education. Within this setting,

1) A clear goal of increasing external funds was stated.

2) The goal of acquiring external funds was emphasized and communicated.

3) Recognition was provided for acquiring external funds.

4) Resources and an office were provided to assist in acquiring external funds.

5) A research council of principal investigators and representatives from each department was established.

6) A development person was hired to facilitate research funding.

7) Faculty appointments were changed from 12-month to 11-month, with no change in salary, so that faculty could augment their income by funding the additional month from external dollars.

These strategies address many of the desirable features of a highly research-productive organization (e.g., providing clear goals that emphasize research, allocating resources to support these goals, and rewarding the achievement of these goals). Indeed, these mechanisms did lead to substantial and significant increases in external funding, as expected. For example, over 10 years the percent of faculty with external dollars rose from 7% to a final 5-year average of about 38%. But, these changes also resulted in very real, undesirable consequences. The organizational climate of the college collapsed, faculty morale plummeted, and the faculty gave a negative review of the dean, who subsequently resigned.

The study suggests several explanations for the latter outcomes. First, the faculty did not perceive they had been recruited with the understanding that they would be expected to generate external dollars. Second, faculty did not feel they were mentored in how to do this. Third, the study report's authors suggest that, "Perhaps the mechanisms were sound, but the implementation of the mechanisms may have been pursued too vigorously. . . . College admin-istration, buoyed by the realization that the fiscal goals of the organization were being attained, did not sufficiently heed faculty concerns" (pp. 17–18). In other words, it seems that this institution, while successful in implement-ing some elements of the research-productivity model, did not sufficiently address recruitment, mentoring, shared culture, positive group climate, com-munication, and most importantly, participative leadership. These findings demonstrate the necessity of attending to a minimum subset of critical fea-tures if a research-conducive environment is to endure.

Although Having All the Features Is Ideal, There Is a Subset of Seven Features That, in Our Assessment, Are Most Essential—Of These, "Clear Goals" and "Leadership" Stand Out as the Most Important

Certainly, implementing all of the research-facilitating features discussed in this book is the optimal scenario. But the optimum is seldom achieved, sug-gesting that departments can be highly productive in research when only some of the features are present. That being the case, we are often asked, "Is there a subset of features that are more critical than others? If you had to pick, what would you say are the most important features of a highly research-pro-ductive department?"

Below, we offer up a list of what we consider to be the most essential characteristics. Our basis for selection was the frequency—and depth—with which these features were discussed in the literature and in our interviews with academic leaders. These seven features are as follows:

1) Clear organizational *goals* that collectively emphasize research

2) *Leadership* that is research experienced and highly participative

3) *Recruitment and selection* processes that bring in highly skilled, research-driven faculty

4) A positive group *climate* and shared *culture* that together support and highly value faculty research

5) *A mentoring* program that advises faculty on their research activities, socializes them to the department's culture, and connects them with the relevant research establishment

6) *Collaborations* that help faculty to stimulate new avenues for research, answer complex research questions, and advance their careers

7) *Communication* that serves to nurture faculty's professional networks

The top two features warrant brief discussion. If there is one feature that is absolutely essential, we believe it is having clear, coordinating goals focused on research. Quite simply, if research is not a visible, priority goal of the organization, research productivity will dwindle. Recall that two of the academic leaders who participated in our interview study were in organizations that had relatively recently transitioned from being a less research-productive unit to a highly research-productive one (General College and the School of Nursing). The first action taken by these units to initiate this move—and the one reported most important—was for research to be made a priority goal and for this emphasis to be reflected in public statements, reward systems, and recruitment (Chapter 3).

A close second for the most important research-facilitating feature is the leader (Chapter 14). As mentioned in Chapter 1, all of the features necessary for a highly research-productive organization are influenced by the leader. If the leader is not research oriented or is ineffective, it is unlikely the other features will be present, or, if initially present, will be maintained. Leaders internalize the group's research-focused mission and keep the research emphasis clear to the group. They also embody the values and culture of academe (e.g., preeminence in research, excellence in teaching). This was confirmed by the consistent profile that emerged for the department heads/chairs in our study. They are themselves research successful; they use a participative leadership approach; they also recognize the impact their behaviors have, and thus are reflective and purposeful about their leadership behaviors.

Constant Vigilance Is Required to Maintain an Enduring Research-Conducive Environment

Another summative lesson that emerged from our qualitative work and the prior literature is that departments with a long history of being research productive have done so not just by design, but by perseverance as well. Yes, they have successfully initiated most or all of the features. But beyond that, they take great care to regularly attend to the vitality of these features, to ensure that their research-conducive environment does not atrophy. For example:

- They take note of exceptional trainees, visiting scholars, and other colleagues, such that when it comes time for hiring new faculty they have an immediate network from which to draw excellent candidates (Chapter 2)—including candidates who will provide the desired diversity in expertise, experience, problem-solving approaches, etc. (Chapter 13).

- They protect their initial investment in faculty by providing them with the resources and time to do research (Chapters 8 and 10), by rewarding their achievements (Chapter 11), and by brokering opportunities for them to develop in their careers (Chapter 12).

- They preserve their local culture and climate (Chapter 4)—even as new faculty are hired and senior faculty retire—through such means as active mentoring (Chapter 5) and a governance structure that promotes a strong sense of ownership in the organization (Chapter 14).

- They revisit, reaffirm, and readjust their research goals so as to stay aligned with their shifting environment (e.g., available funding streams; institutional, regional, national/international priorities; needs of the discipline) (Chapter 3).

In short, research productivity can not be taken for granted. A research-conducive infrastructure can be chipped away by many forces such as dwindling resources, leadership shifts, or a pressing need to vigorously attend to other key areas of the academic mission. If departments rest on their laurels without frequently evaluating and ministering to their research mission, they could easily slip into a state of research stagnancy. Like keeping a body physically fit, a department's research excellence needs constant attention, is easily lost, and takes significant effort to regain.

By Formally Assessing the Presence and Strength of the Research-Facilitating Features, Departments Can Identify Areas Needing Special Attention

The idea of preserving research through perseverance leads us directly to another important overarching lesson: Never underestimate the value of a good needs assessment. This is particularly important in the context of research productivity. Because many of the research-facilitating features appear intuitive, some leaders in higher education might be tempted to quickly scan this book's table of contents and mentally, but prematurely, check off each research-facilitating feature as present and accounted for in their setting. It is possible, however, that a formal needs assessment of their environment would yield very different results.

We can share a local example. In 1999 the University of Minnesota Medical School put significant effort into refining and articulating the school's mission and goals. This occurred through extensive faculty retreats and faculty subcommittees. However, in a faculty survey conducted the following year (n = 465), only 27% of faculty respondents perceived that the school had a vision for the next five years, and just 28% thought that their department's goals related to the school's goals (Bland, Seaquist, Pacala, Center, & Finstad,

2002). In a different (nonlocal) study of 250 research and development supervisors, 85% described themselves as matching the profile of an assertive participative leader (i.e., having a leadership style that facilitated autonomy, openness, risk taking, innovation, and self-responsibility), but this perception did not match the behaviors they actually exhibited during videotaped technical problem-solving meetings (Argyris, 1968).

Of course, the news from a needs assessment can also be good. Recall from Chapter 7 the department head who, after asking the faculty to send him the names of their top three to five professional contacts, found himself buried by replies and was amazed at how connected people were to their external networks. In the area of mentoring (Chapter 5), a few department heads/chairs discovered that their faculty saw no need to be formally assigned a mentor, because they took care to initiate mentoring relationships on their own or otherwise found themselves being satisfactorily mentored in nonstructured ways (e.g., through a highly ingrained departmental tradition of faculty having lunch together each week, where substantive discussions occur about the research being conducted, upcoming conferences, and so on).

In any case, it is beneficial to carefully and regularly evaluate the presence/absence of the research facilitating features—and their strength—within your institution. The list of essential characteristics of research environments (Appendix B) that we used in our study could serve as a useful assessment guide. You might use a version of this instrument to assess how well your setting matches the profile of a highly research-productive organization. An evaluation of this type could occur in the context of an already planned internal/external review of your organization, or be incorporated into periodic strategic planning.

Implementation of All the Features Can Occur by Any Number of Specific Strategies, Fine-Tuned to Best Fit the Local Environment

Perhaps the most impressive thing about the departments and schools that participated in our study is that, when it comes to building/sustaining a highly research-productive organization, they really do walk the talk. Faculty and leaders in these settings do not simply discuss the essential features in the abstract. Rather, they find ways to actually bring the features about—to make them happen and then keep them vital—to the point that these characteristics are intricately woven into their institutional fabric.

This observation brings us full circle to the motivation for this book, and our final take-home lesson: Although the basic architecture of the research-productivity model is consistent across environments, there is no standard set of implementation strategies by which a department achieves research excellence. Certainly, the essential features are consistent at their core, and a constructive interplay among them is required; but there are multiple ways to establish and link the features so as to yield a highly research-productive organization. Even within our one institution, we observed that such things as department size, discipline, and the characteristics of the larger setting in which a department resides (e.g., school, campus) will determine what works best.

In creating this book, we aimed to provide readers with possible strategies and ideas for making these features an integral and enduring part of their local environment. Although by no means are the strategies described in these pages all-inclusive, they do add considerable depth to the existing knowledge base in this area—which, as all highly productive researchers know, is the path to discovery. It is our hope that readers will listen to and learn from the voices in this book as they would other experienced members of their professional network.

Study Origins and Methods

Origin of the Study

This book evolved from the work of the University of Minnesota's Joint Senate/Administrative Working Group on Faculty Development. This group, representing administration and faculty across the university's 23 colleges, was established by Richard Goldstein (chair of the Senate Committee on Faculty Affairs) and Robert Jones (vice provost for faculty and academic programs and executive vice president for student development). The members of this working group are acknowledged by name in the Preface.

The working group's charge was to identify strategies for increasing research and scholarly productivity among University of Minnesota faculty. Indeed, this began as a very broad mandate to develop strategies for ensuring faculty vitality in all roles (i.e., research, teaching, outreach). The working group narrowed this down to the more manageable task of identifying ways to ensure research vitality. The rationale was that the university already had several initiatives in place to facilitate effective teaching and outreach, but lacked similar university-wide activities for facilitating research productivity.

In pursuit of this goal, the working group conducted two projects:

> *Project 1:* An exploratory survey study of tenure-track and tenured faculty who had voluntarily left the University of Minnesota for other academic positions in recent years (1997–2000).
>
> Why would successful faculty leave the university? We thought the answer to this question would alert us to factors important for retaining vital faculty members—with particular interest paid to reasons related to their research productivity. What we found is that departmental features (e.g., perceived social climate, sense of collegiality, management effectiveness) were the greatest source of dissatisfaction for faculty who have left the university. (An executive summary of Project 1 is provided in Appendix G. The full report can be viewed at http://www1.umn.edu/usenate/scfa/exitsurveyreport.html.) This key finding undergirded the working group's second project.
>
> *Project 2:* The development of a publication that identifies and describes best practices for facilitating research productivity. Particular attention is to be paid to describing the

environmental features of departments whose faculty excel in research and scholarship.

Our method for identifying these best practices was to interview the heads/chairs of highly research-productive departments at our institution. Importantly, the interviews were designed around the many characteristics the literature finds to be associated with high productivity in research/scholarship. With this literature as our framework, our goal was to learn how these characteristics are actually manifest in particular departments, whether through specific programs, policies, allocation of resources, and so on. Our study methods are detailed next.

Study Methods

The University of Minnesota consists of 23 colleges on four campuses located in the Twin Cities (Minneapolis and Saint Paul), Duluth, Morris, and Crookston. Each college dean was asked to identify up to three highly research-productive departments in his or her college, using the following criteria:

- Impact of the research/scholarship on the respective discipline

- Quantity of the research/scholarship

- Number of research grant dollars acquired

- Reputation as a research/scholarship productive department

Deans were also asked to note if any of these departments had made a dramatic increase in their research/scholarly productivity in the last five years. From this process, 43 highly research-productive departments were identified.

We invited the heads/chairs of these departments to participate in the interview study. Each was also given a brief written survey that listed the characteristics of a highly research-productive department and asked to indicate ones for which they thought their department had strategies to share. A copy of the pre-interview survey is provided in Appendix B. Participants also completed a brief demographic survey, found in Appendix D.

Five of the contacted departments did not participate because of scheduling problems. Only one declined to participate. Thus, our final cohort consisted of 37 departments. The names of the participating departments and interviewed leaders are listed in the preface. Their demographic characteristics are summarized in Appendix E.

Each department head/chair was interviewed by a member of the working group using a standard protocol based on the literature review. The interview protocol is provided in Appendix C. The interview began with the open-ended question:

> "In your assessment of your department, what are the key factors that contribute to the research productivity of your faculty?"

The inclusion and ordering of the remaining protocol questions were determined by 1) the answer to this question, and 2) the individual's responses to the written survey, indicating for which characteristics they had strategies to share. For example, if a department chair/head checked "Clear Goals" and did not discuss that in the response to the opening question, he or she was asked, "Do you have ways of coordinating faculty goals and working with unit goals? Are there priority research areas in the department, and if so, how were these identified? How do you communicate or keep visible the priority goals of your department?"

Each interview was audio recorded and transcribed. Transcriptions were sent to the working group interviewer for corrections and to the department head/chair for corrections or changes. Interviewees were advised that they would not be quoted, nor would identifiable information be used, without their permission.

Following the interview, each participating department head/chair was sent a brief survey requesting demographic information about the department. A copy of this survey is in Appendix D and Appendix E summarizes the demographic information gathered.

The interview data resulted in more than 1,000 pages of double-spaced text. Within each transcript, responses were coded and assigned to a theme. NVivo Qualitative Research Software was used to sort the coded information across transcripts into the study themes.

The themes were written into the chapters found in this book. Specific quotes included in the chapters were reviewed again and approved by the person quoted. To complete the chapters, the interview data were placed in the context of the broader research literature in that area. Hence each chapter has a literature review section and a section on best practices.

We remind readers to consider the following methodological features of our work when reading about and applying our results:

- First, our study was qualitative, with only minimal quantitative data collected in the pre-interview and demographic written surveys. Thus, the chapters represent our summary of the most dominant strategies and practices offered up by the department leaders responding to a structured interview protocol.

- Second, these data come from one source: the opinions of department heads, chairs, and in a few cases, college deans. Different results may have emerged if other faculty or even staff in the departments were included in the study.

- Third, our results represent a snapshot in the overall history of these departments. By the time you read this book, many of the department chairs and heads will no longer hold these positions and some of the strategies reported here may have changed. It is more likely though, that most of these strategies will have remained in place, since many of these practices were ingrained in the department more by culture than by governance.

Pre-Interview Survey

Characteristics and Approaches for Research Productivity

NAME _____

(By "research" we mean all scholarly or creative work that contributes new information or products.)

For each characteristic below please indicate:

1) the extent to which each describes your department, and

2) if you have an effective approach with regard to this characteristic that you would share with the Working Group.

Scale: Not at all (0), Barely (1), Minimally (2), Somewhat (3), Very Closely (4), Completely (5)

Characteristics of Research Environments	Characteristic Describes Your Department						Have Approach to Share	
	Not at all	Barely	Minimally	Somewhat	Very Closely	Completely	Yes	No
	0	1	2	3	4	5	Y	N
1 *Career Development/Adult Development.* Needs are met of faculty who differ across career level (e.g., assistant professors focus on finding mentors and achieving tenure, full professors seek broader roles and leadership) or by adult development level (e.g., senior faculty are often more interested in writing larger works rather than multiple, single articles.)								
2 *Clear Goals That Serve a Coordinating Function.* Clear organizational goals exist, and people have articulated personal goals that are compatible with the organizational ones. Unit goals serve to coordinate unit activities as well as to significantly influence the other characteristics of the environment such as recruitment, climate, and culture.								

Characteristics of Research Environments	Characteristic Describes Your Department						Have Approach to Share	
	Not at all	Barely	Minimally	Somewhat	Very Closely	Completely	Yes	No
	0	1	2	3	4	5	Y	N
3 *Research Emphasis.* Places priority on research or puts no less emphasis on research than on other goals. This emphasis on research mission serves to focus the climate, culture, resources, and faculty of high research potential as well as to guide the communication, collaboration, and service responsibilities of the faculty.								
4 *Culture.* Has a distinctive organizational culture that bonds its members, provides a group identity, defines common values and practices, and creates a "safe" home in which to experiment.								
5 *Group Climate.* Has high morale and a positive climate. Indicators of a positive climate include: a spirit of innovation, dedication to work, receptivity to new ideas, frequency of substantive interactions, a high degree of cooperation, low faculty turnover, good leader/member relationships, and open discussion of disagreements.								
6 *Assertive Participative Governance.* Has formal mechanisms and expectations for all members to contribute to decision-making. High-quality information is readily available, members feel their ideas are valued, and they have a sense of ownership as well as an important role in the future of the organization.								
7 *Decentralized Organization.* Has an effective flat, decentralized structure. This does not mean anarchy, however; rather, decentralization is matched with clear, commonly understood goals and values and leadership that uses assertive participative governance and has feedback systems to track quasi-autonomous parts.								

Characteristics of Research Environments	Characteristic Describes Your Department						Have Approach to Share	
	Not at all	Barely	Minimally	Somewhat	Very Closely	Completely	Yes	No
	0	1	2	3	4	5	Y	N
8 *Communication.* Consists predominantly of faculty who have frequent, substantive (not merely social) impromptu and formal, inter- and extra-unit communication.								
9 *Resources.* Has essential resources including human (colleagues, assistants, technical consultants, graduate students, research knowledgeable leaders), time, funding, facilities, and libraries. Especially important are productive colleagues. However, the key feature to adequate resources is the members' perceptions of there being accessible, useable resources.								
10 *Productive Local Peer Support.* Has research-productive peers. The same researcher publishes more when placed among productive researchers than when in a department where colleagues publish less. These peers provide continued reinforcement and recognition of work by colleagues, which stimulates productivity.								
11 *Size/Age/Diversity.* Department is relatively large and comprised of faculty who have been together for quite a while. Also, the group includes members with different approaches to problems, degree levels, and discipline backgrounds.								

Characteristics of Research Environments	Characteristic Describes Your Department						Have Approach to Share	
	Not at all	Barely	Minimally	Somewhat	Very Closely	Completely	Yes	No
	0	1	2	3	4	5	Y	N
12 *Rewards.* Money is perceived to be distributed in a fair way. Salaries are not substantially lower compared to other units. Other critical rewards are present: being part of a highly regarded organization, seeing one's work applied, recognition by superiors or peers, public recognition, promotion, opportunities for responsibility, intellectual stimulation, and socially significant work. Members can access rewards differently when their reward needs change.								
13 *Brokered Opportunities.* Continued success of faculty members of all ages and career stages is facilitated by proactively creating and brokering opportunities for professional development (e.g., fellowships, sabbaticals, team teaching, non-traditional assignments, opportunities for specific training on new research equipment).								
14 *Recruitment and Selection.* Extraordinary time and effort is spent recruiting members with specific training, socialization, commitment, and goals that match the organization.								
15 *Leadership.* The leader is highly research oriented and is (or was) a highly skilled scholar/scientist. He or she uses this background to: provide technical help to members to facilitate members' contacts and networks, maintain a positive climate and strong academic culture, build a shared vision, and develop effective career ladders and reward systems. The leader facilitates group productivity through the pairing of common goals and some structure with highly assertive participative governance.								

	Characteristic Describes Your Department						Have Approach to Share	
Characteristics of Research Environments	Not at all	Barely	Minimally	Somewhat	Very Closely	Completely	Yes	No
	0	1	2	3	4	5	Y	N
16 *Personal Motivation.* Most faculty in the department are driven to explore, understand, and follow their own ideas, and believe they have a responsibility to advance and contribute to society through innovation, discovery, and creative works.								
17 *In-depth Knowledge of Their Research Area.* Most faculty in the department are familiar with all major published works in the area, current major projects being conducted, differing theories, key researchers, and predominant funding sources.								
18 *Basic Research Skills as Well as Advanced Ones Applicable to Their Research Area.* Most faculty in the department are comfortable with basic statistics, study design, data collection methods, and with specific advanced statistics design and data collection strategies commonly used in their disciplines.								
19 *Socialization.* Most faculty in the department embrace the values, norms, expectations, and sanctions affecting established faculty researchers. Dominant values of scholars include, for example, serving society through objectivity, truthfulness, beneficence, and academic freedom. The senior faculty facilitate the socialization of newcomers.								
20 *Advisor/Mentor Functioning.* Most faculty in the department are adept at receiving assistance from and collaborating with established scholars. Senior faculty support future, beginning, and mid-level faculty in their research and connect them with the relevant research establishment. Such help is tangible and specific, and occurs before, during, and after training.								

Characteristics of Research Environments	Characteristic Describes Your Department						Have Approach to Share	
	Not at all	Barely	Minimally	Somewhat	Very Closely	Completely	Yes	No
	0	1	2	3	4	5	Y	N
21 *Work Habits.* Most faculty in the department maintain productive scholarly habits established early in their careers, such as blocking time for research and staying connected with colleagues.								
22 *Professional Network.* Most faculty in the department maintain contact with a network of research colleagues both within and outside the institution. These networks enable researchers to build their knowledge base, to critique and replicate work, and to ensure the quality of work in the field.								
23 *Simultaneous Projects.* Most faculty in the department are engaged in multiple simultaneous projects. If one project stalls or fails, another may prove successful, and faculty are thus buffered against the disillusionment that can occur when roadblocks appear during a difficult research project.								
24 *Sufficient Work Time.* Most faculty in the department have significant periods of uninterrupted time to devote to scholarly activities: 10%-80% of their total time to research, ideally over 40%.								
25 *Orientation.* Most faculty in the department are committed to both external and internal activities. External orientation involves attending regional and national meetings and collaborating with colleagues. Internal orientation requires involvement within one's own organization, including curriculum planning, institutional governance, and similar activities.								

Characteristics of Research Environments	Characteristic Describes Your Department						Have Approach to Share	
	Not at all	Barely	Minimally	Somewhat	Very Closely	Completely	Yes	No
	0	1	2	3	4	5	Y	N
26 *Autonomy/Commitment.* Most faculty in the department are able to plan their own time and set their own goals. They also have a meaningful role within their organization and are valued as important contributors to the organization.								
27** *Teaching.* It is understood that good researchers must also be good teachers—these are not mutually exclusive roles; in fact, teaching can lead to greater research productivity. Teaching is expected and rewarded. Faculty are helped to effectively balance their teaching and research roles and are provided with opportunities to develop their teaching skills.								
28** *Collaboration.* Interdisciplinary collaboration is both encouraged and proactively facilitated through purposeful efforts at the departmental or institutional level (e.g., creating interdisciplinary research centers, hiring faculty on joint appointments, offering financial incentives to new collaborative initiatives).								

*Items 1–26 were adapted from: Bland, C. J., & Ruffin, M. T., IV. (1992). Characteristics of a productive research environment: Literature review. *Academic Medicine, 67*(6), 385–397 and Bland, C. J., & Schmitz, C. C. (1986, January). Characteristics of the successful researcher and implications for faculty development. *Journal of Medical Education, 61,* 22–31. See also Bland, C. J., & Bergquist, W. H. (1997). *The vitality of senior faculty members: Snow on the roof—fire in the furnace* (ASHE-ERIC Higher Education Report, 25[7]). Washington, DC: George Washington University, Graduate School of Education and Human Development, p. 40. The studies reviewed in these articles and book were done primarily in life and social sciences. Thus, the generalizability to arts and humanities is unclear.

** Items 27 and 28 were not part of the original questionnaire, but were added to our list after the analysis of our qualitative data, which indicated that department leaders place high value on these two features.

Semi-Structured Interview Protocol

Interview Questions for Highly Research-Productive Departments

Thank you for agreeing to be part of our study on faculty satisfaction and research productivity at the U of M. As we mentioned in our letter, the Faculty Development Working Group is investigating the question of how to best support our faculty in increasing the overall research productivity at the U of M. By "research" we mean all scholarly or creative work that contributes new information or products. We are seeking to gather information from the University's most research-productive departments (such as yours) to learn about the methods productive departments use to facilitate research activity.

Before we start, do you have any questions about this study?

We will start with a general question and then ask specific questions developed from our review of the literature on characteristics that predict research productivity.

A. General Lead Question for All Interviews

1) In your assessment of your department, what are the key factors that contribute to the research productivity of your faculty?

[The inclusion and ordering of the remaining categories of questions is determined by the answer to the first question as well as the individual's responses to the survey.]

B. Main Body of Interview Questions

1) *Career Development/Adult Development.* Productive units meet the needs of faculty who differ by career level (e.g., assistant professors focus on finding mentors and achieving tenure—senior full professors seek broader roles and leadership) or by adult development level.

    1.1. How do you maintain research productivity of faculty throughout their career, especially after they become full professors?

    1.2. Do you have initiatives specifically aimed at maintaining or increasing the research productivity of senior faculty, women, or faculty of color? (Ex: Nominating senior, women, or faculty of color for growth opportunities, prestigious organizations, or leadership positions.) Please describe.

1.3. How do you foster development of leadership skills among your faculty?

2) *Clear Goals That Serve a Coordinating Function.* Productive units have clear organizational goals and people within the units who have articulated personal goals that are compatible with the organizational ones. Unit goals serve to coordinate unit activities as well as to significantly influence the other characteristics of the environment such as recruitment, climate, and culture.

   2.1. Do you have ways of coordinating faculty goals and work with unit goals, and unit goals with institutional goals? Please describe, especially on goals related to research productivity.

      2.1.A. How do you communicate or keep visible the priority goals of your department?

      2.1.B. Are there priority research areas in the department?

      2.1.C. Could we receive a copy of your unit's goals?

3) *Research Emphasis.* The productive unit places priority on research or puts no less emphasis on research than on other goals. This emphasis on research mission serves to focus the climate, culture, resources, and faculty of high research potential as well as to guide the communication, collaboration, and service responsibilities of the faculty.

   3.1. Is there a high expectation in your department that faculty will be research productive?

   3.2. If so, how is that communicated?

4) *Culture.* The productive unit has a distinctive organizational culture that bonds its members, provides a group identity, defines common values and practices, and creates a "safe" home in which to experiment.

   4.1. How do you maintain a culture that highly values research productivity?

      4.1.A. Publicly recognize research accomplishments

      4.1.B. Personally recognize research accomplishments (e.g., notes to PI)

5) *Group Climate.* Productive units are more likely to have high morale and a positive climate. Indicators of a positive climate include: a spirit of innovation, dedication to work, receptivity to new ideas, frequency of substantive interactions, a high degree of cooperation, low faculty turnover, good leader/member relationships, and open discussion of disagreements.

      5.1. How do you maintain good morale and a positive climate?

      5.2. How are disagreements handled?

6) *Assertive Participative Governance.* Productive units have formal mechanisms and expectations for all members to contribute to decision-making. High-quality information is readily available, members feel their ideas are valued, and they have a sense of ownership as well as an important role in the future of the organization.

      6.1. What authority do leaders of subdivisions have? (Are there layers of bureaucracy to get a decision?)

      6.2. What is the governance structure of the department? (Committee structures, how established, standing, rotating . . .)

      6.3. How does decision-making typically occur within this department in department level matters?

      6.4. Would faculty in your department say they have a meaningful voice in important decisions?

      6.5. What is the mechanism for faculty to have input into important decisions?

7) *Decentralized Organization.* Flat, decentralized structures are correlated with productive research groups. This does not mean anarchy, however. The effectiveness of decentralization is found where there are clear, commonly understood goals and values with leadership that uses assertive participative governance and has feedback systems to track quasi-autonomous parts.

      7.1. What is the structure of your department, e.g., divisions?

      7.2. Are there aspects to your structure that especially facilitate research?

      7.3. What authority do leaders of subdivisions have? (Are there layers of bureaucracy to get a decision?)

      7.4. What is the governance structure of the department? (Committee structures, how established, standing, rotating . . .)

8) *Communication.* Productive units consist predominantly of faculty who have frequent, substantive (not merely social) impromptu and formal, inter- and extra-unit communication.

      8.1. What amount and types of structured communication time do you have in your department? (Department meetings, research group meetings, mentor/mentee meetings, group lunches, newsletters, etc.)

9. *Resources.* Essential resources in productive units include humans (colleagues, assistants, technical consultants, graduate students, research knowledgeable leaders), time, funding, facilities, and libraries. Especially important are productive colleagues. However, the key feature to adequate resources is the members' perceptions of there being accessible, useable resources.

    9.1. Time

    9.1.A. Is there a minimum percentage of time that you expect your faculty to devote to research activities?

    9.1.B. Do you employ strategies to provide faculty members with significant periods of uninterrupted time for research? (Ex: leave time, "no committee" time, a reduced teaching load) Please describe.

    9.2. Technical assistance

    9.2.A. What kinds of technical assistance are provided for research?
    (Probes)

    - grant writing workshops or grant writers
    - assistance with survey design
    - assistance with data analysis
    - editing
    - research assistants
    - peer review of grants before submitted

    9.3. Staff

    9.3.A. Do you have enough secretarial assistance to support faculty members' clerical work?

    9.3.B. Do you have ample research assistants to support faculty members' activities?

    9.4. Access

    9.4.A. How do your faculty access these resources for uninterrupted time, and technical and clerical assistance?

    9.5. Funding assistance

    9.5.A. Does your department assist faculty in obtaining funding for research?
    (Examples)

- small department or institutional grants
- private/public partnerships
- university liaisons to state and federal legislature
- fundraising to support departmental priority research areas
- facilitate interdisciplinary research
- facilitate intra-institutional collaboration (travel or conference dollars)

9.6.   Space

   9.6.A.   Do your faculty have sufficient space and equipment to conduct their research?

   9.6.B.   Are your faculty geographically arranged to facilitate research? If not, how do you overcome this?

10) *Productive Local Peer Support.* The productivity of peers sets the norm for others. The same researcher publishes more when placed among productive researchers than when in a department where colleagues publish less. Productive units provide continued reinforcement and recognition of work by colleagues, which stimulates productivity.

   10.1.   Is there a high expectation in your department that faculty will be research productive?

   10.2.   If so, how is that communicated?

11) *Size/Age/Diversity.* In general, productivity increases with the size of the group. As for age, it helps to have a group together for quite a while. The trend is toward more productivity when the group includes members with different approaches to problems, degree levels, and discipline backgrounds.

   11.1.   Does your department make an effort to maintain diversity within your faculty in terms of discipline backgrounds, degree levels, ways of approaching problems, etc.? If so, please explain how.

   11.2.   Does your department have priority research areas with a critical mass of faculty in each one?

   11.3.   If so, how do you ensure that critical mass is maintained?

   11.4.   Do you have enough faculty to cover teaching and outreach obligations such that faculty have adequate time for research?

   11.5.   How do you promote cooperation among faculty to achieve goals of the department in research?

11.5.A. Have your faculty submitted large multi-investigator proposals?

11.5.B. Multidisciplinary proposals?

11.5.C. What has been effective in facilitating the development and funding of these proposals?

12) *Rewards.* Money is only one motivating factor, but it particularly operates under circumstances such as great inequities or low salaries compared to other unit members or other units. Other critical rewards include: being part of a highly regarded organization, seeing one's work applied, recognition by superiors or peers, public recognition, promotion, opportunities for responsibility, intellectual stimulation, and socially significant work. Research-conducive environments not only align the preferred rewards, but also enhance a member's ability to access rewards differently when his or her reward needs change.

12.1. Does your department celebrate and recognize research achievements in non-monetary ways? Please describe.

(Examples)

- public recognition (provide detail)
- peer review and recognition
- systematically nominating faculty for prestigious positions, e.g., National Academy of Sciences.
- career development awards
- sabbatical leave

12.2. Does your department celebrate and recognize research achievements in monetary ways? Please describe.

(Examples)

- raises
- bonuses
- promotion
- providing (or making contingent) research assistant money or faculty
- recruitment money for research productive units
- returning some indirect dollars to the principal investigator

13. Brokered Opportunities. Stuckness results in low productivity, disillusionment, and disengagement. Getting stuck early in a career has a particularly negative impact on productivity. But it is also a concern for senior

faculty who see their options decreasing and need to continually upgrade their knowledge and technical skills. Productive units facilitate continued success by proactively creating and brokering opportunities for professional development (e.g., fellowships, sabbaticals, team teaching, nontraditional assignment, opportunities for specific training on new research equipment, etc.).

13.1. How do you ensure continuity research success of your faculty?

      13.1.A. Do you nominate your faculty for career development opportunities? Please identify.

      13.1.B. Do you nominate your faculty for opportunities within the university? Please identify.

      13.1.C. Are you an advocate of sabbatical leaves?

      13.1.D. How many of your faculty have taken a sabbatical leave in the last three years?

      13.1.E. Do you nominate your faculty for rewards? Which ones?

      13.1.F. Do you nominate your faculty for assignments to university committees?

      13.1.G. What is the motivation for making nominations? (Department influence, faculty development)

13.2. How do you foster the development of leadership skills among your faculty?

14) *Recruitment and Selection.* Productive units spend extraordinary time and effort recruiting members with specific training, socialization, commitment, and goals that match their organization.

14.1. What strategies do you use to recruit highly productive research faculty?

14.2. What do you do to increase the odds that you will attract a person with these qualities?

(Probes)

- Recruit from a site proven to produce productive researchers
- Recruit people who have trained with highly regarded researchers
- Recruit people who have had post-doc training
- Recruit people who already have publications or grants or recognized works of arts, etc.

15) *Leadership.* This is a critical environmental factor since the leader affects all of the other organizational characteristics. The effective leader is highly research oriented and is (or was) a highly skilled scholar/scientist. He or she uses this background to: provide technical help to members to facilitate members' contacts and networks, maintain a positive climate and strong academic culture, build a shared vision, and develop effective career ladders and reward systems. This experience also establishes a basis of power or influence built on competence, experience, and admiration. The leader facilitates group productivity through the pairing of common goals and some structure with highly assertive participative governance.

15.1. What do you think are the most important things you do as a leader of this department (and that other department leaders do) to support the research productivity of your faculty?

16) *Personal Motivation.* Productive units consist predominantly of faculty who are driven to explore, understand, and follow their own ideas, and who believe they have a responsibility to advance and contribute to society through innovation, discovery, and creative works.

16.1. When searching for a faculty member you expect to be highly research productive, what features do you look for?

(Probes)

- In-depth knowledge?
- Possesses basic research skills?
- Already well connected in the field?

17) *In-depth Knowledge of Their Research Area.* Productive units consist predominantly of faculty who are familiar with all major published works in the area, current major projects being conducted, differing theories, key researchers, and predominant funding sources.

17.1. When searching for a faculty member you expect to be highly research productive, what features do you look for?

(Probes)

- In-depth knowledge?
- Possesses basic research skills?
- Already well connected in the field?

18) *Basic Research Skills as Well as Advanced Ones Applicable to Their Research Area.* Productive units consist predominantly of faculty who are comfortable with basic statistics, study design, data collection methods,

and with specific advanced statistics design and data collection strategies commonly used in their disciplines.

    18.1. When searching for a faculty member you expect to be highly research productive, what features do you look for?

        (Probes)

- In-depth knowledge?
- Possesses basic research skills?
- Already well connected in the field?

19) *Socialization.* Productive units consist predominantly of faculty who learn the values, norms, expectations, and sanctions affecting established faculty researchers. Dominant values of scholars include, for example, serving society through objectivity, truthfulness, beneficence, and academic freedom. The senior faculty facilitate the socialization of newcomers.

    19.1. When you bring in new faculty, what are the ways that you as a department show them the ropes? (Let them know what's expected of them.)

    19.2. Orientation: Do you have specific departmental information sessions or materials that are distributed to new faculty to help orient them to their roles as researchers and let them know your expectations of them? (If there is mention of written materials, ask for a copy.)

20) *Advisor/Mentor Functioning.* Productive units consist predominantly of faculty who are adept at receiving assistance from and collaborating with established scholars. Senior faculty support future, beginning, and mid-level faculty in their research and connect them with the relevant research establishment. Such help is tangible and specific, and occurs before, during, and after training.

    20.1. Mentoring: Do you have a way of teaming new faculty with your more seasoned researchers, who then serve as mentors or research advisors? Please describe.

21) *Work Habits.* Productive units consist predominantly of faculty who establish and maintain productive scholarly habits early in their careers, such as blocking time for research and staying connected with colleagues.

    21.1. Networking: Do you employ strategies that help new faculty meet and interact with research colleagues within your department?

        21.1.A. Outside your dept.?

        21.1.B. Outside the U of M? Please describe.

    21.2. Time: Is there a minimum percentage of time that you expect your faculty to devote to research activities?

        21.2.A. Do you employ strategies to provide faculty members with significant periods of uninterrupted time for research? (Ex: leave time, "no committee" time, a reduced teaching load.) Please describe.

22) *Professional Network.* Productive units consist predominantly of faculty who maintain contact with a network of research colleagues both within and outside the institution. These networks enable researchers to build their knowledge base, to critique and replicate work, and to ensure the quality of work in the field.

    22.1. Networking: Do you employ strategies that help new faculty meet and interact with research colleagues within your department?

        22.1.A. Outside your dept.?

        22.1.B. Outside the U of M? Please describe.

    22.2. Do you employ strategies that help established faculty meet and interact with research colleagues within your department?

        22.1.A. Outside your dept.?

        22.1.B. Outside the U of M? Please describe.

23) *Simultaneous Projects.* Productive units consist predominantly of faculty who are engaged in multiple simultaneous projects. If one project stalls or fails, another may prove successful, and faculty are thus buffered against the disillusionment that can occur when roadblocks appear during a difficult research project.

    23.1. Are there expectations as to how many projects a given faculty member is managing at any given time?

24) *Sufficient Work Time.* Productive units consist predominantly of faculty who have significant periods of uninterrupted time to devote to scholarly activities. Productive research faculty should devote approximately 10%–80% of their total time to research, with the ideal being about 40% (most researchers being productive at 40% and up).

    24.1. Time: Is there a minimum percentage of time that you expect your faculty to devote to research activities?

        24.1.A. Do you employ strategies to provide faculty members with significant periods of uninterrupted time for research? (Ex: leave time, "no committee" time, a reduced teaching load.) Please describe.

25) *Orientation.* Productive units consist predominantly of faculty who are committed to both external and internal activities. External orientation involves attending regional and national meetings and collaborating with colleagues. Internal orientation requires involvement within one's own organization, including curriculum planning, institutional governance, and similar activities.

25.1. Orientation: Do you have specific departmental information sessions or materials that are distributed to new faculty to help orient them to their roles as researchers and let them know your expectations of them? (If there is mention of written materials, ask for a copy.)

26) *Autonomy/Commitment.* Productive units consist predominantly of faculty who have academic freedom and the ability to work independently to plan their own time and set their own goals. They also have a meaningful role within their organization and are valued as important contributors to the organization.

26.1. How are faculty goals and time assignments determined?

C. Final Global Questions for All Interviews

1) Are there important contributors to research productivity in your department that we have not yet discussed? (Please elaborate.)

2) We've focused so far on departmental features that facilitate research productivity. What college or core institutional features do you think have facilitated your department's research productivity?

3) Are there college or institutional features that have served as barriers to research productivity?

Demographic Information
Number of full-time

___ professors   ___ associate professors   ___ assistant professors

Number of part-time

___ professors   ___ associate professors   ___ assistant professors

___ Number of civil service

___ Number of P&A

How does the average salary compare to peer institutions?

How many master's students? ___

How many Ph.D. students? ___

How many undergraduate majors? ___

What is the total annual budget? ___

What percent of the revenues are:

    ___ tuition ___ other central support ___ external direct dollars
    ___ indirect dollars ___ gifts ___ other

What is the square footage of the department? _____

Department Leader

    How is the department leader selected?

    How long does that individual typically serve?

    How long have you served?

Senate Working Group Project on Research Productivity

Department Demographic Information

Thank you again for allowing us to interview you! Even if you are not currently the department head/chair, we would still like you to complete this form, responding as though you are still the department head/chair. Please answer the following demographic questions about your department with your best estimates. It is not necessary that you have the exact figures.

Department Name:

Department Head Name:

Person Completing the Survey:

Phone Number: _____ Email:_____

1) Number of:
   _____ Master's students
   _____ Ph.D. students
   _____ Advanced professional students (e.g., medical or veterinary residents)
   _____ Other graduate students (e.g., certificate, fellowship, postdoctoral fellows)

2) How does the average faculty salary in your department compare to peer institutions? (Please check one)
   _____ Significantly higher
   _____ Somewhat higher
   _____ Comparable
   _____ Somewhat lower
   _____ Significantly lower

3) What was the total 2000–2001 budget of your department? $

4) Please share the sources for your total budget by telling what percent of the revenues for your department are from each of the following:
   _____ Central support (tuition, state, indirect dollars)
   _____ External direct dollars
   _____ Gifts
   _____ Other (specify)
   _____
   100% (total budget)

5) Where are offices of the majority of your faculty located?
_____ All in one building on one floor
_____ All in one building on different floors
_____ In different closely located buildings
_____ In different buildings far apart from each other

6) How does your department rank nationally among public institutions with regard to research? By research we mean all scholarly or creative work that contributes new information or products. (Please check one)
_____ Top 5%
_____ Top 10%
_____ Top 20%
_____ Top 30%
_____ Top 50%
_____ In the lower 50%

7) What is the basis for this rank estimate (e.g., National Research Council rankings, *U.S. News & World Report* rankings, etc.)? If there is no common system for ranking departments in your field and your estimate is based on personal observation, please state this.

8) Do you use the term department head or department chair in your department? (Please check one)
_____ Department head
_____ Department chair
_____ Other (specify)

9) How is the department head/chair selected?

10) How long does your department head/chair serve?

10a) If terms are not time limited, on average how long does a department head/chair serve in your department?

11) In your discipline, how highly regarded is your department head/chair for his/her research (current and/or past)? (Please check one)
_____ Extremely high
_____ High
_____ Average
_____ Below average
_____ Very below average

12) Some faculty in your department may be on appointment types that do not require research. For faculty on appointment types where research is expected, what is the expected percent of time they are to spend on the following. (If there is no formal or commonly understood expectation, check here, then go to 12a.) ____

____ % Teaching
____ % Service
____ % Other
_____-

100 % Time

12a) On average, what percent of time do you think these faculty actually spend on research? ____ %

13) Your department was selected for this project because your dean viewed it as highly productive in research/scholarship (e.g., high publication rate, grant getting success, faculty with research/scholarly awards). Please indicate on the line below how long (e.g., how many years) your department has been highly research productive:

0—1—2—3—4—5—6—7—8—9—10—over 10 years
        (Years)

Thank you for completing this form. Please return by January 24, 2002, in the enclosed envelope to:

Carole Bland, Ph.D.
Family Practice and Community Health
306 Bell Museum
10 Church Street SE
Minneapolis, MN 55455
Phone: 612-624-2622 Fax: 612-624-25

Demographic Survey Results of Participating Departments (n = 32)

Number of:	Valid n	Mean	Median	Std. Dev.	Min	Max
Master's students	28	52.9	8.5	88.3	0	300
Ph.D. students	28	43.0	26.0	53.8	0	200
Advanced professional students	28	47.3	0	153.2	0	750
Other graduate students	28	10.1	0	19.2	0	75

What was the total 2000–2001 budget of your department?
(Reported in millions of dollars)

Valid n	Mean	Median	Std. Dev.	Min	Max
26	12.8	8.8	14.5	.80	55

Please share the sources for your total budget by telling what percent of the revenues for your department are from each of the following:

	Valid n	Mean	Median	Std. Dev.	Min	Max
Central support (Tuition, state support, indirect dollars)	27	53.5	44.0	31.6	8.0	100
External direct dollars	27	32.1	35.0	29.8	0	90
Gifts	27	5.6	2.0	9.4	0	39
Other	27	8.8	0	15.2	0	50

For faculty on appointment types where research is expected, what is the expected percent of time they are to spend on the following:

	Valid n	Mean	Median	Std. Dev.	Min	Max
Teaching percent	23	38.7	40.0	10.9	15	60
Service percent	18	14.3	10.0	6.7	5	33
Research percent	30	46.2	50.0	14.1	10	85
Other percent	6	28.0	26.5	16.2	5	50

Please indicate how many years your department has been highly research productive:

	Valid n	Mean	Median	Std. Dev.	Min	Max
	32	10	11	2.5	2	11

Department: Faculty and Staff

	Valid n	Mean	Median	Std. Dev.	Min	Max
Total full-time faculty	37	28.22	22	19.81	11	101
Professors	37	11.84	10	7.39	3	34
Associate professors	37	6.78	5	4.52	1	20
Assistant professors	36	8.81	6	9.92	1	46
Other instructor/ regents professors	16	2.38	1	2.39	1	10
Total part-time faculty	23	5.52	2	8.53	1	35
Professors	15	2.00	1	1.81	1	8
Associate professors	11	5.82	3	9.88	1	35
Assistant professors	5	4.80	4	3.56	1	9
Other instructor/ regents professors	7	1.29	1	0.49	1	2
Administrative and support staff						
Full-time: Civil service and bargaining unit	37	33.03	18	47.70	1	216
Full-time: Professional and administrative staff	35	17.17	14	13.36	1	51
Part-time: Civil service and bargaining unit	29	7.34	2	15.18	1	66
Part-time: Professional and administrative staff	29	5.24	3	6.98	1	36

How does the average faculty salary in your department compare to peer institutions?

Significantly higher	Somewhat higher	Comparable	Somewhat lower	Significantly lower
0	3	13	12	4

Where are the offices of the majority of your faculty located?

All in one building on one floor	All in one building on different floors	In different closely located buildings	In different buildings far apart from each other
8	13	8	3

Do you use the term department head or department chair

Department head	Department chair	Other
15	12	4

In your discipline, how highly regarded is your department head/chair for his/her research?

Extremely high	High	Average	Below average	Very below average
13	11	5	1	0

How does your department rank nationally among public institutions with regard to research?

Top 5%	Top 10%	Top 20%	Top 30%	Top 50%
9	14	3	0	1

What is the basis for this rank estimate?
    National Institutes of Health ranking (n = 3)
    U.S. News & World Report (n = 9)
    Natonal Research Council data (n = 5)
    Independent study (n = 2)
    Personal observation (n = 6)
    Other data (n = 11)

Brief, Narrative Description of the University of Minnesota[1]

As described in the preface and in Appendix A, the study reported in this book took place entirely at the University of Minnesota. Thus, the reader might wonder, how generalizable are the findings to other settings, to my setting? Because our findings are highly congruent with the literature on research productivity, we believe much of the information is generalizable to other settings. Further, the University of Minnesota is a highly diverse institution with 20 colleges on four campuses. While it is a research-intensive university, it is also a major provider of undergraduate education, graduate, and professional education. Its colleges range from a two-year school (General College) dedicated to preparing students for successful transfer to degree-granting university colleges, to a rural four-year liberal arts college, to a medical school. Also, in presenting this information at national meetings, we have always asked the participants: "Is this information useful to you in your college or university?" The response has consistently been "yes." It is not that all the findings are perfectly generalizable, but again and again participants would point out several that they could immediately take home and use as presented or how they would adapt the information for their culture or how a finding caused them to think about an entirely different strategy that would work in their setting. It is our hope that this is what happens for each reader of this book.

The following brief description of the University of Minnesota is provided for the reader wishing more information on the context of the study reported in this book. More detailed information can be found at http://www.umn.edu.

University of Minnesota
The University of Minnesota was established in 1851, seven years before the territory of Minnesota became a state. With its four campuses, it is one of the most comprehensive universities in the country and ranks among the most prestigious universities in the United States. It is both the state land grant university, with a strong tradition of education and public service, and a major research institution, with scholars of national and international reputation.

The University of Minnesota, Twin Cities
The University of Minnesota, Twin Cities, is a classic Big Ten campus in the heart of the Minneapolis–St. Paul metropolitan area. The largest of the four

campuses, it is made up of 20 colleges and offers 161 bachelor's degrees, 218 master's degrees, 144 doctoral degrees, and 5 professional degrees in medicine, law, pharmacy, veterinary medicine, and dentistry. It has a host of nationally recognized, highly ranked programs. In 2001 and 2002, the university's Twin Cities campus was ranked among the top three public research universities in the nation (University of Florida study).

The University of Minnesota, Duluth

The University of Minnesota, Duluth (UMD) offers 11 bachelor's degrees in 70 majors. Its School of Medicine offers a two-year basic science program leading to an MD through the Twin Cities Campus Medical School. In addition, UMD offers graduate programs in 18 different fields. UMD ranks among the top midwestern universities according to *U.S. News & World Report.*

The University of Minnesota, Morris

The University of Minnesota, Morris (UMM), offers baccalaureate degrees in 30 majors and course work in seven preprofessional areas. UMM's distinctive mission and strong academic quality have repeatedly received national recognition in feature articles in *Money Magazine, U.S. News & World Report,* and *Kiplinger's Changing Times* and high rankings in *Peterson's Guide to Competitive Colleges* and the *Fiske Guide to Colleges.*

The University of Minnesota, Crookston

The University of Minnesota, Crookston (UMC), offers bachelor's degrees in 20 programs and associate's degrees in 13. UMC is internationally recognized for its technology initiatives, which have provided individual laptop computers to all full-time students since 1993. Named a *U.S. News & World Report* "Best College" for the past three consecutive years, UMC also has been featured as a national leader in innovative polytechnic education by Microsoft, IBM, and *PC Week Magazine.*

In the Rochester area, the University of Minnesota, through a partnership with the Minnesota State Colleges and Universities, extends upper-division undergraduate and postbaccalaureate degree programs to people in southeastern Minnesota.

Other important parts of the university are institutes, stations, and centers such as the Supercomputing Institute, the Hormel Institute, the Forestry and Biological Stations, the Horticultural Center, the Cancer Center, and the Landscape Arboretum. Through the Extension Service, the university is present in each of Minnesota's 87 counties.

The university consistently ranks among the top 20 public universities in the nation, based on sources such as the National Research Council, *U.S. News & World Report,* and other rankings. Several programs rank among the top 10 in the nation such as chemical engineering, geography, psychology, mechanical engineering, economics, forestry, applied mathematics, management information systems, pharmacy, public health, education (educational psychology, special education, vocational/technical education, and counseling/personnel services), and health services administration.

Based upon the most recent survey of the National Research Council, the scholarly quality of the University of Minnesota's faculty ranks among the top 10 public institutions in the nation.

The university received nearly $455.2 million in contract and grant awards in fiscal year 2000. In fiscal year 2002, the university filed 89 patent applications, receiving 38 new patents from the U.S. Patent and Trademark Office. In 2000, the U of M spun off 11 companies from its discoveries, ranking it fourth among 142 research universities.

Examples of research accomplishments of the faculty include such things as

- Continuing success of the world's leading kidney transplant center
- Release of over 80 new crop varieties that have increased yields worldwide
- Development of the taconite process
- Invention of the flight recorder (black box) and the retractable seat belt for cars
- Eradication of many poultry and livestock diseases
- Invention of the heart-lung machine and its use in the world's first successful open-heart surgery
- Isolation of uranium 235 (in a prototype mass spectrometer)
- Invention of the first heart pacemaker
- Development of the widely used Minnesota Multiphasic Personality Inventory (MMPI)
- Development of hundreds of cold-hardy plant varieties including fruits, vegetables, flowers, and shrubs
- Invention of a drug to treat HIV infections

Total student enrollment in 2000 was 59,185 (45,481 were on the Twin Cities campus). There were 3,409 full-time faculty. The budget for 1999–2000 was $1,873,055,500.

What all these facts and statistics add up to for the researcher at the University of Minnesota is an environment that emphasizes research, but because of its land grant status and history, also emphasizes teaching and outreach. It is also an environment where there are excellent researchers, students, and facilities in nearly any field, literally right next door.

Within this larger context, each college and each department shapes the environment as best it can to facilitate the research for its faculty members. So, while there are many common strategies used to facilitate research across the institution, there are also unique strategies, for example, that are best for fields such as chemical engineering where the faculty work on collaborative projects that are primarily externally funded and there are unique strategies for fields such as cultural studies and comparative literature where scholarly work is primarily done alone or with one or two colleagues and done largely without external funding. For this reason, in the preceding chapters, when we describe research-facilitating practices or quote directly from an interviewee, we consistently alert the reader to the field from which these are drawn.

Endnote

[1]Portions of this description were drawn from the "About the U" section of the University of Minnesota web site © 2003 Regents of the University of Minnesota. Reprinted with permission.

Leaving the University of Minnesota: Results of an Exploratory Survey of Departed Faculty, 1997–2000[1]

Executive Summary
December 2001

Recognizing the need for better information on faculty research productivity at the University of Minnesota, the University Senate and the Office of the Vice Provost for Faculty and Academic Personnel initiated a task force to address this concern. The task force began its work in the 2000–2001 academic year. As part of that effort, the task force requested an exploratory survey of tenure-track and tenured faculty who had voluntarily left positions at the institution for other academic positions in recent years. The request from the task force was in keeping with an earlier recommendation from the Board of Regents that the administration more aggressively examine the reasons for faculty departures from the university. The goal of the survey was to examine the factors associated with faculty leaving the university and to glean from the findings potential policy and practice implications for the university. Forty-three faculty who departed in 1997–2000 responded to the survey. Among the most significant findings were the following:

- Although there is very little published research on faculty departures in higher education, many institutions (including Penn State, Michigan State, and Iowa) conduct regular exit interviews or surveys of their departing faculty, and well-established models exist for these efforts.

- Given the opportunity, former University of Minnesota, Twin Cities, faculty will respond to requests that they provide information on the circumstances of their departures.

- Departing University of Minnesota, Twin Cities, faculty for the period 1997 to 2000 reported mean overall satisfaction scores just above "moderately satisfied."

- Individual considerations, such as salary and course assignments, were of moderate importance and satisfaction to departing faculty.

- Departmental factors, such as the perceived social climate, management effectiveness, and sense of collegiality in the unit, were very important to departing faculty and were the greatest source of dissatisfaction among respondents.

• University and college policies and practices, such as the perceived commitment to disciplinary and interdisciplinary areas, were very important to departing faculty, but had only moderate associations with faculty satisfaction levels.

• University/college items that did have such associations were those most connected to individual departments and disciplines.

• Departing faculty were very satisfied with community life in the Twin Cities and this factor did not seem to be critical in decisions to depart.

• A majority of departed faculty reported having received a retention offer from the university before leaving the institution.

The findings of this analysis must, of course, be viewed very cautiously. Only tenured or tenure-track faculty leaving for tenured or tenure-track positions elsewhere were in the sample. There is no simple way to discern in these data which faculty among those leaving the institution were most valued and productive and which faculty were encouraged to leave the university and perhaps were better suited for positions at other institutions. Analysis of the most productive faculty leaving the university would be more useful than aggregate analysis across all departing faculty. One major college chose not to provide forwarding information for its departed faculty. The survey was sent as much as six months to three years after departure, rather than simultaneously with departure. Only faculty from the Twin Cities campus were included, so no generalizations to other campuses of the University of Minnesota are warranted. The small size of the sample precluded separate analyses for significant subgroups (e.g., faculty of color, faculty from individual colleges). The sample was too small for intensive multivariate analysis, so descriptive data and simple correlations drive the conclusions, without adequate controls for confounding factors. Thus, causation cannot be inferred from the data presented here. Finally, although every effort was made to increase the validity and reliability of the responses, there is no assurance that individuals' responses reflected accurately the full reasons for their departures. For all of these reasons, the findings do not lead definitively to recommendations for administrative actions at either the unit or the central levels.

The analysis here was exploratory, and many limitations apply. Nevertheless, the early evidence presented here can ideally help guide further investigations of ways the university can do a better job in retaining its most valued faculty.

Endnote

[1]This project was conducted at the request of the University of Minnesota Faculty Development Working Group. The primary contributors to the report are James C. Hearn, Susan K. Jensen, and Karin L. Gustafson. The authors gratefully acknowledge the helpful suggestions of Carole Bland, Carol Carrier, Darwin Hendel, and Virginia Seybold on earlier versions of this report. A complete copy of the report is available at http://www1.umn.edu/usenate /scfa/exitsurveyreport.html.

Related Works

Many excellent books are available which, in broadly addressing issues of leadership for department chairs, are useful complements to this book on research productivity practices. Below is a sample list of these related publications.

Creswell, J. W., Wheeler D. W., Seagren, A. T., Egly, N. J. & Beyer, K. D. (1990). *The academic chairperson's handbook.* Lincoln, NE: University of Nebraska Press.

The Department Chair: A Resource for Academic Administrators. Published quarterly by Anker Publishing Company, Inc., P.O. Box 249, Bolton, MA 01740–0249. This periodical contains practical information, useful advice, and other resources that can be readily applied. To view a sample go to http://www.ankerpub.com/news.html

Hecht, I. W. D., Higgerson, M. L., Gmelch, W. H., & Tucker, A. (1999). *The department chair as academic leader.* Phoenix, AZ: American Council on Education/Oryx.

Henkel, M. (2000). *Academic identities and policy change in higher education.* London, England: J. Kingsley.

Knight, P. T., & Trowler, P. R. (Eds.). (2001). *Departmental leadership in higher education.* Philadelphia, PA: Society for Research into Higher Education, Open University.

Leaming, D. R. (1998). *Academic leadership: A practical guide to chairing the department.* Bolton, MA: Anker.

Leaming, D. R. (Ed.). (2003). *Managing people: A guide for department chairs and deans.* Bolton, MA: Anker.

Lucas, A. F. (Ed.). (1989). *New directions for teaching and learning: No. 37. The department chairperson's role in enhancing college teaching.* San Francisco, CA: Jossey-Bass.

Lucas, A. F., & Associates. (2000). *Leading academic change: Essential roles for department chairs.* San Francisco, CA: Jossey-Bass.

Seagren, A. T., Creswell, J. W., & Wheeler, D. W. (2000). *The department chair: New roles, responsibilities, and challenges.* San Francisco, CA: Jossey-Bass.

Tierney, W. G. (Ed.). (1999). *Faculty productivity: Facts, fiction, and issues* (Garland Series in Higher Education, Vol. 15). New York, NY: Routledge-Falmer.

Tucker, A. (1984). *Chairing the academic department: Leadership among peers* (2nd ed.). New York, NY: American Council on Education/ Macmillan.

Walvoord, B. E., Carey, A. K., Smith, H. L., Soled, S. W., Way, P. K., & Zorn, D. (2000). *Academic departments: How they work, how they change* (ASHE-ERIC Higher Education Report, 27[8]). San Francisco, CA: Jossey-Bass.

Wergin, J. F. (2003). *Departments that work: Building and sustaining cultures of excellence in academic programs.* Bolton, MA: Anker.

Bibliography

Allen, M. (1995, February). *Research productivity and positive teaching evaluations: Examining the relationship using meta-analysis.* Paper presented at the Western Communication Association Convention, Portland, OR. (ERIC Document Reproduction Service No. ED379705)

American Association for Higher Education Task Force on Professional Growth. (1984). *Vitality without mobility: The faculty opportunities audit* (Current Issues in Higher Education No. 4). Washington, DC: American Association for Higher Education.

Andrews, F. M. (Ed.). (1979). *Scientific productivity: The effectiveness of research groups in six countries.* Cambridge, England: Cambridge University Press.

Aran, L., & Ben-David, J. (1968). Socialization and career patterns as determinants of productivity of medical researchers. *Journal of Health and Social Behavior, 9,* 3–15.

Argyris, C. (1968). On the effectiveness of research and development organizations. *American Scientist, 56,* 344–355.

Austin, A. E., & Baldwin, R. G. (2000). *Faculty collaboration: Enhancing the quality of scholarship and teaching.* San Francisco, CA: Jossey-Bass. (Original work published 1991)

Bailey, J. G. (1994). Influences on researchers' commitment. *Higher Education Management, 6*(2), 163–177.

Baird, L. (1986). What characterizes a productive research department? *Research in Higher Education, 25,* 211–225.

Baldwin, R. G. (1990). Faculty career stages and implications for professional development. In J. H. Schuster & D. W. Wheeler (Eds.), *Enhancing faculty careers: Strategies for development and renewal* (pp. 20–40). San Francisco, CA: Jossey-Bass.

Balog, C. (1979). Multiple authorship and author collaboration in agricultural research publications. *Journal of Research Communication Studies, 2,* 159–169.

Bayer, A. E., & Smart, J. C. (1988, April). *Author collaborative styles in academic scholarship.* Paper presented at the annual meeting of the American Educational Research Association, New Orleans, LA.

Bean, J. P. (1982, March). *A causal model of faculty research productivity.* Paper presented at the annual meeting of the American Educational Research Association, New York, NY.

Beaver, D. deB., & Rosen, R. (1978). Studies in scientific collaboration, Part I: The professional origins of scientific co-authorship. *Scientometrics, 1*(1), 65–84.

Beaver, D. deB., & Rosen, R. (1979a). Studies in scientific collaboration, Part II: Scientific co-authorship, research productivity and visibility in the French scientific elite, 1799-1830. *Scientometrics, 1*(2), 133–149.

Beaver, D. deB., & Rosen, R. (1979b). Studies in scientific collaboration, Part III: Professionalization and the natural history of modern scientific co-authorship. *Scientometrics, 1*(3), 231–245.

Bellas, M. L., & Toutkoushian, R. K. (1999). Faculty time allocations and research productivity: Gender, race, and family effects. *Review of Higher Education, 22*(4), 367–390.

Bensimon, E. M., Neumann, A., & Birnbaum, R. (1989). *Making sense of administrative leadership: The "L" word in higher education.* Washington, DC: Association for the Study of Higher Education.

Berelson, B. (1960). *Graduate education in the United States.* New York, NY: McGraw-Hill.

Bergquist, W. H. (1992). *The four cultures of the academy: Insights and strategies for improving leadership in collegiate organizations.* San Francisco, CA: Jossey-Bass.

Bergquist, W. H., Greenburg, E. M., & Klaum, G. A. (1993). *In our fifties: Voices of men and women reinventing their lives.* San Francisco, CA: Jossey-Bass.

Biglan, A. (1973). Relationships between subject matter characteristics and the structure and output of university departments. *Journal of Applied Psychology, 57*(3), 204–213.

Birnbaum, P. H. (1983). Predictors of long-term research performance. In S. R. Epton, R. L. Payne, & A. W. Pearson (Eds.), *Managing interdisciplinary research* (pp. 47–59). New York, NY: John Wiley & Sons.

Blackburn, R. T. (1979). Academic careers: Patterns and possibilities. In J. B. Francis (Ed.), *Faculty career development* (pp. 25–27). Washington, DC: American Association for Higher Education.

Blackburn, R. T., Behymer, C. E., & Hall, D. E. (1978). Research note: Correlates of faculty publications. *Sociology of Education, 51,* 132–141.

Blackburn, R. T., & Lawrence, J. H. (1986). Aging and the quality of faculty job performance. *Review of Educational Research, 56*(3), 265–290.

Blackburn, R. T., & Pitney, J. A. (1988). *Performance appraisal for faculty: Implications for higher education* (Technical Report 88-D-002.0). Ann Arbor, MI: National Center for Research to Improve Postsecondary Teaching and Learning. (ERIC Document Reproduction Service No. ED316066)

Bland, C. J. (1997). Beyond corporate downsizing: A better way for medical schools to succeed in a changing world. *Academic Medicine, 72*(6), 13–19. With permission of *Academic Medicine.*

Bland, C. J., & Bergquist, W. H. (1997). *The vitality of senior faculty members: Snow on the roof—fire in the furnace* (ASHE-ERIC Higher Education Report, 25[7]). Washington, DC: George Washington University, Graduate School of Education and Human Development.

Bland, C. J., Center, B. A., Finstad, D. A., Risbey, K. R., & Staples, J. G. (2004). *The impact of appointment type on the productivity and commitment of full-time faculty in research and doctoral institutions.* Minneapolis, MN: University of Minnesota Medical School, Department of Family Practice and Community Health. Manuscript submitted for publication.

Bland, C. J., Center, B. A., Finstad, D. A., Risbey, K. R., & Staples, J. G. (in press). A theoretical, practical, predictive model of research productivity. *Academic Medicine.*

Bland, C. J., Hitchcock, M. A., Anderson, W. A., & Stritter, F. T. (1987). Faculty development fellowship programs in family medicine. *Journal of Medical Education, 62,* 632–641.

Bland, C. J., & Holloway, R. I. (1995). A crisis of mission: Faculty roles and rewards in an era of health-care reform. *Change, 27*(5), 30–35.

Bland, C. J., & Ruffin, M. T., IV. (1992). Characteristics of a productive research environment: Literature review. *Academic Medicine, 67*(6), 385–397.

Bland, C. J., & Schmitz, C. C. (1986, January). Characteristics of the successful researcher and implications for faculty development. *Journal of Medical Education, 61,* 22–31.

Bland, C. J., Seaquist, E., Pacala, J. T., Center, B., & Finstad, D. (2002). One school's strategy to assess and improve the vitality of its faculty. *Academic Medicine, 77*(5), 368–376.

Bland, C. J., Starnaman, S. M., Hembroff, L., Perlstadt, H., Henry, R. C., & Richards, R. W. (1999). Leadership behaviors for successful university-community collaborations to change curricula. *Academic Medicine, 74*(11), 1227–1237.

Blau, J. R. (1976). Scientific recognition: Academic context and professional role. *Social Studies of Science, 6,* 533–545.

Bohen, J. S., & Stiles, J. (1998). Experimenting with models of faculty collaboration: Factors that promote their success. In S. H. Frost (Ed.), *New directions for institutional research: No. 100. Using teams in higher education: Cultural foundations for productive change* (pp. 39–55). San Francisco, CA: Jossey-Bass.

Boice, R. (1986). Faculty development via field programs for middle-aged, disillusioned faculty. *Research in Higher Education, 25*(2), 115–135.

Boice, R. (1993). Primal origins and later correctives for mid-career disillusionment. In M. L. Finkelstein & M. W. LaCelle-Peterson (Eds.), *New directions for teaching and learning: No.55. Developing senior faculty as teachers* (pp. 115–135). San Francisco, CA: Jossey-Bass.

Bowen, H. R., & Schuster, J. H. (1986). *American professors: A national resource imperiled.* New York, NY: Oxford University Press.

Bozeman, B., & Lee, S. (2003, February). *The impact of research collaboration on scientific productivity.* Paper presented at the annual meeting of the American Association for the Advancement of Science, Denver, CO.

Brand, M. (2000). Changing faculty roles in research universities: Using the pathways strategy. *Change, 32*(6), 42–45.

Braskamp, L. A., & Associates. (1982, March). *Faculty development and achievement: A faculty's view.* Paper presented at the annual meeting of the American Educational Research Association, New York, NY. (ERIC Document Reproduction Service No. ED216626)

Braxton, J. M. (1983). Teaching as performance of scholarly-based course activities: A perspective on the relationship between teaching and research. *Review of Higher Education, 7*(1), 21–33.

Braxton, J. M. (1996). Contrasting perspectives on the relationship between teaching and research. In J. M. Braxton (Ed.), *New directions for institutional research: No. 90. Faculty teaching and research: Is there a conflict?* (pp. 1–15). San Francisco, CA: Jossey-Bass.

Business–Higher Education Forum. (2001). *Working together, creating knowledge: The university–industry research collaboration initiative.* Washington, DC: American Council on Education and the National Alliance of Business.

Byrne, M. W., & Keefe, M. R. (2002). Building research competence in nursing through mentoring. *Journal of Nursing Scholarship, 34*(4), 391–396.

Cameron, S. W., & Blackburn, R. T. (1981). Sponsorship and academic career success. *Current Issues in Higher Education, 52,* 369–377.

Cascio, W. F. (1993). Downsizing: What do we know? What have we learned? *Academy of Management Executive, 7*(1), 95–104.

Cascio, W. F., & Morris, J. R. (1996). *The impact of downsizing on the financial performance of firms.* Denver, CO: University of Colorado–Denver, College of Business and Administration and Graduate School of Business Administration.

Center for the Study of Higher and Postsecondary Education & Center for the Education of Women. (1999). *University of Michigan faculty work-life study report.* Ann Arbor, MI: The Regents of the University of Michigan.

Cini, M. A. (2001, Spring). Group newcomers: From disruption to innovation. *Group Facilitation: A Research and Applications Journal, 3,* 3–13.

Clark, S. M., & Lewis, D. R. (Eds.). (1985). *Faculty vitality and institutional productivity: Critical perspectives for higher education.* New York, NY: Teachers College Press.

Cole, S., & Cole, J. (1967). Scientific output and recognition: A study in the operation of the award system in science. *American Sociological Review, 32,* 377–390.

Collins, J. C., & Porras, J. I. (1994). *Built to last: Successful habits of visionary companies.* New York, NY: HarperCollins.

Corcoran, M., & Clark, S. M. (1984). Professional socialization and contemporary career attitudes of three faculty generations. *Research in Higher Education, 20*(2), 131–153.

Corcoran, M., & Clark, S. M. (1985). The "stuck" professor: Insights into an aspect of the faculty vitality issue. In C. Watson (Ed.), *The professoriate: Occupation in crisis* (pp. 57–81). Toronto, Canada: Ontario Institute for Studies in Education.

Crane, D. (1972). *Invisible colleges: Diffusion of knowledge in scientific communities.* Chicago, IL: University of Chicago Press.

Creswell, J. W. (1985). *Faculty research performance: Lessons from the sciences and social sciences.* Washington, DC: Association for the Study of Higher Education. (ERIC Document Reproduction Service No. ED267677)

Creswell, J. W. (2002). *Educational research: Planning, conducting, and evaluating quantitative and qualitative research.* Upper Saddle River, NJ: Pearson Education.

Creswell, J. W., & Bean, J. P. (1996). Research output, socialization, and the Biglan model. *Research in Higher Education, 15,* 69–89.

Creswell, J. W., Wheeler, D. W., Seagren, A. T., Egly, N. J., & Beyer, K. D. (1990). *The academic chairperson's handbook.* Lincoln, NE: University of Nebraska Press.

Culpepper, L., & Franks, P. F. (1984). Family medicine research: Status at the end of the first decade. *Journal of the American Medical Association, 249*(1), 63–68.

Curtis, P., Dickinson, P., Steiner, J., Lanphear, B., & Vu, K. (2003). Building capacity for research in family medicine: Is the blueprint faulty? *Family Medicine, 35*(2), 124–130.

Denton, J. J., & Hunter, F. A. (1997). The multiple effects of influencing external funding productivity. *Research Management Review, 9*(1), 37–50.

Diamond, A. (1985). The money value of citations to single-authored and multiple-authored articles. *Scientometrics, 8*(5–6), 315–320.

Dill, D. D. (1982). The management of academic culture: Notes on the management of meaning and social integration. *Higher Education, 11*(3), 303–320.

Dill, D. D. (1985). Theory versus practice in the staffing of R & D laboratories. *R & D Management, 15*, 227–241.

Dill, D. D. (1986a, April). *Local barriers and facilitators of research.* Paper presented at the annual meeting of the American Educational Research Association, San Francisco, CA.

Dill, D. D. (1986b). Research as a scholarly activity: Context and culture. In J. W. Creswell (Ed.), *Measuring faculty research performance* (pp. 1–23). San Francisco, CA: Jossey-Bass.

Dohm, F. A., & Cummings, W. (2002). Research mentoring and women in clinical psychology. *Psychology of Women Quarterly, 26*(2), 163–167.

Drew, D. E. (1985). *Strengthening academic science.* New York, NY: Praeger.

Drotar, D., & Avner, E. D. (2003). Critical choices in mentoring the next generation of academic pediatricians: Nine circles of hell or salvation? *Journal of Pediatrics, 142*(1), 1–2.

Dundar, H., & Lewis, D. R. (1998). Determinants of research productivity in higher education. *Research in Higher Education, 39*(6), 607–631.

Eckert, R. E., & Stecklein, J. E. (1961). *Job motivations and satisfactions of college teachers: A study of faculty members in Minnesota colleges* (Cooperative Research Report No. 7). Washington, DC: U.S. Department of Health, Education, and Welfare.

El-Khawas, E. (1991). Senior faculty in academe: Active, committed to the teaching role. *Research Briefs, 2*(5), 1–12.

Engebretson, J., & Wardell, D. W. (1997). The essence of partnership in research. *Journal of Professional Nursing, 13*(1), 38–47.

Epton, S. R., Payne, R. L., & Pearson, A. W. (Eds.). (1983). *Managing interdisciplinary research.* New York, NY: John Wiley & Sons.

Fairweather, J. S. (2002). The mythologies of faculty productivity: Implications for institutional policy and decision-making. *Journal of Higher Education, 73*(1), 26–48.

Feldman, K. A. (1987). Research productivity and scholarly accomplishment of college teachers as related to their instructional effectiveness: A review and exploration. *Research in Higher Education, 26*(3), 227–298.

Finkelstein, M. (1984). *The American academic profession: A synthesis of social scientific inquiry since World War II.* Columbus, OH: Ohio State University Press.

Finkelstein, M. J. (1996). Faculty vitality in higher education. In *Integrating research on faculty: Seeking new ways to communicate about the academic life of faculty* (pp. 71–80). Conference report: Results of a forum sponsored by the National Center for Education Statistics, the Association for Institutional Research, and the American Association of State Colleges and Universities, January 10–11, 1994. Washington, DC: U.S. Department of Education, National Center for Education Statistics, NCES 96 849.

Finkelstein, M. J., & Schuster, J. H. (2001). Assessing the silent revolution: How changing demographics are reshaping the academic profession. *AAHE Bulletin,* 3–7.

Fox, M. F. (1991). Gender, environmental milieu, and productivity in science. In H. Zuckerman, J. R. Cote, & J. T. Bruer (Eds.), *The outer circle: Women in the scientific community* (pp. 188–204). New York, NY: W.W. Norton.

Fox, M. F. (1992). Research, teaching, and publication productivity: Mutuality versus competition in academia. *Sociology of Education, 65,* 293–305.

Fox, M. F., & Faver, C. A. (1984). Independence and cooperation in research: The motivations and costs of collaboration. *Journal of Higher Education, 55*(3), 347–359.

Fox, K. J., & Milbourne, R. (1999). What determines research output of academic economists? *Economic Record, 75*(230), 256–267.

Gappa, J. M. (1996). *Off the tenure track: Six models for full-time, nontenurable appointments* (AAHE Working Paper Series 10). Washington, DC: American Association for Higher Education. (ERIC Document Reproduction Service No. ED424820)

Gething, L., & Leelarthaepin, B. (2000). Strategies for promoting research participation among nurses employed as academics in the university sector. *Nurse Education Today, 20*(2), 147–154.

Gibbons, M. (1998, October). *Higher education relevance in the 21st century.* Paper prepared as a contribution to the United Nations Educational, Social, and Cultural Organization World Conference on Higher Education, Paris, France.

Gmelch, W. H., & Miskin, V. D. (1993). *Leadership skills for department chairs.* Bolton, MA: Anker.

Goffman, W., & Warren, K. S. (1980). *Scientific information systems and the principle of selectivity.* New York, NY: Praeger.

Green, R. G., Bellin, M. H., & Baskind, F. B. (2002). Results of the doctoral faculty publication project: Journal article productivity and its correlates in the 1990s. *Journal of Social Work Education, 38*(1), 135–152.

Gustad, J. W. (1960). *The career decisions of college teachers: A report of the southern region* (SREB Research Monograph Series No. 2). Atlanta, GA: Southern Regional Education Board. (ERIC Document Reproduction Service No. ED000261)

Hargens, L. L. (1978). Relations between work habits, research technologies, and eminence in science. *Sociology of Work and Work Occupations, 5*(1), 97–112.

Hearn, J. C. (1999). Pay and performance in the university: An examination of faculty salaries. *Review of Higher Education, 22*(4), 391–410.

Hearn, J. C., & Anderson, M. S. (2001). Clinical faculty in schools of education: Using staff differentiation to address disparate goals. In W. Tierney (Ed.), *Faculty work in schools of education: Rethinking roles and rewards for the twenty-first century* (pp. 125–149). Albany, NY: State University of New York Press.

Hecht, I. W. D., Higgerson, M. L., Gmelch, W. H., & Tucker, A. (1999). *The department chair as academic leader.* Phoenix, AZ: American Council on Education/Oryx Press.

Hemphill, J. K. (1955). Leadership behavior associated with the administrative reputation of college departments. *Journal of Educational Psychology, 46*(7), 385–401.

Hitchcock, M. A., Bland, C. J., Hekelman, F. P., & Blumenthal, M. G. (1995). Professional networks: The influence of colleagues on the academic success of faculty. *Academic Medicine, 70*(12), 1108–1116.

Hodder, P. (1979). Limits to collaborative authorship in science publishing. *Journal of Research Communication Studies, 2,* 169–178.

Howard, A. (1984). *Cool at the top: Personality characteristics of successful executives.* Unpublished manuscript.

Hoyt, D. P., & Spangler, R. K. (1978). *Administrative effectiveness of the academic department head: II. Correlates of effectiveness* (Research Report #42). Manhattan, KS: Kansas State University, Office of Educational Research. (ERIC Document Reproduction Service No. ED171215)

Hutchens, J. (1998). Research and professional development collaborations among university faculty and education practitioners. *Arts Education Policy Review, 99*(5), 35–40.

The Institute for Research on Higher Education. (2000, March/April). Why is research the rule? The impact of incentive systems on faculty behavior. *Change, 32*(2), 53–56.

Johnston, R. (1994). Effects of resource concentration on research performance. *Higher Education, 28*, 25–37.

Jones, R. F., & Gold, J. S. (2001). The present and future of appointment, tenure and compensation policies for medical school clinical faculty. *Academic Medicine, 76*(10), 993–1004.

Jordan, J. M., Meador, M., & Walters, S. (1988). Effects of department size and organization on the research productivity of academic economists. *Economics of Education Review, 7*(2), 251–255.

Kalivoda, P., & Sorrell, G. R. (1994). Nurturing faculty vitality by matching institutional interventions with career-stage needs. *Innovative Higher Education, 18*(4), 255–272.

Kanter, R. M. (1979). Changing the shape of work: Reform in academe. *Current Issues in Higher Education, 1*, 3–10.

Kapel, D. E., & Wexler, N. (1970). Faculty attitude toward research in an emergent college. *Journal of Experimental Education, 38*(3), 44–47.

Katerndahl, D. A. (2000). Effect of attendance at an annual primary care research methods conference on research productivity and development. *Family Medicine, 32*(10), 701–708.

Katz, J. S., & Martin, B. R. (1997). What is research collaboration? *Research Policy, 26*, 1–18.

Katz, R. L. (1978). Job longevity as a situational factor in job satisfaction. *Administrative Science Quarterly, 23*, 204–223.

Kellett, C. E. (1999). Transformation in the university and the community: The benefits and barriers of collaboration. *Journal of Family and Consumer Services, 91*(2), 31–35.

Kelly, M. E. (1986). Enablers and inhibitors to research productivity among high and low producing vocational education faculty members. *Journal of Vocational Education Research, 11*(4), 63–80.

Knight, P. T., & Trowler, P. R. (Eds.). (2001). *Departmental leadership in higher education.* Philadelphia, PA: Society for Research into Higher Education, Open University.

Knight, W. H., & Holen, M. C. (1985). Leadership and the perceived effectiveness of department chairpersons. *Journal of Higher Education, 56*(6), 678–690.

Knorr, K., Mittermeir, R., Aichholzer, G., & Waller, C. (1979). Individual publication productivity as a social position effect in academic and industrial research units. In F. M. Andrews (Ed.), *Scientific productivity: The effectiveness of research groups in six countries* (pp. 55–94). Cambridge, England: Cambridge University Press.

Kotrlik, J. W., Bartlett, J. E., II, Higgins, C. C., & Williams, H. A. (2001, December 12). *Factors associated with research productivity of agricultural education faculty.* Paper presented at the 28th annual National Agricultural Education Research Conference, New Orleans, LA. Retrieved February 19, 2004, from http://aaaeonline.ifas.ufl.edu/NAERC/2001/Papers/kotrlik.pdf

Kuh, G., & Hu, S. (2001). Learning productivity at research universities. *Journal of Higher Education, 72*(1), 1–28.

Latham, G. P., & Mitchell, T. R. (1976). *Behavioral criteria and potential reinforcers for the engineer/scientist in an industrial setting.* Washington, DC: American Psychological Association.

Latham, G. P., & Wexley, K. N. (1981). *Increasing productivity through performance appraisal.* Reading, MA: Addison-Wesley.

Lawani, S. M. (1986). Some bibliometric correlates of quality in scientific research. *Scientometrics, 9*(1-2), 13–25.

Lawrence, J. H., & Blackburn, R. T. (1985). Faculty careers: Maturation, demographic, and historical effects. *Research in Higher Education, 22*(2), 135–154.

Lawrence, J. H., & Blackburn, R. T. (1988). Age as a predictor of faculty productivity: Three conceptual approaches. *Journal of Higher Education, 59*(1), 22-38.

Leaming, D. R. (1998). *Academic leadership: A practical guide to chairing the department.* Bolton, MA: Anker.

Lee, T. H., Ognibene, F. P., & Schwartz, J. S. (1991). Correlates of external research support among respondents to the 1990 American Federation for Clinical Research survey. *Clinical Research, 39*(2), 135–144.

Lewis, D. R., & Becker, W. E. (Eds.). (1979). *Academic rewards in higher education.* Cambridge, MA: Ballinger.

Lightfield, E. T. (1971). Output and recognition of sociologists. *American Sociologist, 6,* 128–133.

Linsky, A. S., & Straus, M. A. (1975). Student evaluations, research productivity, and eminence of college faculty. *Journal of Higher Education, 46*(1), 89–102.

Locke, E. A., Fitzpatrick, W., & White, F. M. (1983). Job satisfaction and role clarity among university and college faculty. *Review of Higher Education, 6*(4), 343–365.

Long, J. S., & McGinnis, R. (1981). Organizational context and scientific productivity. *American Sociological Review, 46,* 422–442.

Lucas, A. F. (Ed.). (1989). *New directions for teaching and learning: No. 37. The department chairperson's role in enhancing college teaching.* San Francisco, CA: Jossey-Bass.

Lucas, A. F., & Associates. (2000). *Leading academic change: Essential roles for department chairs.* San Francisco, CA: Jossey-Bass.

Mainous, A. G., III, Hueston, W. J., Ye, X., & Bazell, C. (2000). A comparison of family medicine research in research intense and less intense institutions. *Archives of Family Medicine, 9*(10), 1100–1104.

Manis, J. G. (1951). Some academic influences upon publication productivity. *Social Forces, 29,* 267–272.

McCarthy, M. J. (1972). *Correlates of effectiveness among academic department heads.* Manhattan, KS: Manhattan State University.

McGee, G. W., & Ford, R. C. (1987). Faculty research productivity and intention to change positions. *Review of Higher Education, 11,* 1–16.

McWilliam, C. L., Desai, K., & Greig, B. (1997). Bridging town and gown: Building research partnerships between community-based professional providers and academia. *Journal of Professional Nursing, 13*(5), 307–315.

Meagher, B. M., & Gray, D. O. (2002, November). *Faculty outcomes from industry–university collaboration: A multivariate predictive study.* Paper presented at the meeting of the Fourth Triple Helix Conference, Copenhagen, Denmark–Lund, Sweden.

Melicher, R. W. (2000, Spring/Summer). The perceived value of research and teaching mentoring by finance academicians. *Financial Practice and Education, 166–174.*

Meltzer, L. (1956). Scientific productivity in organizational settings. *Journal of Social Issues, 12,* 32–40.

Mervis, J. (1999). Cheap labor is key to U.S. research productivity. *Science, 285*(5433), 1,519.

Michalak, S. J., Jr., & Friedrich, R. J. (1981). Research productivity and teaching effectiveness at a small liberal arts college. *Journal of Higher Education, 52*(6), 578–597.

Miles, M. W., & Huberman, A. M. (1994). *Qualitative data analysis: An expanded sourcebook.* Thousand Oaks, CA: Sage.

Mills, O. F. (1995, March). Factors associated with research productivity in family practice residencies. *Family Medicine, 27*(3), 188–193.

Mitchell, J. E., & Rebne, D. S. (1995). Nonlinear effects of teaching and consulting on academic research productivity. *Socio-Economic Planning Sciences, 29*(1), 47–57.

Moed, H. F., de Bruin, R. E., & Straathof, A. (1992). *Measurement of national scientific output and international scientific cooperation in CEC-related areas of science during 1985–1990: Updating the study "Measurement of scientific cooperation and co-authorship in CEC-related areas of science" by F. Narin and E. S. Whitlow.* Luxembourg: Commission of the European Committees, Directorate-General, Telecommunications, Information Industries and Innovation.

Morton, J. A. (1964, May). From research to technology. *International Science and Technology, 29,* 82–92.

Mundt, M. H. (2001). An external mentor program: Stimulus for faculty research development. *Journal of Professional Nursing, 17*(1), 40–45.

National Center for Education Statistics. (2002). *Tenure status of postsecondary instructional faculty and staff: 1992-1998.* Washington, DC: U.S. Department of Education, National Center for Education Statistics. (NCES 2002-210)

Norbeck, J. S. (1998). Teaching, research, and service: Striking the balance in doctoral education. *Journal of Professional Nursing, 14*(4), 197–205.

Noser, T. C., Manakyan, H., & Tanner, J. R. (1996). Research productivity and perceived teaching effectiveness: A survey of economics faculty. *Research in Higher Education, 37*(3), 299–321.

Nudelman, A. E., & Landers, C. E. (1972). The failure of 100 divided by 3 to equal 33-1/3. *The American Sociologist, 7*(9), 9.

Nyiendo, J., Lloyd, C., & Haas, M. (2001). Practice-based research: The Oregon Experience. *Journal of Manipulative and Physiological Therapeutics, 24*(1), 25–34.

Okrasa, W. (1987). Differences in scientific productivity of research units: Measurement and analysis of output inequality. *Scientometrics, 12*, 221–239.

Olsen, D., & Simmons, A. (1996). The research versus teaching debate: Untangling the relationships. In J. M. Braxton (Ed.), *New directions for institutional research: No. 90. Faculty teaching and research: Is there a conflict?* (pp. 31–39). San Francisco, CA: Jossey-Bass.

Pao, M. L. (1980). Co-authorship and productivity. In *Proceedings of the 43rd American Society for Information Science,* 17 (pp. 279–281). Washington, DC: American Society for Information Science.

Pao, M. L. (1981). Co-authorship as communication measure. *Library Research,* 2, 237–238.

Paul, S., Stein, F., Ottenbacher, K. J., & Liu, Y. (2002). The role of mentoring on research productivity among occupational therapy faculty. *Occupational Therapy International, 9*(1), 24–40.

Pellino, G. R., Boberg, A. L., Blackburn, R. T., O'Connell, C. (1981). *Planning and evaluating growth programs for faculty* (Monograph Series No. 14). East Lansing, MI: Michigan State University, Center for the Study of Higher Education. (ERIC Document Reproduction Service No. ED219022)

Pelz, D. C. (1967). Some social factors related to performance in a research organization. *Administrative Science Quarterly, 11,* 311–325.

Pelz, D. C., & Andrews, F. M. (1966). *Scientists in organizations: Productive climates for research and development.* New York, NY: John Wiley & Sons.

Perkoff, G. T. (1986). The research environment in family practice. *Journal of Family Practice, 21*(5), 389–393.

Perry, R. P., Clifton, R. A., & Menec, V. H., Struthers, C. W. & Menges, R. J. (2000). Faculty in transition: A longitudinal analysis of perceived control and type of institution in the research productivity of newly hired faculty. *Research in Higher Education, 41*(2), 165–194.

Peters, T. J., & Waterman, R. J., Jr. (1982). *In search of excellence: Lessons from America's best-run companies.* New York, NY: Harper & Row.

Pfeffer, J., & Langton, N. (1993). The effect of wage dispersion on satisfaction, productivity, and working collaboratively: Evidence from college and university faculty. *Administrative Science Quarterly, 38*(3), 382–407.

Pineau, C., & Levy-Leboyer, C. (1983). Managerial and organizational determinants of efficiency in biomedical research teams. In S. R. Epton, R. L. Payne, & A. W. Pearson (Eds.), *Managing interdisciplinary research* (pp. 141–163). New York, NY: John Wiley & Sons.

Pravdic, N., & Oluicvukovic, V. (1986). Dual approach to multiple authorship in the study of collaboration scientific output relationship. *Scientometrics, 10*(5-6), 259–280.

Price de Solla, D. J. (1963). *Little science, big science.* New York, NY: Columbia University Press.

Price de Solla, D. J., & Beaver, D. (1966). Collaboration in an invisible college. *American Psychologist, 21,* 1011–1018.

Project on Faculty Appointments at the Harvard Graduate School of Education. (1999). *Faculty Appointment Policy Archive* (Version 2.1) [CD-ROM]. Cambridge, MA: Author.

Reichheld, F. F., & Teal, T. A. (1996). *The loyalty effect: The hidden force behind growth, profits, and lasting value.* Boston, MA: Harvard Business School Press.

Reif-Lehrer, L. (1982). *Writing a successful grant application.* Boston, MA: Science Books International.

Reskin, B. F. (1977). Scientific productivity and the reward structure of science. *American Sociological Review, 42,* 491–504.

Reynolds, P. P., Giardino, A., Onady, G. M., & Siegler, E. L. (1994). Collaboration in the preparation of the generalist physician. *Journal of General Internal Medicine, 9*(4), S55–S63.

Rice, R. E., & Austin, A. E. (1988). High faculty morale: What exemplary colleges do right. *Change, 20*(2), 50–58.

Rice, R. E., & Austin, A. E. (1990). Organizational impacts on faculty morale and motivation to teach. In P. Seldin (Ed.), *How administrators can improve teaching: Moving from talk to action in higher education* (pp. 23–42). San Francisco, CA: Jossey-Bass.

Rice, R. E., & Finkelstein, M. J. (1993). The senior faculty: A portrait and literature review. In M. J. Finkelstein & M. W. LaCelle-Peterson (Eds.), *New directions for teaching and learning: No. 55. Developing senior faculty as teachers* (pp. 7–19). San Francisco, CA: Jossey-Bass.

Roberts, K. (1997). Nurse academics' scholarly productivity: Framed by the system, facilitated by mentoring. *Australian Journal of Advanced Nursing, 14*(3), 5–14.

Rogers, J. C., Holloway, R. L., & Miller, S. M. (1990). Academic mentoring and family medicine's research productivity. *Family Medicine, 22*(3), 186–190.

Rovegno, I., & Bandhauer, D. (1998). A study of the collaborative research process: Shared privilege and shared empowerment. *Journal of Teaching in Physical Education, 17*(3), 357–375.

Scherger, J. E., Rucker, L., Morrison, E. H., Cygan, R. W., & Hubbell, F. A. (2000). The primary care specialties working together: A model of success in an academic environment. *Academic Medicine, 75*(7), 693–698.

Schrier, R. W. (1997). Ensuring the survival of the clinician-scientist. *Academic Medicine, 72*(7), 589–594.

Schweitzer, J. C. (1988, July). *Personal, organizational and cultural factors affecting scholarly research among mass communication faculty.* Paper presented at the 71st annual meeting of the Association for Education in Journalism and Mass Communication, Portland, OR. (ERIC Document Reproduction Service No. ED295268)

Seagren, A. T., Creswell, J. W., & Wheeler, D. W. (2000). *The department chair: New roles, responsibilities, and challenges.* San Francisco, CA: Jossey-Bass.

Sindermann, C. J. (1985). *The joy of science: Excellence and its rewards.* New York, NY: Plenum Press.

Skipper, C. E. (1976). Personal characteristics of effective and ineffective university leaders. *College and University, 51,* 138–141.

Smart, J. C., & Elton, C. F. (1975). Goal orientations of academic departments: A test of Biglan's model. *Journal of Applied Psychology, 60,* 580–588.

Smith, C. G. (1971). Scientific performance and the composition of research teams. *Administrative Science Quarterly, 16*(4), 486–496.

Smith, S. L., Baker, D. R., Campbell, M. E., & Cunningham, M. E. (1985). An exploration of the factors shaping the scholarly productivity of social work academicians. *Journal of Social Service Research, 8*(3), 81–99.

Snyder, I. (1992). "It's not as simple as you think!" Collaboration between a researcher and a teacher. *English Education, 24,* 195–211.

Stack, S. (2003). Research productivity and student evaluation of teaching in social science classes: A research note. *Research in Higher Education, 44*(5), 539–556.

Staehnke, S. (1997, July 2). Kick out witless managers [Letters to the Editor]. *Star Tribune,* p. A28.

Steiner, G. A. (Ed.). (1965). *The creative organization.* Chicago, IL: University of Chicago Press.

Stinchcombe, A. L. (1966). On getting "hung-up" and other assorted illnesses. A discourse concerning researchers, wherein the nature of their mental health problems is discussed and illustrated. *Johns Hopkins Magazine, 28,* 25–30.

Taylor, J. S., Friedman, R. H., Speckman, J. L., Ash, A. S., Moskowitz, M. A., & Carr, P. L. (2001). Fellowship training and career outcomes for primary care physician-faculty. *Academic Medicine, 76*(4), 366–372.

Taylor, M. S., Locke, E. A., Lee, C., & Gist, M. E. (1984). Type A behavior and faculty research productivity: What are the mechanisms? *Organizational Behavior and Human Decision Processes, 34,* 402–418.

Tenenbaum, H. R., Crosby, F. J., & Gliner, M. D. (2001). Mentoring relationships in graduate school. *Journal of Vocational Behavior, 59*(3), 326–341.

Teodorescu, D. (2000). Correlates of faculty publication productivity: A cross-national analysis. *Higher Education, 39,* 201–222.

Terenzini, P. T., & Pascarella, E. T. (1994). Living with myths: Undergraduate education in America. *Change, 26,* 28–32.

Tierney, W. (1987). Facts and constructs: Defining reality in higher education organizations. *Review of Higher Education, 11*(1), 61–73.

Tosti-Vasey, J. L., & Willis, S. L. (1991). Professional currency among midcareer college faculty: Family and work factors. *Research in Higher Education, 32*(2), 123–139.

Trower, C. A. (Ed.). (2000). *Policies on faculty appointment: Standard practices and unusual arrangements.* Bolton, MA: Anker.

Tschannen-Moran, M., Firestone, W. A., Hoy, W., & Johnson, S. M. (2000). The write stuff: A study of productive scholars in educational administration. *Educational Administration Quarterly, 36*(3), 358–390.

Tucker, A. (1984). *Chairing the academic department: Leadership among peers* (2nd ed.). New York, NY: American Council on Education/Macmillan.

Turney, J. R. (1974). Activity outcome expectancies and intrinsic activity values as predictors of several motivation indexes for technical-professionals. *Organizational Behavior and Human Performance, 11,* 65–82.

Visart, N. (1979). Communication between and within research units. In F. Andrews (Ed.), *Scientific productivity: The effectiveness of research groups in six countries* (pp. 223–252). Cambridge, England: Cambridge University Press.

Votruba, J. C. (1990). Strengthening competence and vitality in professional development. In S. L. Willis & S. S. Dubin (Eds.), *Maintaining professional competence: Approaches to career enhancement, vitality, and success throughout a work life* (pp. 214–232). San Francisco, CA: Jossey-Bass.

Walker, J. A. (1988, Winter). Often difficult—but worth it. *Journal of Extension, 26*(4). Retrieved May 2, 2002, from http://www.joe.org/joe/1988 winter/a1.html

Walvoord, B. E., Carey, A. K., Smith, H. L., Soled, S. W., Way, P. K., & Zorn, D. (2000). *Academic departments: How they work, how they change* (ASHE-ERIC Higher Education Report, 27[8]). San Francisco, CA: Jossey-Bass.

Wanner, R. A., Lewis, L. S., & Gregorio, D. I. (1981). Research productivity in academia: A comparative study of the sciences, social sciences and humanities. *Sociology of Education, 54*(4), 238–253.

Wheeler, D., & Creswell, J. (1985, March). *Developing faculty as researchers.* Paper presented at the annual meeting of the Association for the Study of Higher Education, Chicago, IL. (ERIC Document Reproduction Service No. ED259649)

Williams, R. G., Dunnington, M. D., & Folse, R. (2003). The impact of a program for systematically recognizing and rewarding academic performance. *Academic Medicine, 78*(2), 156–166.

Wilson, P. P., Valentine, D., & Pereira, A. (2002). Perceptions of new social work faculty about mentoring experiences. *Journal of Social Work Education, 38*(2), 317–333.

Wispe, L. G. (1969). The bigger the better: Productivity, size, and turnover in a sample of psychology departments. *American Psychologist, 24*, 662–668.

Zuckerman, H. (1977). *Scientific elite: Nobel laureates in the United States.* New York, NY: Free Press.

Author Index

Subject Index